THE
PERFECTIONIST
and Other Plays

THE PERFECTIONIST

and Other Plays

JOYCE CAROL OATES

THE ECCO PRESS

THE ECCO PRESS
100 West Broad Street, Hopewell, New Jersey 08525
Published simultaneously in Canada by
Penguin Books Canada Ltd., Ontario
Printed in the United States of America
Designed by Debby Jay
FIRST EDITION

"The Interview" was commissioned by and performed at the McCarter Theatre, Princeton, N.J., January 1994, and was published in *Boulevard*, Winter 1994. It is included in *The Best American Short Plays 1994*. "Gulf War" premiered at the Ensemble Studio Theatre, May 1992. It was published, in another form, in *Boulevard*, Fall 1992. "The Rehearsal" premiered at the Ensemble Studio Theatre, June 1993, and was published in *Ontario Review*, Fall/Winter 1993. "Ontological Proof of My Existence" premiered at the Cubiculo Theatre, February 1972, and was published in *Partisan Review*, Vol. 37, 1970. "Black" premiered at Williamstown Theatre Festival, Williamstown, Mass., July 1992, and was published, in an earlier version in *Twelve Plays by Joyce Carol Oates* (Dutton, 1991). "The Perfectionist" premiered at the McCarter Theatre, Princeton, New Jersey, September 1993. "The Sacrifice" was published in *American Poetry Review*, May–June 1993. "Here She Is!", "Negative", and "The Sacrifice" are scheduled to premiere in Philadelphia in April 1995 under the auspices of the Philadelphia Festival Theatre for New Plays. "Homesick" was commissioned by the McCarter Theatre, Princeton, for a festival of one-act plays scheduled for June 1995. It was published in *The Missouri Review*, Fall 1994.

Library of Congress Cataloging-in-Publication Data

Oates, Joyce Carol, 1938–
    The perfectionist and other plays / Joyce Carol Oates.
        p. cm.
    I. Title.
PS3565.A8P47   1995
812'.54—dc20   94-17484
   ISBN 0-88001-400-8
The text of this book is set in Sabon.

for Patti Bosworth and Tom Palumbo

CONTENTS

THE INTERVIEW   1

GULF WAR   13

NEGATIVE   35

HERE SHE IS!   49

THE SACRIFICE   65

THE REHEARSAL   79

ONTOLOGICAL PROOF OF MY EXISTENCE   101

HOMESICK   129

BLACK   141

THE PERFECTIONIST   185

THE INTERVIEW ❧

A Play in One Act

Cast

THE IMMORTAL — an elderly, white-haired aristocratic gentleman
THE INTERVIEWER — a youngish man, in his thirties
KIMBERLY — a young woman, in her twenties

Setting

A contemporary hotel room with a suggestion of luxury. Minimal furnishings: a sofa, a table, a pitcher and a glass of water.

An elegant Mozart string quartet is issuing from a cabinet.

Lights up. Lighting is subdued at the start of the play, then gradually increases in intensity. By the end, it is as bright and pitiless as possible.

THE IMMORTAL *is seated on an antique sofa, head high, hands clasped on his knees, in a posture of imperturbable dignity. His eyes are half shut as if he is contemplating a higher reality. He is dressed with Old World formality—a dark suit with a vest, a white flower in his lapel. Brilliantly polished black shoes.*

A rapping at the door. IMMORTAL *serenely ignores it.*

INTERVIEWER   Hello? Hello? Is anybody there? It's—me.

Frantic rapping. IMMORTAL *takes no heed.*

INTERVIEWER *(Voice, desperate)*   It's the eleven o'clock interviewer—am I late—?

On the word "late" THE INTERVIEWER *pushes open the door, which is unexpectedly unlocked. He stumbles inside the room dropping his heavy duffel bag out of which spill a tape recorder, a camera, and several books.* INTERVIEWER *is casually dressed in jeans, jacket, jogging shoes; hair in a pony- or pigtail. He is breathless and apologetic.*

INTERVIEWER   Oh!—oh, my God! It's—you. *(Approaching* IMMORTAL *reverently)* I—I'm—jeez, excuse me! *(Staring)* It is—you?

IMMORTAL *remains unperturbed. Music continues.*

INTERVIEWER *(Nervous chattering as he fumblingly picks up his things)* I c-can't tell you, sir, what an honor this is. The honor of a lifetime. And here I am late! *(Angry, incredulous laughter at himself)* Held up in traffic for half an hour—plus my assistant Kimberly screwed up on the time—not that there's any excuse to be late for an interview with you, sir. I hope you will—forgive me? *(Craven)*

IMMORTAL *remains imperturbed. Music continues.*

INTERVIEWER *(Awkward, nodding)* I, um—well, yes. Right. *(Fussing with tape recorder; drops a cassette, retrieves it)* That's right, sir. *(Nervous laugh)* That music—it's real high class. I—sort of thought—listening out in the hall—you might be playing it, yourself. You were trained as a classical musician, sir—in addition to your other talents—weren't you?

IMMORTAL *remains imperturbed. Music continues.*

INTERVIEWER *(First hint of his self-importance)* Your publisher explained who I am, sir, I hope? *(Pause)* I began with a modest Sunday books column for the Detroit News—within eighteen months was promoted to the editorial page—where my column HEAR THIS! ran the gamut from high culture to low controversy! *(Laughs)* No, seriously, I never shrank from any subject. I ran my own photos, interviewed both "big" and "little" folks, soon became syndicated in over a hundred dailies—whiz bang zap zolly!—here I am: lead columnist for *America Today,* circulation fifty-seven million daily. *(Breathless)* Interviewing, in depth, men and women of the stature, sir, of *you.*

IMMORTAL *remains imperturbed, unimpressed. Music continues.*

INTERVIEWER *(Smiles, rubs hands, ebullient)* Well, now! The editors of *America Today* are asking five hundred of the world's leading men and women in all the creative arts—at the cutting edge of science—politics—culture: What do you prophecize for the year 2000? *(Pause, jokes) Will we make it? (Laughs)*

IMMORTAL *remains as before.*

INTERVIEWER *(Respectfully)* You, sir, having been born in 1798—Oops! *(Checks notes)*—1898—have lived through virtually the entire twentieth century—so my first question will be— Will you *make it? (Laughs)*

IMMORTAL *remains as before, stiff and unresponsive;* INTERVIEWER *ceases laughing, embarrassed.*

INTERVIEWER Umm—just a little joke. I'm known for my, um—sense of humor. *(Pause)* "Irreverent"—"refreshing"—"wacko in all the right ways"— *(Pause)* Bill Clinton said that, sir. About my column. *(Pause)* What Hilary said, I don't know. *(Awkward laugh)*

IMMORTAL *as before.*

INTERVIEWER *(Slightly abashed, but taking a new tack)* Well, *now!* Here we go in earnest! *(With tape recorder)* You don't mind these, sir, I hope? *(Punching buttons)* Jeez if I tried to take notes the old, literate way, I'd really screw up. My handwriting's like Helen Keller's in an earthquake. *(Laughs)*

IMMORTAL *as before.*

INTERVIEWER *(Slightly abashed, defensive)*   Helen Keller was an old blind deaf dumb *genius*—I guess. You'd've gotten along real well together, sir.

INTERVIEWER *fusses with his recorder, muttering under his breath. Voices emerge squealing and squawking, unintelligible.*

FEMALE VOICE *(High-pitched squeal)*   No no no no no you stop that!

INTERVIEWER   Oops! *(Punches a button, fast-forwarding)* That's an oldie—Barbara Bush.

INTERVIEWER'S VOICE *(On tape, volume loud)*   —prophecize for the year 2000, sir?

MALE VOICE *(Evangelical-sounding)*   The Second Coming—the Resurrection of the Body—"And all ye shall rejoice, and see God"—

INTERVIEWER *abruptly cuts off cassette, rewinds.*

INTERVIEWER   We'll just tape over that. *(Condescending)* One of those nuts—hitting all the TV talk shows last week—his book's a number one bestseller—real lowbrow crapola, not highbrow, sir, like *you.* *(Kneeling at* IMMORTAL'S *feet, fussing with the recorder)* You, sir—I reverence you. First time I read your work, sir, I was in sixth grade. Yeah, I was precocious! *(Chuckles)* That sure does bring problems, sir, doesn't it?—precocity?—peers get Goddamned *jealous.* As you'd know, sir, eh?—your first book was published when you were eighteen? Wow. *(Pause)* Or am I thinking of—whosis—Rambo? *(Pause)* Hey, before we get going— *(Brings over a stack of books for* IMMORTAL *to sign)* Would you sign these, please, sir? I know it's a nuisance—being so renowned—autograph seekers hounding you constantly—but I'd appreciate it so much, sir! Here's my card, sir, so you get the name right.

IMMORTAL *signs books in a pompous manner, his head still held stiffly high.* INTERVIEWER *gives him a pen, opens books and positions them on his lap, chatting all the while.*

INTERVIEWER   Here, sir—please use this pen. It's a Mont Blanc—a little token from Samuel Beckett when I interviewed him. Last interview that great man gave. We really hit it off, Sam and me. I may be from Detroit but I can sure yuk it up with you immortals! *(Chuckles, then peers at books)* Um, sir—excuse me—would you date your signature, please? And, um—you might say "New York City" below, too— Thank you! Immensely! *(Checks the signatures, chuckles)* Your handwriting's like Helen Keller's in an earthquake, sir! *(Nudges IMMORTAL in the ribs)*

The flower falls from IMMORTAL's lapel.

IMMORTAL *"comes alive" though retaining, at least intermittently, certain of his pompous mannerisms.*

IMMORTAL   Qu'est-ce que c'est? Qui êtes vous?

INTERVIEWER   Say what? *(Atrocious accent)* Non parlez-vous français here, sir! Nossir!

IMMORTAL *(Stiff alarm, distaste)*   Vous êtes—americain?

INTERVIEWER *(Loudly, as if IMMORTAL is deaf)*   Weewee! I zetes americain!

IMMORTAL *(Elderly confusion)*   Mais, pourquoi—

INTERVIEWER   Sir, parlez English, eh? *(Checks PR sheet)* It says here you're "septo-lingual"—speak seven languages with equal fluency—so let's have it for English, eh? *(Joking)* I didn't know there were seven languages left in Europe.

IMMORTAL *(Now in Italian, haltingly)*   Non capisco . . . Che cosè? Mi sono perso . . . ? *(I don't understand. What is it? Am I lost?)*

INTERVIEWER *(Loudly)*   Ing-lese, sir! ING-LESE! You know it, for sure. You're in the U.S. of A. now.

IMMORTAL   Per favore—aiuto! Mi sento male . . . *(Please, help! I feel ill.)*

INTERVIEWER   C'mon, sir! ING-LESE! AMER-I-CAN!

IMMORTAL   Who are you? Have you come to help me?

INTERVIEWER   Terrifico!—English. *(Starts recorder)* You had me worried there for a minute, sir!

IMMORTAL *(Dazed, tragic voice)*   I want—to live again. *(Pause)* I want to die.

INTERVIEWER *(Cheerfully, holding microphone)*   Can't do both, sir! Not at the same time. Comment, sir what do you prophecize for the upcoming millennium?

IMMORTAL   My beloved Marguerite, where are you—

INTERVIEWER *(Rattling off choices)*   "End of the world"—"things better than ever"—"more of the same?"

IMMORTAL *(Wildly)*   Marguerite! Help me—

INTERVIEWER *(As if humanly struck)*   That's touching, sir. My goodness. Could you expand upon—?

IMMORTAL *(Squinting at INTERVIEWER, tragic "classical" voice)*   Please help me, have you been sent to help me? I am in pain. Where is the light?

INTERVIEWER Light? Nah, there's plenty of light in here, it's pouring through the window. Plus I got a flash camera. *(Pause)* Enough of this, though— *(Strides over to a cabinet, switches off the Mozart abruptly)* That artsy stuff gets on your nerves after a while.

IMMORTAL Marguerite, my dear one—

INTERVIEWER *(Peering at PR sheet)* Um—"Marguerite"—"wife of"— "deceased, 1923"—"Christiane"—"wife of"—"deceased 1939"— "Pilar"—"wife of"—deceased 1961"—"Claudia"—"wife of"— "deceased 1979"—"Chantal"—"wife of"—"deceased 1987"— Wow, sir! I mean—*wow*. I hate to tell you, though—you got some catching up to do.

IMMORTAL Why am I—alone?

INTERVIEWER *(Reading from sheet of paper)* Let's move on, sir, to more provocative issues. What's your frank opinion of American civilization, as viewed from your side of the Atlantic are we a nation of coarse philistines, illiterates, and wannabee capitalist swine, or a "Brave New World?"

IMMORTAL *(Confused)* "Brave New World?"

INTERVIEWER *(Enthusiastically)* Right! I think so, too. One thing pisses me off it's that hypocritical bullshit, we Americans are crass and uncultured. Screw that! Every God-damn country in the world including your homeland, excuse me, sir, emulates us, and wants our dough. Any comment?

IMMORTAL I—feel such cold. Where is this terrible place?

INTERVIEWER *(Consulting notes briskly)* Um-hum—moving right along now— Sir, in your Nobel Prize acceptance speech you stated: "As a youth I had wished to emulate—"

IMMORTAL *(Overlapping with unexpected passion, clarity; hand gestures)* "As a youth I had wished to emulate Homer—Dante—Goethe— Balzac—setting myself the task of creating a great epic commensurate with the spirit of mankind. Immortalizing the heritage of the West. The most ambitious work of the twentieth century. The tragedy of Nazism unleashed the terror that history and civilization could be annihilated—and so it remains for *us* to bear witness—unflinchingly."

INTERVIEWER *(Clapping)* Wow! That's telling 'em, sir!

IMMORTAL *(Continuing, gesturing)* "The future of humankind is legislated by its spiritual leaders—its artists—"

INTERVIEWER *(Cutting right in)* Um-hum! Well, my editor's gonna make me cut all this back pretty much. *America Today* is reader-friendly— our paragraphs are never more than a single sentence. *(Briefest of pauses, no transition, abruptly and brightly)* Changing the subject somewhat, sir, moving from the lugubrious to the caluminous—is it true that you plagiarized your early dramas from Pirandello?

IMMORTAL *(Shocked, agitated)* What! I! Plagiarize!

INTERVIEWER *America Today*'s readers just want the simple truth, sir: *yes* or *no*?

IMMORTAL H-He—stole from *me*—

INTERVIEWER *(Checking notes)* One of you is the author of the immortal classic *Five Characters in Search of an Author* and the other is the author of the immortal classic *Six Characters in Search of an Author*—so, which came first?

IMMORTAL *(Spitting gesture)* Pirandello!—a shallow, meretricious talent! A mere mimicry of—

INTERVIEWER *(Consulting notes)* You had a scandalous love affair with—Colette? Who threw you over publicly for—Franz Liszt? Wow!

IMMORTAL *(Incensed)* How dare you! Whoever you are, how—

IMMORTAL *is so agitated, his hearing aid falls from his ear.*

INTERVIEWER Uh-oh! We're getting a little hyper, sir, are we? *(Retrieves the hearing aid which has fallen to the floor)* What's it—oh, a hearing aid. Jeez, you scared me, I thought it was part of your *brain* falling out. *(Laughs)* That'd be weird, eh? Terrific story, but weird. Let me— *(Tries to fit the hearing aid into* IMMORTAL's *ear, but it slips back out)* Damn! *(Tries again, jamming it in;* IMMORTAL *flinches with pain, but the hearing aid slips out anyway)* Fuck it! These "miracles of modern technology!" *(Tries other ear)* Uh-oh! There's already one in this ear. *(Hearing aid falls to the floor and is apparently broken;* INTERVIEWER *picks it up, chagrined)* Ooops! Looks like it's, um, a little cracked. Shit, am I sorry!

IMMORTAL *reaches for the hearing aid, but* INTERVIEWER *stuffs it into* IMMORTAL's *pocket.*

INTERVIEWER For safekeeping, sir! Wouldn't want you to lose the damn thing. *(Consulting notes)* Ummm, yes: how does it feel, sir, to be a great artist?—a "classic?"— the oldest living "immortal" of the French Academy *and* the oldest living Nobel Prize laureate since what's-his-name, that Bulgarian, croaked last year? Our audience yearns to know, sir: how does it feel to have "made it?"

IMMORTAL *(High, quavering voice)* So lonely. My loved ones, my friends—gone. My enemies—gone. *(Clutching at* INTERVIEWER's *arm)* I had wanted to outlive my enemies—and I have.

INTERVIEWER Terrific! That's sure candid stuff. *(Takes up camera)* Lemme take a few quick shots, and we can wrap this up. *(Blinding flash)* Little smile, sir? C'mon, little smile? You can do better than that, sir, come *on. (Aggressively close, as* IMMORTAL *flinches)*

IMMORTAL   What—place is this? Who are you?

INTERVIEWER *(Taking photos)*   Tell our audience about your friendship with the great Nabokov, sir. *He* plagiarized *you*—that's the scuttle-butt, eh?

IMMORTAL   Why am I—here?

INTERVIEWER *(Chuckling)*   You "esthetes"—any truth to the rumor you and Nabokov, um, got it on together upon occasion?

IMMORTAL   Nabokov?

INTERVIEWER   Those were the days, eh?—"Gay Nineties"—"Roaring Twenties"—"Lost Generation"—no "safe sex" for you, eh? *(Suddenly realizing, strikes forehead and consults notes)* Uh-oh! Shit! You *are* Nabokov!

IMMORTAL *(Trying to escape but falling back weakly onto the sofa in ter-ror)*   I know you! I know you! Go away!

INTERVIEWER *(Incensed)*   What the hell, Mr. Nabokov, I'm slotted in for thirty minutes! That's bottomline *rude.*

IMMORTAL   I know your face—you are Death.

Pause. INTERVIEWER *is standing rigid, camera in hand.*

INTERVIEWER   Excuse me, Mr. Nabokov, but that's insulting.

IMMORTAL   Death! Come for me! But I am not ready! My soul is not ready! Go away!

IMMORTAL *lunges suddenly at* INTERVIEWER, *trying to snatch his camera from him. The flash goes off.*

IMMORTAL   Oh!

As if the flashbulb has been a gunshot, IMMORTAL *collapses onto the sofa and lies limp.*

INTERVIEWER'S *hair has come loose in the struggle, altering his appear-ance. He stands straight and tall and does indeed have the frightening aura of an agent of Death.*

INTERVIEWER   You Immortals—all alike. Guys like *me*, we got your num-ber. *(Packs up his things into duffel bag, muttering to himself)* Where's he get off, calling *me* Death! Me with a syndicated readership of fifty-seven million!—second only to "Dear Abby."

Flurried knocking at the door. KIMBERLY *runs in, aghast.*

KIMBERLY *(Biting thumbnail)*   Oh! oh God! oh you're going to be mad at me, oh I just know it!

INTERVIEWER   What?

KIMBERLY *(Little-girl, pleading)* Oh I just know you are! I know you are!

INTERVIEWER Kimberly, what the hell—? I've had it up to here with fucking obfuscation this morning!

KIMBERLY Promise you won't be mad at me . . .

INTERVIEWER *(Shouting)* I promise! I won't be mad at you!

KIMBERLY I, uh—um—this is the wrong hotel. This is the Plaza, and you're supposed to be at the Saint Regis. Whoever *he* is—he's the wrong person.

INTERVIEWER *(Louder)* What? Wrong hotel? Wrong person? *What?*

KIMBERLY *(Little-girl manner, softly)* You promised you wouldn't get mad.

INTERVIEWER You're responsible for me wasting my entire morning? And I'm not supposed to be *mad?*

KIMBERLY *(Pleading)* It wasn't my fault—the FAX from the office is so smudged. See— *(She shows him the FAX, which he snatches from her fingers)*

INTERVIEWER *(Peering at it)* Holy shit! I *am* supposed to be at the Saint Regis! I'm twenty minutes late already! *(In a fury, takes out his recorder, erases cassette)* There! ERASE! God*damn.*

As INTERVIEWER *moves to exit,* KIMBERLY *notices* IMMORTAL *whom she approaches with concern.*

KIMBERLY Oh! This gentleman! Is he—?

INTERVIEWER *(Breezy, sarcastic)* He says he's Nabokov.

KIMBERLY *(Impressed)* Oh!—"Nab-o-kov"—that famous dancer? The one who deflected from the Soviet Union when it was still Communist?

INTERVIEWER *(Exiting)* Defected.

KIMBERLY *approaches* IMMORTAL. *(A strain of romantic music might be used here.)*

KIMBERLY Mr. Nabokov? Are you—alive? *(Pause)* I never saw you dance, but—my grandmother did, I think. She said you were— *(Pause)* —fantastic. Mr. Nabokov?

IMMORTAL *begins to stir, moaning.* KIMBERLY *helps him sit up; unbuttons his collar, loosens his tie, etc. She dips a handkerchief or scarf into the glass of water and presses it against his forehead.*

KIMBERLY Mr. Nabokov, I guess you had a little fainting spell! I'd better call the hotel doctor.

IMMORTAL *(Reviving slowly)* No—no, please.

KIMBERLY *(Thumb to mouth)* You're sure? You look kind of—pale.

IMMORTAL *(Staring at* KIMBERLY*)* My dear one! Is it—*you?*

KIMBERLY Who?

IMMORTAL *(Hoarse whisper)* Not Marguerite, but—Chantal? Returned to me?

KIMBERLY "Chantal"—?

IMMORTAL *(With elderly eagerness)* My dear! Darling! Don't ever leave me again!

KIMBERLY Gosh, Mr. Nabokov, I'm afraid I—

IMMORTAL I will die in this terrible place if you leave me. *(Takes her wrist)*

KIMBERLY —afraid there's been some—

IMMORTAL My darling, I'm so lonely. They call me a "living classic"—an "immortal"—but without *you,* I am nothing.

KIMBERLY But you're so famous, Mr. Nabokov!

IMMORTAL Chantal, please—don't leave me again, ever. I seem to have grown old, I know—but it's only an illusion.

KIMBERLY *(Embarrassed)* Gee, I hate to say this but you're a little . . . confused, Mr. Nabokov. I'd better call the doctor—

IMMORTAL *You're* still young, and I, in my heart, in my soul—I am unchanged.

KIMBERLY You are? *(Pause, sees flower on floor)* Oh!—is this yours? *(Picks it up, restores it to his lapel)* There!

IMMORTAL Chantal, my dear one—you won't leave me, will you? Say you won't!

KIMBERLY I'm, uh, not "Chantal" but "Kimberly." I'm the assistant of that man who just—

IMMORTAL *(Pleading)* My "Chantal *des fleurs*"—my dear one? You won't abandon me in this terrible place?

KIMBERLY I—don't know. How long do you want me to stay, Mr. Nabokov? *(Checks watch)* I guess I could skip lunch.

IMMORTAL pulls at KIMBERLY's arm; she sits beside him on the sofa.

IMMORTAL *(Reverently)* You are—Life. Restored to me. My Chantal! The only woman I ever loved. *(Pause)* You can order up from room service anything you want, dear. This is America—all my expenses are being paid.

KIMBERLY *(A new idea)* Oh!—Mr. Nabokov, can *I* interview you? Nobody ever gives me a chance but I know I'm a thousand times more emphatic—empathetic?—than *he* is.

IMMORTAL Of course, my darling. Anything! Only don't ever leave me again.

KIMBERLY takes out her tape recorder, sets it going briskly.

KIMBERLY   Oh, Mr. Nabokov, I sure won't. I promise. *(Sudden professional tone)* Mr. Nabokov, will you share with our readers your reflections on the imminent year 2000? When you deflected from the Soviet Union, did you ever guess *all this would be coming to pass?*

Lights very bright then fade rapidly.

Lights out.

THE END

GULF WAR ❧
A Play in One Act

Cast

NICOLE BELL—late twenties, very attractive, rather stiffly poised
STUART BELL—her husband, about thirty, tall, solidly built, an aggressive
  and ambitious young stockbroker
MITZIE WIDMARK—early sixties, attractive
DEFORREST WIDMARK—about sixty-five, morose, lip-chewing, slump-
  shouldered

Setting

The BELLS' house, new, sparely furnished, contemporary in design, sophis-
ticated and sterile. The rooms in which the action occurs (bedroom, family room, outdoor deck) can be represented by simple space divisions on
the stage. The time is January 1991.

SCENE 1

The BELLS' *bedroom. Early evening.* NICOLE *and* STUART *are dressing for cocktails.* NICOLE *is wearing a stylishly short skirt (in stark white or black) and is fumbling with the many buttons of a long-sleeved silk blouse.* STUART, *newly returned from his office, is changing his shirt, and then knots a floral print tie briskly about his neck. He whistles cheerfully. He regards himself in a full-length mirror with critical exactitude.*

NICOLE *stands facing us, her back to* STUART. *She addresses the audience conspiratorially, urgently. We must get the distinct impression that* NICOLE *is utterly sincere even as we sense her weakness.*

NICOLE Tonight—I will tell him. I must. I've waited so long . . .

NICOLE *glances back at* STUART *to make sure she isn't being observed. She takes a glass (gin-and-tonic) out of its hiding place, perhaps in a dresser drawer or behind a vase; sips from it gratefully; winces; returns the glass to its hiding place.* STUART *seems unaware.*

NICOLE *(With resolution)* Now we're living in this new house, this house *without memory* . . . *(A pause)* Sometimes it's easiest to speak what's in your heart . . . before witnesses.
STUART *(Calling over, pleasantly)* When you called the Whitbecks, darling, I hope you explained why we haven't had them over in some time?—moving into the new house, and all.
NICOLE *(Confused, but tries to maintain poise)* The—Whitbecks? Isn't it the Witkes who are coming for drinks?
STUART *(Still pleasantly)* The Whit*becks*—it's written in my date book. Didn't you call them?
NICOLE *(Nervously)* I don't think so, Stuart. I thought you did.
STUART I'm sure *you* did, Nicole. Our social engagements are your responsibility, sweetie!

NICOLE   But our friends are all yours . . .

STUART *(Without irony)*   They aren't my friends, they're my business associates. My distinguished elders.

NICOLE *(As if trying to make a joke, "feminine," hoping to charm her husband)*   They all seem to look alike! I can't keep them straight.

STUART *chuckles, kisses* NICOLE *on the forehead, then reverts to somewhat dogmatic tone.*

STUART *(As if reciting a platitude)*   You can measure your success by the ages of your social acquaintances. If they're your elders, you're doing just fine. *(Laughs, shakes head)* If your prime-time Saturday nights are spent with old college friends, or the neighbors—forget it!

NICOLE *(Slowly)*   It's good, we've moved here . . . no one knows us here. *(Pause)* I don't think we have any neighbors here. "Fox Hollow Hills" is so spread out.

STUART   Fox Hills *Hollow. A Planned Residential Community.*

NICOLE *(Blankly)*   It's so . . . beautiful here. A view from all the windows. *(As if peering out a window)*

STUART *(Good-natured, critical)*   And one of these days you might even find time to do a little shopping for the house . . . we need carpeting, more furniture, lamps . . .

NICOLE *(Quickly)*   I've been to the mall. And I . . . it's so . . . big.

STUART *(Good-natured)*   I don't mind the rooms with an actual *echo,* but our friends are going to wonder!

NICOLE   We'll take the Witkes into the family room. There's enough furniture there.

STUART *(Laughing, exasperated)*   The Whit*becks,* Nicole. Not the Wit*kes.* The Whitbecks are more crucial right now than the Witkes— we'll do the Witkes another time.

NICOLE *(To herself)*   Not Wit*kes* but Whit*becks.* Yes! I see.

STUART   I wish I could believe you, that you *do. (Frowning at her)* You haven't been drinking, Nicole, have you?

NICOLE *(Guiltily)*   How . . . would I be drinking? *(Hurt, pouting)* Why would I drink . . . alone! *(Disdain)* That would be like—making love alone!

STUART   You do eat, don't you, during the day?—and take the vitamins the doctor prescribed? *(When* NICOLE *nods, annoyed)* You still haven't gained back that weight.

NICOLE   I have!—some of it. *(Self-conscious beneath his scrutiny)* Stuart, don't look at me!—like that.

STUART *(Trying to make light of it)*   You're a beautiful woman, why shouldn't I look at you? *(Laughs)* How do you think I fell in love with you? *(Pause)* "Love enters through the eyes."

NICOLE *(Uneasily)*   If it *is* the Whitbecks who are coming . . . I think *you* must have called them, Stuart. Not me.

STUART   When?

NICOLE   When did you call them? How would I know, sweetie!

STUART   It's possible, I suppose, that they called us.

NICOLE   And you invited them over?

STUART   Hell, they may have invited themselves over. You know what they're like.

NICOLE   I . . . mix them up with the others.

STUART *(Cheerfully)*   Pushy, aggressive. Are they ever! *(A whistling noise as of grudging admiration)* But kind, basically.

STUART slips on a sports coat, peers at himself in the mirror.

STUART Shit! My hair . . . I should have had it trimmed today . . . but I worked right through lunch.

NICOLE   I thought you just had it trimmed.

STUART   That was Monday. This is Friday. It must be my Goddamn adrenaline, my hair *grows*.

NICOLE *(An effort at maintaining some kind of control)*   I think you look—perfect. "The handsomest youngest man in the room."

STUART *(Not to be co-opted)*   I don't *want* to look perfect—perfection doesn't inspire trust. Like this— *(Adjusts shirt cuffs to make one just perceptibly more visible than the other; moves tie just to left of center, combs hair to make it appear slightly ruffled, boyish)* "Trust enters through the eyes." *(Now assessing NICOLE, who has finally buttoned her blouse)* And you: how many times have I told *you* . . . Glamour isn't the style in Fair Haven, not in our set. *(He musses NICOLE's hair just a little; goes to a bureau, returns with a necklace of chunky amber beads)* How's this?

NICOLE   That doesn't go with this outfit.

STUART   It doesn't *go*, but it gives the right touch. Sort of—pretty but clunky. Like, maybe, Judy Whitbeck's daughter, say she's got a daughter your age, might wear.

STUART lowers the necklace over NICOLE's head. She starts a little, involuntarily; has to restrain herself from pushing from him.

STUART   What's wrong?

NICOLE   The floor tilted just now.

STUART   The *floor*—? *(Exasperated)* Maybe if we get some wall-to-wall carpeting in here, it *won't*. *(A pause)* Do you have something you want to tell me, Nicole?

A pause. NICOLE *looks helplessly at* STUART. *She does have something to say, but has not the courage to say it at this moment.*

NICOLE   Tell you . . . ? How?
STUART *(Briskly, turning away)*   Then *don't.*

Lights down.

SCENE 2

NICOLE, *alone in the bedroom. As if embarrassed, apologetic for her failure of courage. Addresses audience earnestly, in tone and manner conspicuously different from previous scene.*

NICOLE   I've been married for six and a half years, and I've been in love at least that long. *(Pause)* Or longer! *(Pause)* You don't chose your fate. I used to think you did—we did—but we *don't.* Fate chooses *us.* *(Pause)* I used to be the "weather girl" for South Orange, New Jersey cable TV channel 39—but that was a long time ago. I drew mixed notices from the viewers: O.K. with the good, sunny weather, "smiles too much" with the bad. They see through you if you smile wrong, but they sure don't like you if you don't *smile.* *(Pause)* Stuart's right: whatever it is, it "enters through the eyes." *(Pause, as if bitterly)* That's our fate.
There's the "Gulf War" going on right now—in the TV downstairs in the family room. This is the time of the "Gulf War"—but I'm not political. *(Pause)*
You can be *not political* like you can be . . . *not a mother,* for instance. *(Pause)*
I am *not political* and have no interest in the Gulf War or in any war. I lack the spirit of . . . optimism. *(Pause)* A depletion of optimism. *(Pause)* "Depletion of oxygen"—did I say? *(More firmly)* "Depletion of optimism." *(Pause)*
I was eleven years old when the Vietnam War officially ended without my knowing it and I was through with my schooling including three semesters at Connecticut College by the time "an awakened interest in the Vietnam War became a trendy phenomenon in American education and entertainment"—that goes for the Holocaust, too. *(Pause)* I do not care for war movies, of any era.
STUART *(Voice off-stage, words need not be audible)*   Nicole, where the hell are you? It's six thirty!

NICOLE hurriedly locates her gin-and-tonic, drains the glass, returns it to its hiding place. Begins to exit stage right, fluffing up her hair, adjusting the amber beads, etc. Laughs, suddenly dizzy.

NICOLE   Damn floor. It *does* tilt.

Lights out as NICOLE exits.

SCENE 3

In a neutral space, presumably the foyer of their house, the BELLS are looking out at their arriving guests. STUART in particular is agitated, amazed.

STUART   Good Christ! It isn't the Whitbecks, it's the—Widmarks? *(Incredulous)* The Widmarks—for drinks?
NICOLE   Oh, dear! Do I know them?
STUART   *(Staring out window, muttering)* DeForrest Widmark—the "kiss-of-death" at Crawson, Hinney, Flaux, & Roe. The firm's most loyal, uncomplaining employee—decades of hard work and devotion—never made a partner—salary frozen for the past five years— "priceless resource"—well-liked—kind, generous—pitied, shunned, despised—*so* helpful to junior staff—"avoid old Widmark like the plague"— *(Furious at NICOLE)* Of course you know them, they had us to dinner back in November! And I told told *told* you never to accept another invitation from them again!
NICOLE   *(Faltering)*   But, this . . . isn't an invitation of theirs. Is it? This is our house . . . isn't it?
STUART   Who invited them here, if not you?
NICOLE   But I don't even know them . . .
STUART   Are you suggesting *I* invited them?—*I*, who know them?

As the WIDMARKS ring the doorbell, STUART completely transforms himself. He becomes an exuberant young host, welcoming his elders inside, effusive in greetings, handshakes, etc. NICOLE, though less confident, is surprisingly capable of transforming herself too. She becomes the smiling, happy, welcoming young hostess.

The WIDMARKS may be imagined as a nightmare version, or vision, of the BELLS; the physical resemblances, etc., should be suggested rather than too blatantly stated. MITZIE is a still-pretty but overly made-up woman wearing clothes that are a bit too youthful for her; she teeters in·high-heeled shoes that resemble NICOLE's. DEFORREST *is the very image of failure—yet a droll, self-aware, not overly embittered failure; "American Dad" of a kind—in a suit past its prime, long-sleeved white shirt, a "colorful" neck-tie. Lip-chewing, slump-shouldered, balding, with an expression that seems to suggest, "I know, I know, I'm pathetic, even laughable—but please like me all the same."*

The WIDMARKS *must be shorter than the* BELLS. MITZIE *may be very petite.*

Greetings at the door are general, effusive. Much overlapping.

STUART   Come in! Welcome! So great to see you! Mitzie, DeForrest! Wow! It's been a while! Come right in! Any trouble finding the house?

NICOLE   Hello! Mitzie, DeForrest! Come in, please! Is it cold outside? Is it raining outside? Oh, come *in*.

MITZIE *is not content with merely shaking the* BELLS' *hands warmly, but must kiss them on the cheeks, smudging lipstick on both. In the moments following, at a convenient juncture, the* BELLS *indicate to each other that there is lipstick on their cheeks, and wipe it off with a tissue. If the gesture can be done without being too obtrusive,* NICOLE *can wipe off the smudge on* STUART's *cheek.*

MITZIE *(Overlapping with the preceding)*   Hello, hello! Oh, how lovely this is! Dear Stuart! Dear—is it Nicole? So sweet of you to invite us! Are we too early? Are we *late*? We did get lost a bit, DeForrest took a wrong turn of course, but—here we are!

DEFORREST *(Shambling, mumbling, somber smile)*   Hello, Stuart my boy. Hello, dear. So kind of you. My, yes!

STUART *(Ushering them forward)*   This—through here—our "family room"—watch the steps!

MITZIE *(Teetering in high heels, leaning on* STUART's *arm)*   Ohhh these itty-bitty steps going *down*, going *up*—all the houses of today have them!

DEFORREST *(Somber)*   Yes indeed it seems to be . . . the thing.

Lights down.

Lights immediately up. No break in action as the four enter the "family room."

MITZIE *(Effervescent)*   How lovely *this* is!—such a spacious room! A true *family* room, my yes! Isn't it, DeForrest?

DEFORREST *(Polishing bifocals)*   Indeed, yes. *(Puts on glasses, blinking)* Indeed.

NICOLE   Thank you. We're very . . . happy here.

STUART *(As if* NICOLE's *response is too weak)*   We *love* it here. *(Rubbing hands together)* Now, drinks! Mitzie, DeForrest—what would you like?

MITZIE Mmmm well!—I *could* be tempted. Just a teeny bit of dry white wine maybe with ice?

DEFORREST *(Mumbling)* S'chonnaruksson.

MITZIE DeForrest, love, speak *up*.

DEFORREST *(Louder mumble)* Scotch on the rocks, son. Thank you.

STUART *(Zestfully)* Coming right up!

MITZIE Oh, um . . . maybe I change my mind? A, um, Bloody Mary, instead? *(Giggling)* This is a fun evening!

STUART Absolutely positively, Mrs. Widmark.

MITZIE *(Lightly poking him)* "Mitzie"—please.

STUART *(Charming smile)* Mitzie—of course. *(To NICOLE)* Club soda, honey? Tonic water?

NICOLE Tonic water, with a splash of gin. *(Nervous laugh)* Oh, I'll make my own.

STUART *(Pleasantly)* No trouble dear—I'll make it.

NICOLE *(Gaily)* No trouble—*I'll* make it.

STUART *prepares drinks for the* WIDMARKS *and for himself;* NICOLE *prepares her own.*

NICOLE *sips her drink, disguising her relief.* STUART *nudges her as if to warn her against drinking too much and she blinks up at him open-eyed, innocent.*

MITZIE *is prodding* DEFORREST *to look about the room, in admiration.*

MITZIE *(Little-girl ruefulness)* Look here, DeForrest—exactly the kind of fireplace we always wanted! Authentic fieldstone.

DEFORREST *(Mumbling)* So it is! Very nice.

MITZIE And, here—this beautiful streamlined *glass*-topped table!

DEFORREST *Very* nice.

MITZIE Oh, what a handsome big television set! *(To the* BELLS, *a faint wail) Our* lives just slid by, DeForrest's and mine, as on greased roller skates. *We* live amid boring old tasteful *antiques. (Accepts drink from* STUART*)* Oh, my, thank you. This is so much fun, isn't it, DeForrest?

DEFORREST *(Accepting drink from* STUART*)* Thank you, son. Very good of you.

STUART *(Raising glass)* Here's to—many happy occasions in the future!

NICOLE *(Gaily)* *Many* happy!

DEFORREST *(Mumbling)* Very kind . . . thoughtful young people.

MITZIE *(Puckishly)* There can't be *many*, you know—at our age! *(Drinks)* My, I haven't had so delicious a drink in a long long time, have I, DeForrest?

DEFORREST *(Drinking, mumbling)* Um . . . very nice.

STUART Shall we be seated?

NICOLE *(Graciously, calmer now that she has a drink)* Yes, please! Mrs. Widmark—

MITZIE remains on her feet, the better to keep attention on herself.

MITZIE *(A quick retort)* "Mrs. Widmark is *his* mother"—I used to say. *(Laughing)* But, these days, I *can't*—the poor old dear has been dead, how long, DeForrest?

DEFORREST is just about to draw STUART aside for a confidential chat.

DEFORREST Ummm, Mitzie?

MITZIE *(Loudly)* Your poor dead mother, lovey. How long?

DEFORREST *(Cupping hand to ear)* I didn't quite hear, Mitzie . . .

MITZIE *(Brightly, to NICOLE)* You must feel the same way, dear—when people call you "Mrs. Ball." A young wife can never quite believe that's *her.*

NICOLE *(Apologetically)* Actually, his name—our name—is "Bell."

MITZIE That's what I said: "Ball."

NICOLE *(Earnestly)* B - E - L - L. *Bell.*

MITZIE "Bell." *(Savoring the sound)* "Bell." I *like* it.

DEFORREST *(A heavy hand on STUART's arm, as if in a surreptitious aside)* Son, *very* fine work on the Scattergood account! But—mum's the word, eh! *(Forefinger to lips)*

STUART is at once excited, eager to hear more; but manages to restrain himself.

STUART You—heard? Already?

DEFORREST *(Laying his forefinger alongside his nose, slyly)* Um—news travels fast at Crawson-Hinney-Flaux-and-Roe. *(The firm's name rattles off his lips mechanically)*

STUART But, I just handed the material in this afternoon to Mr. Hinney—

DEFORREST Hmmm mmm mmm! No business talk tonight, son! The ladies will be bored.

NICOLE has seen that STUART is aglow with pleasure, and has come to slip an arm through his: the supportive wife.

NICOLE Oh, I'm never bored! The brokerage world is fascinating.

STUART *(Not wanting the subject to slip away)* Was it Mr. Hinney who—?

MITZIE *(Gaily chiding)* DeForrest, you promised! No shoptalk tonight!

DEFORREST *(As if confidentially to STUART)* Bix and I go back a long way, son. *(Nodding)* My, yes. A long way.

MITZIE *(Wagging finger)* Now, DeForrest!

DEFORREST *(Maudlin reminiscence; a sigh)* To the pioneer-days, don't you know. *(Envisioning sign, gesturing)* When the sign out front was *Crawson-Flaux.* And we were in the old building, on Union Street.

STUART I've seen that building!

DEFORREST *(To STUART)* For now, son—mum's the word, eh!

STUART has indicated that DEFORREST sit down, which he does, heavily; MITZIE prefers to remain on her feet. STUART and NICOLE sit, a bit uneasily. (NICOLE has been taking small consoling sips of her drink.)

MITZIE Is this Fox Hollow Hills, or Fox Hills Hollow?—we were in both, tonight. *(Laughs, but with an edge)* Poor DeForrest, faced with two roads, will *invariably* choose the wrong one—

NICOLE *(Impulsive friendliness)* Oh, Stuart is like that, too—with road maps.

STUART *(Stung)* What? I most certainly am *not.*

MITZIE *(Ominously, to NICOLE)* That's how it begins, with road maps. From there, it metastasizes.

DEFORREST *(Mumbling)* Mmmm uhhh bhrragg. My, yes!

MITZIE Speak up, DeForrest!

DEFORREST Um, just to say—*very* nice. *(Indicates his drink)*

MITZIE *(Sharply)* Well, nurse it: you're not having another.

NICOLE *(Searching for a subject)* Mrs. Widmark—Mitzie—that was such a lovely dinner party at your house. Stuart and I were so grateful to be invited.

STUART My, yes!

MITZIE *(A bit coolly)* And yet, since then—silence. At this end.

NICOLE *(Apologetically)* Oh, we've been so busy—moving here.

MITZIE has conspicuously snapped open her purse (Which may be an eye-catching shade of red patent leather) to take out a piece of paper which she hands to NICOLE.

NICOLE Oh, thank you!—what?

MITZIE My recipe for *boeuf bourguignonne.* You said you wanted it.

NICOLE Oh! Oh yes. Thank you.

MITZIE You *do* cook, dear, don't you?—some of these young wives don't seem to have time.

NICOLE Oh, I do! I do.

STUART Nicole's a great cook! Terrific.

DEFORREST *(Mumbling, enthusiastically)* Mmmmsmllgdd, my yes!

STUART *(Cupping hand to ear)* Excuse me, sir?

DEFORREST *(Nodding)* Smells good! Delicious!

As NICOLE *and* STUART *exchange panicky glances,* MITZIE *snorts in derision and pats* DEFORREST *condescendingly on the cheek.*

MITZIE   Lovey, we're not invited for *dinner* here tonight. *(With an air of one hurt, yet making light of it; smiling)* Only for *drinks.*

NICOLE *(Flustered, apologetic)*   Oh, we hope—another t-time—

STUART   —when things get settled—

MITZIE *(Sniffing)*   I don't smell anything.

NICOLE   Actually there, there isn't—any dinner. I mean—

MITZIE   Just as well. You can't let the men ride roughshod over you, you know. American men have cast-iron stomachs and, you know, they can't be filled. A woman tries, her entire life, to fill just one of those stomachs, and— *(A gesture as of dropping something down a bottomless chasm)* —it's like the Grand Canyon. Can't be filled. *(Pause; more brightly)* I want a tour of this house! That's what *I* want!

STUART *and* NICOLE *rise obediently;* DEFORREST *remains sitting.*

STUART *(Quick smile)*   Of course, Mitzie!

MITZIE *(Poking* DEFORREST*)*   Lovey, c'mon! We're going on a tour of the Balls' beautiful house.

DEFORREST *wakes with a little snort, nods and murmurs with alacrity, heaves himself to his feet.*

DEFORREST   Yes, that's so! Just what I was thinking.

The BELLS *and* MITZIE *leave the family room, and* DEFORREST *trots behind. All four carry their drinks. (*NICOLE *may have unobtrusively replenished her drink.)*

DEFORREST *(Loud murmur)*   Just what I was thinking.

SCENE 4

As close to a montage as possible, as STUART *leads the others through the rooms of the house. They will end up on the outdoor deck, stage left.*

Voices may overlap considerably.

STUART   Through here—watch the steps!—the living room—here—dining room— *(Laughs)* We haven't gotten around to furnishing the house much, yet—

MITZIE   Itty-bitty steps! Do watch out, DeForrest! Oh, how spacious how lovely! My, my! On a junior executive's salary, oh *my*!

NICOLE *(Apologetically)*   What you hear is—an echo, actually—

DEFORREST *(Mumbling)*   Very nice, very!

MITZIE   An echo adds—adds, what, DeForrest?—*dignity* to a house. I *like* an echo.

STUART   Through here—now—*up* the steps! The "country" kitchen—

MITZIE   How lovely it is! And so deserving! *(Pause, corrects herself)* You are so deserving! Such an attractive young couple!

STUART   And now—up these stairs—

DEFORREST wanders in the wrong direction, MITZIE *takes his arm.*

MITZIE   This way, sweetie! We're going *upstairs.*

DEFORREST *(Mumbling)*   Quite right.

STUART   Through here—the master bedroom—

MITZIE *(Flirtatious aside to NICOLE)*   We know who's "master," don't we!

STUART   And here—adjoining—

MITZIE   —a nursery! Why, of course. *(Cooing to NICOLE)* No need to identify *this* room, is there!

STUART *(Quickly)*   And through here—watch the steps, Mr. Widmark!— our redwood deck. *My* design.

At stage left, the outdoor deck upon which the four gather.

MITZIE   Oh, what a lovely view! Is that a *lake?*

STUART *(Proudly)*   Fox Hollow Lake—"use restricted to residents."

NICOLE   Actually, it's an artificial pond. *(Pause)* Oh, but it's lovely.

DEFORREST, panting from the stairs, sits on the railing at extreme stage left.

MITZIE *(Poking him)*   DeForrest, *are* you all right? *(Mild bitterness)* The last time we had a fun evening, oh it was so long ago!—DeForrest had to ruin it all, with angina pains in his chest. So, naturally, we wound up in the emergency room of the hospital for *hours.*

NICOLE *(Concerned)*   Do you have a heart condition, Mr. Widmark?

STUART *(Overlapping)*   —a heart condition, Mr. Widmark?

MITZIE *(Sharply)*   No, he does not. *(Pokes DEFORREST, who is wheezing)* Do you, lovey?

DEFORREST   What's that?—ummm yes I *would.* *(Raises empty glass)* If you others are, I mean. *(Mumbled aside to STUART)* Very high quality Scotch, son.

MITZIE *(Pouting)*   Sometimes I think DeForrest hasn't any heart at all.

NICOLE   Oh, I think Mr. Widmark is—sweet!

MITZIE *(Jokey repartee)*   Do *you* want him, then?

NICOLE *(Taking it seriously)*   I . . . have my own.

STUART has gravitated to stand with DEFORREST and NICOLE and MITZIE are together, in the foreground.

STUART *(Pointing)*   See those birches?—our property goes that far.

DEFORREST *(Mumbling)*   Uhhmmm!

MITZIE   Your children will be so happy here! This is a dream life, dear! *(Corrects herself)* —house, I mean. Dream house.

STUART *(Calling over)*   We have no children, yet, Mrs.—Mitzie.

MITZIE *(Coquettishly)*   I'm sure you will! *(To NICOLE, in a modified voice; squeezing her hand)* With such a, um, vigorous husband, I'm sure you will.

NICOLE   We had one, once. But we let him die. *(Giggles, then hiccups)*

MITZIE *(Not seeming to hear)*   My, what a lovely necklace! Amber, is it! *(She fingers NICOLE's necklace)* I do love amber. It's so . . . true to its name.

NICOLE speaks the following as if meditating aloud, even as MITZIE continues admiring the necklace. MITZIE murmurs "Pretty! So pretty!" etc.

NICOLE   I was the one to discover him lying on his face in his crib. So still! He always woke us with his crying, never let us sleep for more than three hours at a time, so . . . when he let us sleep past six o'clock I knew something was wrong. *(Pause)* He was four months old. *(Pause, hiccups)* It was just such a . . . surprise. *(Pause)* Stuart prefers no one know, who need not know. He figures this way— *(Pause)* — the subject won't come up. *(Giggles)*

MITZIE *(Laughing)*   Oh, sorry!—I'm tickling you.

MITZIE has been fingering the amber beads, and has in fact tickled NICOLE.

NICOLE   Oh, it's all right! I'm just too sensitive.

MITZIE   *We* women are, around the breasts. *(A pause)* Mine was named Dondi. *(Forefinger to lips, with bitterness)* "Mum's the word!"

NICOLE   Donnie?—Donna?

MITZIE *(Angry zestfulness)*   "Mum's the word, eh!"

MITZIE and NICOLE look over at STUART and DEFORREST, who have been talking together.

STUART *(Speaking rapid-fire)*   Scattergood estate—such a mess!—the old widow, she—

DEFORREST *(Rapid-fire)*   —I made my name on just such an account, son—oh my yes—years ago—

STUART   —it's the God damned lawyers who—

DEFORREST   —nineteen percent capital gains, seventy-seven percent investment futures—

STUART   —Treasury refinancing—industrial average—IBM—GM—GE—

DEFORREST   —Big Board—skittish—Dow Jones—Treasury securities—

STUART   —S & E—NCNB—Trump Taj Mahal—bankrupt—

MITZIE *(To NICOLE)*   DeForrest admires your husband so much, dear! His word, you know, counts heavily—very!—with the partners.

NICOLE   That's so kind of him.

MITZIE   It seems every time I turn around DeForrest is shaking his head, marveling— *(MITZIE has raised her voice, so that the men can hear)*— "Young Ball will go far in this firm, mark my words!"

STUART and DEFORREST move to re-enter the house.

DEFORREST *(Murmur, embarrassed)*   Now, Mitzie!

MITZIE   Well, it's the truth. "Young Ball will go far in the firm. Mark my words."

As STUART and DEFORREST exit the deck, MITZIE grasps NICOLE's arm as if to steady herself.

MITZIE *(Into NICOLE's ear)*   And that's exactly how DeForrest talks, even around the house—like a pompous old fart. *Exactly.*

Lights out.

SCENE 5

The family room. NICOLE, MITZIE, DEFORREST are seated. STUART is handing around fresh drinks; then takes a seat, facing DEFORREST.

NICOLE tastes her drink, decides it isn't quite potent enough; unobtrusively rises to pour a little more gin into it. As STUART glances over at her, NICOLE smiles and nods, a finger to her lips as if to indicate there's no problem.

This action occurs simultaneously with MITZIE's and DEFORREST's lines.

MITZIE *(Sipping)*   This is the most . . . potent . . . Bloody Mary of my life! Mmmm thank you, "Young Ball." *(Drunken flirtatious giggle)*

DEFORREST *(Mumbling)*   Nnnnyp'zent u'verse d'kmttr . . .

MITZIE   Lovey, speak *up.*

DEFORREST *(Clearing throat loudly)*   Ninety percent of the universe is "dark matter" . . . invisible . . . and you can't prove it's *there. (Emphatically; we realize he is mildly drunk)* Even the astapyzz— astapyzzists—astrophiacists—

MITZIE   As tro phy si cists.

DEFORREST *(Quick mumble)* Astapyzzists—*(At normal pace, raised voice)* —don't know what the hell it *is*. *(Nods emphatically as if he has made a point; drinks)*

STUART *(Boyish enthusiasm, leaning forward with elbows on knees)* No, it's ninety percent of all animal species that have ever lived on earth, that are now extinct. I wonder if that's what you mean, Mr. Widmark?

DEFORREST *(Not at all fazed, to our surprise)* Ninety-*nine* percent of all animal species, son. My, yes! A grim statistic, eh! *(Eloquent, ominous)* God tries a little of this creature, a little of that creature, then He loses interest, and—pouf! *(Bells out his cheeks like the God of the Winter Wind in the old engravings)* Gone! *(Condescending chuckle to STUART)* That's what I mean, son.

DEFORREST has spoken so commandingly, there is a moment's pause. NICOLE is particularly startled.

NICOLE *(Grasping drink with both hands, halfway to mouth)* Oh! Ninety-*nine* percent! *(Shivering, a nervous giggle as she glances down at herself, and at the others)* There's not many of us . . . left.

MITZIE *(Sharply, as if jealous of DEFORREST)* It's just a silly old *statistic*. *(Aside to NICOLE)* He gets those things from *Reader's Digest*.

STUART *(Still the bright schoolboy)* O.K., Mr. Widmark, but—

DEFORREST *(Leaning over to slap STUART's knee)* Nah! "DeForrest" is the name, son! I hope we're on a first-name footing by now! *(Extravagantly)* The hell with "Widmark," eh?—the old fart!

When NICOLE and MITZIE express feminine surprise at this waggish remark, DEFORREST grins, winks lewdly at them.

DEFORREST Eh? Hell with the old fart, eh? *(Hearty laughter)*

STUART *(Trying a new tack)* Sir—DeForrest, I mean—what do you think of our Gulf War strategy?

DEFORREST *(Growing excited)* The United States should use its firepower and bomb Iraq flat—broil Sudan Hassum in his bunker, by God!—he's the aggressor. Move right on into Iran, next—the "Holy Shi-its"—*(Laughs)*—as we should have done, long ago.

STUART *(Playing devil's advocate)* You don't have much faith in sanctions, I guess?

DEFORREST Sanctions only work with civilized men! Try sanctions on Hitler, eh! Those *Holy Shi-its* they want *our* hides, so bomb 'em flat! Teach 'em a lesson! *(Glancing at the women for approval, but NICOLE and MITZIE sit frozen-faced)*

STUART *(Chuckling)* D'ja see how fast the Democrats came around— Congress almost vetoed the war—now, we're winning, and looking pretty damn good, and—

DEFORREST   George Bush is an old C. I. A. hand—"strike first, ask questions afterward"—yessir! Knows how to get the job done.

STUART   I'm just afraid we'll pull back too soon—like in Vietnam.

DEFORREST   Son, we never used our firepower in Vietnam. That's the tragedy. By God, you pay your taxes and there's trillions of dollars going into defense hardware and not one percent of it ever gets used!

STUART   That's what Mr. Flaux was saying the other day at lunch—

DEFORREST   *(Different tone)* Flaux?—lunch? *(A pause, then reverts to bluster)* Well, I say it too: not one percent of our military might ever gets deployed. Money down a rathole.

STUART   Saddam Hussein—you can be sure *he'd* use all the nuclear weapons he could, if he had them.

DEFORREST   And there's that other Hussun—Husine—a pack of 'em named Hassad or Assad or Asshole in—is it Libya? Lebanon? Syria?— thumbing their noses at the U.S. Reagan knew how to deal with Colonel what's-his-name Queerdafi—blew up his son—yessir!—that got the Colonel's attention, eh! *(Wipes face; points to TV)* Whyn't you turn the TV on, son—might as well check in on the war.

STUART rises enthusiastically, but NICOLE protests.

NICOLE   Oh no, wait, Stuart, please! *(As everyone stares)* I . . . have something to say, and I . . . *(Long pause)* The war upsets me.

MITZIE   *(Now quite drunk, vehement)* All a war *is* is damn fool men shooting one another and it's boring as *hell.*

DEFORREST   *(Shocked)* Why, Mitzie!

MITZIE   *(Contemptuously)* They call the weapons by different names, that's all. And *they* have different names . . . 'cause it's a different war. That's *all.*

STUART   But, Mrs. Widmark—

MITZIE   Fuck "Mizzuz Widmark!"

DEFORREST   Mitzie, you can't let a madman like this Hussine run rampage over the white world for God's sake can you?—eh? *(Seems genuinely upset)*

MITZIE   *(Laughing)* Me? What the hell do I have to do with it? What have *you* got to do with it? Sit on your backside flicking through the channels watching TV? That's *your* war!

DEFORREST   *(Setting down drink, overturning glass)* Mitzie, we are leaving. Right now.

MITZIE   Oh no you don't! *I* have something to say, and I wish to say it before witnesses.

DEFORREST   Mitzie, what?

MITZIE   *(Furious, tearful, pointing at DEFORREST, appealing to the BELLS)* He!—him!—this one!—won't let me talk about Dondi. He visited

Dondi's grave *once*. He doesn't give a damn about Dondi!

DEFORREST protests ("Mitzie!" "Mitzie, please!") but MITZIE continues with her accusations unhesitatingly.

MITZIE The poor darling needed a second dialysis to rid his blood of toxins—his poor kidneys were *seventy-eight percent deteriorated!*— and this selfish old man said it cost too much and he let Dondi die and now he refuses to talk about him and—*(As DEFORREST tries to take hold of her arm, savagely)* Don't you touch me, you! *(Slaps him away)* You just don't care. All you care about is stuffing your belly, and hiding in the top-floor men's room to pick up gossip, and I hate you, I hate you and I always did. So there!

MITZIE has lurched to her feet. This is her "scene" and she means to play it to the hilt. DEFORREST struggles to stand, but MITZIE shoves him back down; he sits heavily.

MITZIE Murderer!

DEFORREST Mitzie, please! Darling! You know you don't mean it!

MITZIE I know I *do*. Nasty old hypocrite, I know I *do*.

DEFORREST I . . . miss Dondi too. I loved him too . . .

MITZIE You did not you did not you never did! Hypocrite!

DEFORREST Mitzie, Dondi was only a dog—

MITZIE *(Near-hysterical)* Dondi was not "only a dog!" How dare you! You bastard! What are you—"only a man?" Oh, don't touch me, you—pervert!

DEFORREST Mitzie—

MITZIE As soon as the poor darling died, you—

DEFORREST Mitzie, control yourself—

MITZIE —flushed him from your heart! Oh yes you *did*! *(To NICOLE)* Beware, dear! Oh, beware!

DEFORREST *(To the BELLS, who sit astonished)* Don't pay any attention to Mitzie, don't you know! The poor woman has been under such a strain—

MITZIE Murderer! How do you dare! *(Pause; glances around)* Oh! that echo!

They all listen. Silence.

MITZIE *(Clamping hands over ears)* It's everywhere! *(Teetering in her high heels, MITZIE rushes weeping from the room)*

DEFORREST *(Following after, agitated)* Excuse us, please! We aren't ourselves tonight! Goodnight!—MITZIE!

Through this exchange, NICOLE and STUART have been sitting simply staring.

MITZIE's *red purse has been left behind on the floor, but neither notices.*

STUART *(On his feet)* Mr. Widmark, sir—DeForrest! Mitzie! Thank you for coming! Goodnight!

NICOLE *(On her feet)* Mrs. Widmark—Mitzie—thank you for the recipe!

Lights out.

SCENE 6

Immediately following. NICOLE *and* STUART *are returning, having seen the* WIDMARKS *drive away.* STUART *has an arm around* NICOLE's *shoulders and is leading her back.* NICOLE *wipes at her eyes.*

STUART Don't apologize, sweetie, because there's no need. It was a blunder, it happened. It won't happen again.

NICOLE *nods mutely; eases away from him, and, under cover of tidying up, drains not only her own drink but the remains of* MITZIE's *Bloody Mary.*

STUART *(Not noticing)* Nicole, don't ever say *anything* about this to *anyone!*—not even that those pathetic people were here. *(Pause, shakes head)* Old "Kiss-of-Death" Widmark! I'd be mortified if anyone from the office knew we'd, um, been seeing them socially.

NICOLE, *her back to* STUART, *draining a glass, makes no reply.*

STUART *too drains a glass, quickly. Begins to laugh, recounting the incident; pointing to the seats* MITZIE *and* DEFORREST *had been in for their scene. We see how* STUART *accommodates "emotion"—by reinventing it as anecdotal, comic.*

STUART *She* said—"I wish to say it before witnesses." *He* said—"Only a dog"— *(Laughing)* Then he tried to touch her— Then she—"Only a man" *(Slaps thigh)* "PERVERT!"

NICOLE *hides her face in her hands.*

STUART *(Milking the scene, now a bit crudely)* "Bastard!" "Pervert!" "Murderer!" *(Cupping mouth, parody of* DEFORREST*)* "MIT-ZI!"

STUART *snorts with laughter. Then ceases, abruptly. Silence.*

NICOLE *removes her hands from her face. She appears composed.*

STUART Well. It won't happen again. Will it?

NICOLE *(Quietly)*   Nothing can happen more than once.

STUART *stares at* NICOLE. *He draws his thumb slowly across his lower lip, as if considering. Then, suddenly, he is the amorous husband. He hugs her from behind, arms beneath her breasts; nuzzling her throat.*

STUART   I told you those amber beads would do the trick, eh? So sort of *daughterly. (Fingering beads, and* NICOLE'S *breasts)* Oops!—are we ticklish?

NICOLE *(As if frightened)*   No—stop. *(Pushes him away)*

STUART   Don't be silly. *(Tickles her)* Honeybunch—

NICOLE *(Breathless, wrenching away)*   Stuart, I . . . have something to say.

STUART *(Parodying* MITZIE*)*   "Before witnesses!" *(Pause)* Can't it wait? Let's have dinner, I'm fam-ished.

NICOLE   I've been . . . wanting to tell you.

STUART *(Interrupting)*   Not to be critical, honey, but, y'know, you should have set out *hors d'oeuvres* for our guests. Shrimp-n-dip, veggie platter, salted cashews. Sure it was only the Widmarks but it might have been the Whitbecks, or the Witkes. *(Deep breath)* Or, one day, the Hinneys.

NICOLE   Stuart, I . . . love you. But I—

STUART *(A sort of aggressive boyish enthusiasm)*   God, I love *you*. Honey, I hope you know that. That's the bottom line. *(Pause)*

NICOLE   But I need to—

STUART *(Quickly)*   We're, like, in this together. For the long run. We have a, a past . . . and, uh, a . . . future. *(Seems doubtful)* It's just right now . . . "the present" . . . *(Feeble laugh)* . . . that's a little tricky. *(Pause)*

NICOLE   You laughed at them. Why did you laugh at them. *(Flat, accusing)*

STUART   Huh? Who? —Oh, them. *(Laughs harshly)* Because they're pathetic. I mean, funny. *(Pause)* I *didn't* laugh at them—while they were here. *(Pause)* You laughed, too.

Silence.

NICOLE *(Moving away from him)*   Stuart, I . . . haven't gone to the Mall, actually. I drive to the edge of the parking lot, I sit in the car . . . I cry. And . . . then I come home.

STUART *(Stoically)*   I figured as much. The pills don't help, huh?

NICOLE *(Sharply)*   They're for *sleeping*, not *shopping*.

STUART   Maybe the doctor could prescribe some—estrogen? *(Corrects himself)* Amphetamine?

NICOLE   The problem lies . . . deeper.

STUART *(With distaste)*   Ulcers? *Cysts?*

NICOLE   I . . . don't think I can continue.

STUART   Yes, well—don't push yourself. *(Has moved after her, but awkwardly; as if fearfully)*

NICOLE   I said I can't *continue.*

STUART   We'll, uh, go out to dinner, then. Terrific! There's this new seafood place on Route 1—

NICOLE   *(Hands over ears, looking around)*   Oh! the echo—

STUART   Echo—?

Silence.

STUART   That's—silence.

NICOLE   The echo of silence.

NICOLE *has noticed* MITZIE's *red purse, which has been conspicuous to the audience, but out of the line of vision of the* BELLS, *on the floor beside a chair. She picks it up.*

NICOLE   *(Holding the purse aloft, examining it oddly)*   I'll take this over to her tomorrow.

STUART   Damn! We can mail it.

NICOLE   *(Firmly)*   I'll take it. Tomorrow.

STUART   *(Not wanting a confrontation)*   Well. *(Tries to revive his earlier comic mood, but fails)* "You did not you did not you *never* did!"

NICOLE   And . . . another thing.

STUART   *(Uneasy)*   Oh geez honey, I'm starved . . . *(Boyish laugh)* You know, me and my "cast-iron stomach."

NICOLE *comes slowly forward, holding* MITZIE's *purse; preparing to deliver her much-anticipated speech. But she has not the courage; or, perhaps, does not want to wound* STUART. *So she delivers her substitute lines with displaced anger, even rage, even as she offers the confession as a comic anecdote of "feminine" charm. Her attitude is, "Can you believe this of me? Do you think this is me? If so—here I am." By the end of the little speech she should be communicating a suppressed fury totally at odds with the innocuous contents of the speech.*

NICOLE   Our dinners you say you love . . .

STUART   Why, sure I do!

NICOLE   *(Raising her voice)*   . . . I buy them, secretly, at the Fair Haven Food Emporium. And, in secret, in the privacy of my kitchen with its gleaming luxury appliances, I add ingredients—to make them mine. *(A pause, to allow the significance of this "weighty" revelation to sink in)* Water chestnuts. Tricolored pasta. Tiny asparagus. Extra saffron. *(Pause)* And then, sometimes . . . oh, this is so neurotic! . . . I *panic* Stuart. I *panic.* And try to take the ingredients out, if I can. With a spoon—a sieve. Hoping that you, my husband, won't notice. *(Savage satisfaction)*

STUART *(Choosing to react as a boyish-amorous husband, missing her irony)* Aw honey, I knew, I guess.

NICOLE You knew? All along?

STUART I could tell, sort of. Like, water chestnuts in *coq au vin,* five or six little pasta curls in veal shank risotti . . . And all the aluminum trays and pans squashed flat in the trash can . . .

NICOLE And you . . . forgive me?

STUART Honey, I *love* you.

NICOLE Well. I feel so . . . forgiven.

A pause.

STUART *(Almost shyly)* Maybe we could . . . try again?

NICOLE *(Ironically)* Try again? With the Widmarks? Oh no—the Whitbecks.

STUART slips his arm around NICOLE's shoulders. He takes MITZIE's purse from her and sets it down on a table.

STUART I wasn't thinking of them . . .

NICOLE The Hinneys?

STUART No, not the Hinneys. *(Pause)* Not just yet.

NICOLE Until we get some furniture. Decent carpeting. The echo eradicated.

STUART Yes. Until then. *(Walking NICOLE slowly out of the room, reverts to mimicry, "humor")* She said, "I hate you and I always did!" *He* said, "Mitzie, only a dog!" *(Laughter)* "Pervert!" "Murderer!" *(Laughter)*

A pause before they exit.

STUART *(A sober voice)* Wonder what kind of breed it was.

NICOLE I'll ask.

Lights out as they exit.

THE END

NEGATIVE ❦
A Play in One Act

Cast

MARY—a young Caucasian woman
VERONICA—a young black woman

Setting

The room is sparely furnished: two beds at opposite corners, two desks (one near a window), lamps, chairs, bureaus, a mirror; two closets, doors shut. Clothes have been laid in neat piles across suitcases and cartons of books, shoes, etc., in the center of the room. VERONICA's possessions are considerably more lavish than MARY's; included is a hefty trunk.

In this encounter, racial stereotypes are reversed, as in a photograph negative. The mood and pacing should suggest a comedy of which the participants are unaware.

Lights up. MARY *has just entered the college dormitory room she will be sharing with another freshman woman. She is moderately attractive and modestly dressed; may wear glasses; wears a yellow freshman beanie and a shiny yellow identification button with HI! in black letters.*

MARY *(A naive, childlike tone)* So—this is it! At last! My freshman room! Oh God I'm so excited I can't stand it! The college of my choice—my dreams! And I'm here on a scholarship—*they want me*! *(Pause, hugs herself)* For months I've been dreaming of this moment and now I'm here—alone. My roommate's been here—and gone out again—we haven't met—my folks are driving back to Davenport and I'm—here—alone. *(A touch of panic)* For the first time in my life I will be—*living away from home.* A thousand miles away where no one knows me. Gosh, I'm scared. *(Thumb to mouth)* Oh Mom!—Mommy! Daddy!—come back! *(Pause)* No. I am not scared. I am Mary Strep, Class of 1998. Whooeee! *(Tiptoes over to examine her roommate's things.)* Oh, God!—my roommate must be rich. *(Holds a stylish leather mini-skirt against herself; stares into mirror)* Wow. *(Holds up a dressier costume; sighs)* Oh!—so *pretty.* *(She discovers a framed photograph of* VERONICA *and her family which she stares at, appalled.)* Oh!—oh *no.* Oh *no.* The college has matched me with one of *them.*

VERONICA *strides into the room with a dazzling smile. Very attractive, self-assured. She too is wearing a freshman beanie but wears it with style; also a tight, colorful college T-shirt, an eye-catching skirt. The HI! button is prominent on her breast.*

A beat as MARY *and* VERONICA *stare at each other.*

VERONICA *(Recovering first, exuding "personality")* Well, hi! I'm Veronica Scott, your roommate!
MARY Oh!—h-hi! *(She has almost dropped the photograph; stammers*

guiltily) I was j-just admiring your f-family—

VERONICA *(Warmly extending her hand to shake MARY's)*   Please call me "Ronnie"—all my friends do.

MARY *(Shyly and awkwardly shaking hands, as if it's a new thing for her)* "R-Ronnie"—

VERONICA   "Veronica" is a nice enough name but far too formal, don't you think? *I* believe in informality.

MARY *(Nervous)*   Oh, yes—

VERONICA   *I* believe in egalitarianism.

MARY   "Egali—?" Oh, yes—

VERONICA   And what is *your* name?

MARY   *My* n-name?

VERONICA   Maybe it's on your name tag?

MARY *(Squinting down at the button)*   Oh yes—"Mary Strep."

VERONICA   "Mary Step."

MARY   "Strep."

VERONICA   "Step?"—that's what I said.

MARY   *"Strep."*

VERONICA   With your accent I'm having trouble hearing it. "Mary *Strep*"—?

MARY   Yes.

VERONICA   Hmmm!—"Mary Strep." I *like* it.

MARY *(Faintly incredulous)*   You do?

VERONICA   Oh, yes! You don't hear many names like that. So—exotic. Musical. Is it a name with a legend?

MARY   I guess it's just a, a—name. Like in the telephone directory.

VERONICA   Oooooh no it isn't just a *name,* it's a—an *aura.* It has its own history, I bet.

MARY   My mother's name is "Mary," and so is my grandmother's— "Mary." Back through my father's family everybody is named "Strep."

VERONICA *(Wide-eyed)*   Ooooh see what I mean!

MARY *(A bit too eagerly)*   People call me "Mary"—for short.

VERONICA   Fascinating! And where are all these people?

MARY   Huh?

VERONICA   Sorry, I mean where are you from, Mary?

MARY   Davenport, Iowa.

VERONICA   Ooooh no! You aren't! *(Enunciates words sensuously)* "Davenport, Iowa!"

MARY   What's wrong?

VERONICA   Nothing's *wrong,* it's just you're the first person from Davenport, Iowa, I've ever met.

MARY   Gosh, I'm sorry . . .

VERONICA   Oh, no—it's *fabulous*. "Davenport, Iowa." Such a whole-some *cereal*-sounding kind of place! *(Pause, sighs)* I'm from Green-wich, Connecticut: quintessence of American Suburbia.

MARY   "Greenwich, Connecticut"—I've heard of it, I think. It sounds beautiful. So—green?

VERONICA   And where did you go to high school, Mary?

MARY *(Surprised)*   In Davenport, Iowa.

VERONICA   Oh—there's a school there?

MARY *(Puzzled)*   Sure. Davenport High School.

VERONICA *(Catching on)*   Oh, I see!—public school. You went to public school—of course.

MARY   Where—did you go?

VERONICA *(Airily)*   Oh, Exeter. Eight members of our graduating class are here as freshmen; must be twenty-five Exeter grads on campus. Can't escape us!

MARY   Exeter must be an—exclusive school?

VERONICA   Oooooh no! Not really. We had lots of scholarship students. Exeter is racially mixed, and balanced; two of my closest friends—*and* a roommate, junior year—were white girls. Really.

MARY   That's . . . nice.

VERONICA *(Proudly)*   The president of our senior class was a white boy.

MARY   Oh that's . . . nice.

VERONICA   *And* he was gay; *and* he had psoriasis. We all loved him.

MARY   . . . nice . . .

VERONICA   At least, *he's* not here. *(Pause; rubbing hands together briskly)* Well! Which corner of the room would you prefer, Mary? I was here earlier but I deliberately didn't choose, I thought I'd leave the choice to you.

MARY   To me?

VERONICA   Why, yes!—to you. That corner has the window, and that corner has the, um, corner.

MARY *(Shyly)*   Gosh, I—just don't know.

VERONICA   A view of the bell tower and the historic green where a cli-mactic battle of the Revolutionary War was fought—or a view of the, um, corner?

MARY *(Very hesitantly pointing toward the window)*   Well—maybe—if you don't m-mind—

VERONICA   My, thanks! *(As if MARY has pointed in the reverse direction, VERONICA takes the bed near the window; she speaks sincerely)* Now you're sure, Mary? You don't mind not having the view, or any natu-ral light?

MARY *(Swallowing)*   I guess not . . . Veronica.

VERONICA *(Shaking forefinger, big smile)*   Now, now—"Ronnie!"

MARY   "R-Ronnie."

VERONICA   I'll call you "Mary,"—I *adore* that name!—if you'll call me "Ronnie." *(Places a quilted spread on her bed as if to claim it)* Now: the closets. Which is your preference, Mary?

MARY *(Squinting and groping about)*   It's sort of . . . dark . . . over here. I don't see a closet.

VERONICA   The big, spacious one is back beyond your desk; the absurdly cramped one is over here by mine. But please feel free to choose whichever you wish.

MARY   Oh, now I see it! *(Opens closet door)* Gee, it *is* spacious.

VERONICA   Obviously, I have many more clothes and suitcases than you do, Mary, but—it's your choice.

MARY *(Apologetically)*   It probably makes sense for me to take this one, Ronnie, doesn't it?—since it's—

VERONICA *(Sharply)*   What'd you call me, girl?

MARY   "R-Ronnie"—

VERONICA   Oh, right—I guess I told you to call me "Ronnie." *(Slightly forced smile)* If we're going to be roommates I suppose it's best to be—informal. *(Tapping foot impatiently)* Take your time choosing, Mary. We've got all afternoon.

MARY *(Shyly)*   Well, like I said it probably makes sense for me to take this closet, since it's right beside my—

VERONICA *(Now a sincere dazzling smile)*   Oh, that's sweet of you, Mary!—thanks.

Again VERONICA behaves as if MARY has said exactly the reverse of what she has said. VERONICA begins to hang up her clothes in the larger closet; MARY has no choice but to hang up her clothes in the other closet.

VERONICA   We'll have dinner together, Mary, O.K.? You can join me and my friends from Exeter—and these really cool guys I just met. Unless you have other plans?

MARY *(Quickly)*   Oh no, no—I don't know anyone here. It's such a big place and I—I don't know anyone here.

VERONICA *(Squeezing MARY's hand)*   Well, you know *me*.

As MARY goes to hang up a dress, VERONICA pauses to admire it effusively. It is a quite ordinary plaid wool dress with a white bow, white cuffs.

VERONICA   Ooooh! What is *this*?

MARY *(Shyly)*   My good wool dress . . .

VERONICA   Where'd you find such a style?

MARY   My grandma sewed it for me. For my eighteenth birthday just two weeks ago.

VERONICA   No! Your grandmother *sewed* this?— *(Making a sewing gesture as if plying a needle)* —by *hand?*

MARY   Oh, no, Grandma uses a sewing machine—a Singer. She's had the same identical machine since 1938.

VERONICA   No! You don't say!

MARY   Grandma sewed my senior prom gown, too—sixty yards of pink taffeta and chiffon; and strapless! *(A bit daringly)*

VERONICA   *My* grandmothers, they insist we grandchildren call them "Meredith" and "Tracey"—their first names. They look young as my mother. *(Laughs)* They'd as soon run a sewing machine as a—butter churn. I'm envious! *(Holding* MARY's *dress against herself, admiring)*

MARY   *(Proudly)*   Actually, Grandma sews all my clothes. She sewed these. *(Indicating the nondescript outfit she is wearing.)*

VERONICA   Isn't that sweet! Soooo caring! Must be a folkway, or something? In Indiana?

MARY   *(Shyly)*   What's a—folkway?

VERONICA   *(Airily intellectual)*   Oh, just some species of unexamined ethnic, religious, or regional custom aborigines persist in practicing over the centuries without a clue as to *why.* Claude Levi-Strauss is still the most insightful analyst of the phenomenon. *(Preening before mirror)* You see, Mary, when you wear this, um, most original dress your grandmother sewed for you, you feel *happy* because you feel *loved.* That's a folkway.

MARY   Oh. *(Wipes at eyes)* Gosh, I'm going to m-miss Grandma—so far away!

VERONICA   You see?—emotion of a primitive, visceral, binding nature is generated out of, um, not much. *(Examining dress, turns a sleeve roughly inside out)* How's this sewed together?—oh! *(She has ripped a seam)*

MARY   *(Recoiling as if feeling pain)*   Oh!

VERONICA   *(Sincerely)*   Gee, I'm sorry, Mary.

MARY tries to take the dress from VERONICA, *but* VERONICA *retains it.*

MARY   *(Childlike, accusing)*   You ripped the seam, Veronica . . .

VERONICA   It was an accident, Mary. I said I was sorry.

MARY   You *tugged* at it, I saw you.

VERONICA   I did not *tug,* I was just *looking.* The thread is rotted—see? *(Tugs slightly, and another seam rips)* That's the cause.

MARY   *(Pain)*   Oh! Grandma!—

MARY takes the dress from VERONICA, *staggering to her side of the room; contemplates the dress; hangs it in the closet.*

VERONICA *has located a camera amid her possessions, and approaches* MARY.

VERONICA Mary?—turn here!

MARY *turns, and* VERONICA *takes a quick flash photo.*

VERONICA Thanks, Mary! That's cool.

MARY *(A bit blinded)* W-What did you do that for?

VERONICA *(A bit evasively)* Um—just wanted to. I'm sentimental. This being our first day together, and all. *(Pause, warmly)* Mary, I know! I'll have your dress mended by this wonderful French seamstress who sews my Momma's clothes. She can replace all that rotted old thread with new. And, um, maybe straighten the hemline . . .

MARY *(Quickly)* No, thanks—I'll take the dress home at Thanksgiving, and Grandma can mend it herself. She'd want to.

VERONICA I just hope these quaint old Midwestern folkways don't die out before Thanksgiving!

MARY *(Coolly)* If you mean my Grandma Crockett, she's only eighty-three years old. *Her* mother is still alive and going strong with *her* Singer sewing machine—*(Proudly)* —at the age of one hundred and one.

VERONICA *(Genuinely amazed)* No! You actually have a great-grand-mother, Mary?—one hundred one years old?

MARY Great-grandma Quantril is my *younger* great-grandmother, in fact.

VERONICA Ooooh! I just have to record this! *(She has located a tape recorder amid her possessions; slips in a cassette, sets the machine going)* You say, Mary, you have *two* great-grandmothers?—and how many grandmothers?

MARY *(Staring at recorder)* W-What is that?

VERONICA Oh, probably you don't have these in Indiana—don't pay the slightest heed.

MARY You're—recording what I say? R-right now?

VERONICA No, no it's nothing! Don't mind *me.*

MARY But—

VERONICA Just a little hobby of mine. Like say a guy calls me, I have the recorder hooked up to the phone, I set it going—for fun.

MARY But it makes me n-nervous, Veronica. I wish you'd turn it off.

VERONICA I said—never mind *me, you're* the fascinating one of the two of us, Mary. Rich archival lore! *(Mysteriously)* I see I have much, much to learn this freshman year. Now, about the grandmothers—

MARY *(A bit stiffly)* I'd rather not discuss my grandmothers any more right now, thanks. "Ronnie."

VERONICA Oh, but think of those old pioneer women out there on the great cereal plains of America—*sewing away.* Gives me the shivers!

MARY   Actually . . . Davenport is a city.

VERONICA   "Davenport"—what's that?

MARY   Where I'm from—Davenport, Ohio. I mean—Iowa. It's a city, not a cereal field. *(A bit boastful)* We have a population of over one hundred thousand.

VERONICA *(Skeptical)*   People?

MARY   Yes . . .

VERONICA *(Catching on)*   Oh, you mean *white* people.

MARY *(Noticing tape recorder)*   Gosh, is that thing still *on*?

VERONICA   No! *(Pretends to be switching the recorder off)* There we are: off. *(Teasing)* My, we're a little thin-skinned, Mary, aren't we? That's how Davenportians *are*?

MARY   I'm s-sorry, it just makes me n-nervous—

VERONICA   You know, Mary, your accent is so *interesting*. I've never heard one quite like it before.

MARY   My accent?

VERONICA *(Laughs)*   Hear? The way you say "accent" . . .

MARY   How is it supposed to sound?

VERONICA *(An English intonation)*   "Ac-cent."

MARY *(Nasal)*   "Ac-cent." "Ac-cent."

VERONICA tries to hide her laughter.

MARY *(Hurt)*   What's so f-funny?

VERONICA   Not a thing. I *adore* the way you talk, Mary!

MARY *(Perplexed)*   Up until a few days ago, when we left home to drive East, I never had the slightest accent. Nobody did! I don't know how on earth I got one *here*.

VERONICA *(Hands to mouth but snorting with laughter)*   Oh! There you go again!

MARY   What? What?

VERONICA squeals with laughter as if she's being tickled; then forces herself to become sober.

VERONICA   Mary, look: America is a mosaic of many, many different ways of speech—local customs—"ac-cents"— *(She cruelly imitates MARY's "accent")*—it's a democracy and *we're all equal*.

MARY   We are?

VERONICA stifles laughter again.

MARY *(Miserably)*   Everybody's going to laugh at me here—I know it. My professors, my classmates, my r-roommate—In my dreams, all summer, I'd hear strangers laughing at me—but I didn't know *why*.

VERONICA *(Practicably)*   Well, now you know. That's a gain.

MARY   Maybe you could h-help me, Ronnie? I could learn to talk like you?

VERONICA *(Graciously)*   I have no objections if you try to model yourself after me, certainly. My little, um, white-girl roommate at Exeter tried that, too. It was such *fun.*

MARY   What happened?

VERONICA   Oh, I don't know. We were just roommates a few weeks before she, um, dropped out of school. Vanished without a trace.

MARY *(Grimly)*   That's what I'm afraid of. Scared to death. I'll fail my subjects—drop out—vanish without a trace. Oh gosh-golly!

VERONICA *(Enunciating in the direction of the recorder)*   "Gosh-golly!"

MARY *(Upset)*   Is that recorder-thing still *on?*

VERONICA   It is *not.* I told you I turned it off, didn't I?

MARY   Why is this little wheel still going round?

VERONICA   It's unwinding. Re*lax,* Mary.

MARY would turn back to continue unpacking, but VERONICA detains her. An initial shyness, or a pretense of shyness, on VERONICA's part.

VERONICA   Oh, er . . . Mary? Now we've, um, gotten to know each other so well . . . can I ask you something personal?

MARY *(Guardedly)*   What?

VERONICA   Your hair.

MARY *(Touching hair, alarmed)*   My hair? That's a question?

VERONICA   Promise, now, you won't be miffed?—you're kind of thin-skinned, I've discovered.

MARY   I won't . . . be miffed.

VERONICA   Promise!

MARY *(With dread)*   I promise.

VERONICA   I've always wanted to ask one of you: is your hair naturally that way?

MARY   What way?

VERONICA   Or do you do something to it?

MARY   How—is it?

VERONICA touches MARY's hair with cautious fingers; her expression is one of someone touching an insect.

VERONICA   So sort of—fine. Dry. Ooooh!—sort of *shivery.*

MARY *(Backing off)*   I d-don't do anything to my hair except shampoo it.

VERONICA   Don't you brush it? Comb it?

MARY *(Hotly)*   Of course I brush and comb it! I just don't think about it.

VERONICA *(Faint protest)*   But your hair is—lovely, Mary. It suits *you* perfectly.

MARY   I—I'd better finish packing, I mean unpacking . . . *(Fumblingly returns to her things)*

VERONICA *(Cheerfully)* I'd better finish unpacking. We have a date for dinner, remember?—a big table of us. You'll love my friends, Mary. And I know they'll be crazy about you. *(Pause)*

MARY *is so rattled she drops something;* VERONICA *doesn't notice.*

VERONICA And these two guys I just met—are they *cool.*

MARY *and* VERONICA *are busily hanging up clothes, unpacking suitcases and boxes, etc.*

MARY *(Worried)* These guys, um—are they?—
VERONICA Seniors. Real hunks!
MARY Are they, er—?
VERONICA Good-looking? You bet!
MARY I mean, um—
VERONICA Tall? For sure. *I* don't go out with dwarfs!
MARY *(Miserably nervous)* I, er, was wondering what—r-r-race—
VERONICA *(Surprised)* "Race"—?
MARY I mean, you know—what c-c-color—their skin—
VERONICA "Color?"—"skin?" *(A beat.)* I didn't notice.
MARY Oh.
VERONICA I never notice such superfluities. Race—skin—color: America is a *mosaic,* we're all absolutely *equal,* we're beyond primitive divisions of *us* and *them.*
MARY Yes, but I—I get n-nervous, if— I mean, I don't feel comfortable if— I had this feeling, when my folks and I crossed the quad, and came into the dorm here—p-people were watching us.
VERONICA What kind of people?
MARY The, uh—majority people. *Your* people.
VERONICA Mary, that isn't so! Why'd anybody look at *you?* *(Pause, embarrassed)* Oh, um—I didn't mean that the way it sounded. I just meant—people like you are one hundred percent welcome here—this college has been integrated since 1978! Wasn't that a rousing speech the Chancellor gave this morning?—"Giving a Boost to The Needy." And you "Deficiency Scholars" aren't tagged in any obvious way; it's almost as if you scored high SATs and your folks can pay full tuition like the rest of us. Really.
MARY *(Thumb to mouth)* R-Really?
VERONICA Roommates are warned—I mean, notified—but only so we can help tutor you, if necessary. *I* volunteered to room with one of you, for that purpose.
MARY Gee, you did?
VERONICA Well, it fits in with my Freshman Honors Seminar thesis.
MARY *(Stunned)* You've chosen your topic already? What is it?

VERONICA   Um . . . a photo-journal account. Kind of a personal diary. With anthropological and psychological dimensions, of course.

MARY   You're going to write about . . . me?

VERONICA   Oh no, oh no!—don't be silly, Mary. Not *you*. Not you *personally*.

MARY   Now I feel kind of . . . funny.

VERONICA   Well, you wouldn't, if you didn't take everything so personally! *(Pause)* Just be yourself. Be your natural self. That's *my* philosophy of life.

MARY *(Swallowing hard)*   "Just be yourself." I'll try, Ver-, "Ronnie." Can I model myself after you?

VERONICA   Oooooh is that sweet! *(Gives MARY a quick kiss on the cheek, which quite dazes MARY)* But you should just be *you*, if you know who that is. That's what growing up in America in these enlightened times is all about.

MARY and VERONICA continue unpacking, etc. VERONICA removes her beanie and tosses it onto her bed; MARY, watching her, imitates her—but MARY's beanie misses her bed. VERONICA whistles and moves to suggestive dance music; MARY imitates her, unable to do more than hiss, and moving about most clumsily.

VERONICA   Um—Mary?

MARY *(Eager, yet in dread)*   Y-Yes, "Ronnie?"

VERONICA   Could you do me a favor and carry this trunk downstairs to the storage room?

A beat.

VERONICA *(Radiant smile)*   I'll be happy to pay you, of course!

MARY *(Stunned)*   N-Now?

VERONICA   Well, before dinner. Is five dollars enough?

MARY   I . . .

VERONICA   Ten dollars?

MARY   But I . . .

VERONICA locates her wallet, takes out a ten-dollar bill, lays it on MARY's desk with a flourish.

VERONICA   Thanks so much, Mary. I *appreciate* it. *(Pause)* These suitcases, now—hmmm!—maybe they can fit into your closet?

MARY   S-Suitcases? Gosh, I don't think so—

VERONICA *(Peering into MARY's closet, shoving clothes on hangers roughly aside)*   Well, we can *try*. C'mon, help me. *(VERONICA and MARY push several of VERONICA's suitcases into the closet)* Tight fit, but it's O.K. Thanks!

Some of MARY's *shoes have been forced out of the closet;* MARY, *not know-ing what to do with them, puts them beneath her bed.* VERONICA *is unnoticing.*

MARY *(Plaintively)* But, Veronica, here are my own s-suitcases—

VERONICA You can take them down to the storage with you, along with my trunk. They're made of cardboard, not leather—they won't scratch. What's the problem? *(Seems genuinely puzzled)*

MARY *covers her face with her hands. During this speech of* VERONICA's *she goes into a trance, stares off into space.*

VERONICA *(Shyly boastful)* I didn't want to, um, overwhelm you right away, Mary, but . . . my father is Byron T. Scott. *(Pause; no response from* MARY, *but* VERONICA *behaves as if there is)* Yes, that's right!—I'm the daughter of Byron T. Scott himself. *(Pause)* Daddy is in private practice in Manhattan now, but, in the Sixties, I guess you know, he was a renowned civil rights attorney. A personal friend of John F. Kennedy—and Jackie; and, now, Bill and Hillary. *(Pause; no response from* MARY, *but* VERONICA *behaves as if there is)* Yes, I sure am lucky, Mary! And I know it. Daddy was a champion of integration from the first. In his law firm he always hired whites—not by quota, either. *And* the handicapped. *(Pause)* Physically and mentally challenged—Daddy doesn't discriminate, nor does he allow others to do so. Ooooh *no!* That's how we were brought up.

VERONICA *has tiptoed over to get her camera, unobtrusively.*

VERONICA *(Lyric, sentimental)* Mary, I want to share this with you. One of my earliest memories is of my nanny . . . who was white. *(Pause)* Nellie Fay Cotton, the kindly, obese, diabetic Ozark woman my par-ents hired at the minimum wage to care for me when I was just a baby. Ooooh did I love Nellie Fay! She was ugly as sin, and, ugh, the ugliest *hair*—but her soul was beautiful inside. *(Pause)* Nellie was of welfare stock—had fifteen children by the age of thirty-five—her husband was an unemployed miner with black lung who had nothing to do all day but drink and beat up on her till she finally escaped with her children and fled North—but Nellie never lost her faith in God—never! "The Lord sees into our hearts, He loves us each and every one"—Nellie used to tell me, when I was still in my crib. *(Wiping at eyes, maudlin)* Then, one summer when I was five or six, these sort of snooty relatives of Momma's were visiting, from Boston, and my aunt's sapphire chok-er was missing from her room, and Nellie Fay was the suspect of course, and oh! it was *so* sad!—Nellie Fay was scared and nervous and acted guilty—poor thing! The Greenwich police were called—interrogated Nellie down at the station—did a body check, I guess—didn't find the missing jewelry—but Nellie Fay was dismissed from our household, and went away, and a few days later guess what?—

VERONICA *turns dramatically to* MARY, *who sits as before, staring glassily into space.*

VERONICA   You guessed it, Mary!—the damn old choker was found in the deep end of our swimming pool, when the maintenance men came to clean it. Oh, were Momma and Daddy apologetic! Oh, were they chagrined! Right away they sent for Nellie Fay, but it was too late. Poor dear Nellie had *killed herself*—in shame—swallowed a can of Drano she'd taken out of our kitchen. Oh! the sorrow in our household! the regret! It took Momma weeks and weeks to find an adequate replacement! *(Wipes at eyes; pause; she has the camera ready)* Excuse me, Mary? Could you look up, and *smile*? I'd like an intimate shot of both of us. To commemorate our first day together as roommates. The frontispiece of my photo-journal . . .

Telephone rings. VERONICA *answers it.*

VERONICA   *(Exuding "personality")*   Hi! Yeah! *(Listens)* What?—oh, wow! Cool! Tonight? Dewitt, Evander, Jacey?—and Buchanan? Down from New Haven? Hmmm! How many cars? To Manhattan?—that's an hour and a half. O.K., but when? *(Checks watch)* Wow, that's half-an-hour. *(Listens)* O.K., sure. Count me in. *(Listens)* Buchanan's got his Jaguar? Cool! *(Listens)* No, no—what other plans would I have for tonight? This place is Dullsville. Bye! *(Hangs up)*

VERONICA, *in her upbeat mood, approaches* MARY *who sits catatonic as before.*

VERONICA   *(Adjusts camera, positions it on a desk or table facing* MARY*)* Now!—I set this here—set the timer—O.K.! *(Hurries to get into the picture, sitting beside* MARY *on the bed; her arm around* MARY's *shoulders and her head close beside* MARY's*)* One-two-three SMILE! We're going to have a terrific freshman year!

VERONICA *smiles her dazzling smile;* MARY *remains catatonic but smiles, at last, a ghastly blank wide smile.*

Camera flashes.

Lights out.

THE END

HERE SHE IS! ❦

A Play in One Act

Cast

BARBARA—forty-four
MISS ALABAMA—early twenties; secretly a transvestite
MISS ALASKA—early twenties; secretly part-Inuit (Eskimo)
MISS MICHIGAN—early twenties; black
MISS NEW YORK—early twenties
LIZ—the production manager; any age over thirty
MC—middle-aged or older
STAGEHAND 1—young man
STAGEHAND 2—young man

Setting

BARBARA enters slowly, glancing about in perplexity. She is a suburban woman in the city for the day; her glasses are of a slightly outmoded "stylish" style; she is neatly groomed, moderately attractive, very conventionally dressed; carrying a "good" purse and several packages, predominantly a Bloomingdale's shopping bag.

Lights up. An empty stage with a brief runway. Isolated props. An American flag on a tacky "gold" pedestal, of a kind seen in public school auditoriums.

Enter, crossing BARBARA'S *path without noticing her, deep in conversation,* MISS ALABAMA, MISS ALASKA, *and* MISS MICHIGAN. *The three young women are strikingly attractive, and heavily made up; they wear skin-tight jeans, high-heeled shoes, and showy designer blouses or sweaters; their long nails are polished, their hair dramatic and eye-catching, their jewelry a bit excessive. Their voices are stagey melodic murmurs.*

MISS ALABAMA *(Southern accent)*   I declare, I'm scared *stiff*! You girls all know this part of the country but I never been so far *north* before!

MISS ALASKA *(Holding out her shaky, but very pretty hands)*   I've never been so far *south* before! *I'm* scared petrified!

MISS MICHIGAN *(Cooing "black" cadences)*   Ohhh man, what about *me*? Who's goin to look at me for my*self*? I'm a walkin' talkin' in-yo'-face *political statement*!

Enter MISS NEW YORK, *as the three young women are about to exit.* MISS NEW YORK, *with extravagant long ripply russet-red hair, and a "statuesque" body, is the most glamorous of all. She trips along fetchingly in her high-heeled pumps.*

MISS NEW YORK   Oooohhh! guys!—wait for *me*! You going to rehearse your routines?

MISS ALABAMA   Nah, we're going up the block to the I Can't Believe it's Yogurt. C'mon!

BARBARA *has been staring at the young women in amazement.*

BARBARA *(Calling out belatedly after them)*   Excuse me—?

MISS NEW YORK, MISS ALABAMA, MISS ALASKA, and MISS MICHIGAN exit, arms around one another's waists, giggling happily.

LIZ, *the production manager, enters briskly, having sighted* BARBARA. *She is a practical-minded woman of any age beyond thirty.*

LIZ *(Vexed, relieved)*   Oh, there you are, Miss Utah! We've been looking all over for you.

BARBARA   For me?

LIZ *(Displaying wristwatch)*   Isn't it five twenty-five, Miss Utah?

BARBARA   It *is*, but . . .

LIZ   Where's your production schedule, Miss Utah? Your rehearsal was to begin promptly at five fifteen.

BARBARA   Why do you call me "Miss Utah?" My name is—

LIZ *(Impatiently)*   We don't have time for *names* here, Miss Utah. *Names* come and go every season; *states* abide forever. We're on the air in two and a half hours. *(Staring)* Is *that* your dance costume?

BARBARA   Dance costume?

LIZ *(Snapping fingers, yelling)*   Music up, Jerry! Check out the sound system.

Brisk syncopated music for tap dancing comes on; perhaps a wildly syncopated version of "Tea For Two."

BARBARA   I'm afraid there's been a—misunderstanding? I'm from Katonah, not Utah. I have no connection with Utah. I'm in the city just for today, exchanging some of my daughter's birthday presents, and right now I'm looking for apartment number 13D, the name is Cottler—?

LIZ, *who hasn't been listening, takes the Bloomingdale's bag from* BARBARA, *removes a modish sexy-punky costume. Perhaps a leather mini-skirt, or a black cat-suit. The latest in ephemeral teen fashion.*

LIZ   O.K., Miss Utah, quick-change. We're behind schedule and the boss will be furious if he finds out.

BARBARA   Excuse me—what? C-Change? *(As* LIZ *thrusts the clothes at her)* Here?

LIZ   Honey, you don't want to face our live audience and one hundred million TV viewers raw and unrehearsed, do you? Think of the good folks back in Utah, pinning their hopes on *you*.

BARBARA *(Unaccountably changing her clothes, with desperate swiftness, even as she protests)*   B-But I'm not from Utah, I'm from Katonah, New York! I took the Amtrak in this morning and I'm scheduled to take it back at seven! I thought this was the Atlantic Apartments, 668 West End Avenue?—but where is 13D?—my old Bryn Mawr roommate is expecting me—

LIZ *(Yelling)*   Louder, Jerry!

Music louder.

BARBARA   —and my husband is expecting me home in time to make dinner. He'll be terribly upset if—

LIZ *(Helping BARBARA with costume)*   Wow! This is *chic.*

BARBARA   But—it's Terrill's, a size six. Isn't it a little too—snug—on me?

LIZ   Honey, in our Pageant, *skin* isn't too snug. *(Snapping fingers)* O.K.—one time through.

BARBARA   *Isn't* this the Atlantic Apartments, 668 West End Avenue? Did I step into the wrong building?

LIZ *(About to remove BARBARA's glasses)*   We'll just take these off.

BARBARA *(Resisting firmly)*   Oh, no: I always wear my glasses. They hide the bags under my eyes.

BARBARA begins to tap dance. Hesitant at first; then inspired; surprisingly good. During her brief performance of a minute or two, MISS ALABAMA, MISS ALASKA, MISS MICHIGAN, and MISS NEW YORK enter to watch. They are eating yogurt cones or sundaes and rapidly lose their appetites.

MISS ALABAMA   Ohhhh my Gawd—which one of us is *that?*

MISS ALASKA   Talk about natural talent—wow!

MISS NEW YORK   That's Miss Utah!—ohhh that smooth skin! Those teeth! Eyes! Hair! Glowing with health!

MISS MICHIGAN   —The "natural" look—oh, man!

MISS ALABAMA   Miss Utah makes *me* feel kinda, ohh kinda—synthetic?

MISS ALASKA   She makes *me* feel I better go back and floss my teeth one more time—

MISS NEW YORK   *I* better shampoo my hair one more time—

MISS MICHIGAN   *I* better do my nails one more time—

MISS ALABAMA   *I* better rethink my strategy one more time—

MISS ALABAMA, MISS ALASKA, MISS MICHIGAN, MISS NEW YORK shrink away, exit.

The music has been cut off rudely. BARBARA continues dancing for a beat or two before she realizes.

LIZ *(Sincerely applauding)*   Miss Utah, that's terrific! Since our Pageant was inaugurated in 1921, I've never seen a performance so—heartfelt.

BARBARA *(Suddenly anxious)*   Was I—all right? I'm sort of—out of—practice— *(She is breathless, adjusting glasses, hair, costume, pantyhose)*

LIZ   I mean—*terrific!* You'll win the judges' hearts, I just know.

BARBARA   I w-will? The judges' hearts?

LIZ *(Looking through BARBARA's other shopping bags)*   Where's your evening attire?

BARBARA   Evening attire?

LIZ   Never mind, we've got some extras—left over from previous competitions. *(Exiting, yelling)* Maggie—?

Lights up on the MC. *He is a puffy middle-aged man in a tuxedo with a red satin cummerbund; there is orangish pancake makeup on his face and he wears an obvious toupee. Enters frowning at himself in a pocket mirror; wets and smooths eyebrows, practices puckers and smiles. He should resemble, dream-fashion, the actor Robert Taylor.*

BARBARA   Excuse me, sir—

MC   *(Big glistening smile)*   Ah, hah: Miss—is it Nevada? No! *(Snaps fingers)* Colorado?—no! *(Snaps fingers)* Wyoming?—no!

BARBARA   Utah?

MC   Utah!—of course. Great ol' state.

BARBARA   But I'm not from Utah.

MC   *(Chuckling)*   That's what we all say, when we have stage fright. *(Mimicry of female terror)* "I'm not from Utah!"

BARBARA   I think there's been some confusion—

MC   *(Immediate reaction)*   What? Confusion? Where? Whose? *(Vehemently)* Everything is going smoooothly and professssionally exactly as it has since our first competition in 1921.

BARBARA   Competition?

MC   Well, we don't like to stress *that*, Miss Utah. "Pageant" sounds a whole lot better—kinder.

BARBARA   But I am not from Utah! You're mistaking me for someone else! I was born in Greenwich, Connecticut—I live in Katonah, New York with my husband and two children—I'm in the city just for today—and at the moment I'm looking for apartment 13D?—I'm sure I stepped into the right building—

MC   Hmmm! Which building?

BARBARA   The Atlantic Apartments at 668 West End Avenue—

MC   This is Atlantic *City.*

A beat.

BARBARA   W-What?

MC *(A hearty chuckle)*   It's just stage fright, Miss Utah. I know the symptoms. *(He checks her pulse)* Rapid pulse—*(Touches her forehead)* Feverish skin *plus* cold clamminess—*(Squeezes her hands)* Nerves! You gals are the *crème de la crème* of American womanhood—beauty, brains, sweetness, *goodness*—but out on that runway it's dog-eat-dog, eh?—or do I mean cat-eat-cat?—only one of you will wear a crown tonight. Hell, *I'm* nervous myself— *(Displays his badly shaking hands, smiling broadly)*—even an old show biz pro like *me.*

BARBARA How did I get to Atlantic *City*? I took a cab from Bloomingdale's to 668 West End Avenue—I stepped into the foyer of the Atlantic Apartments—

MC You got here, honey, because you're a *winner*. You already beat out *millions* of rivals and tonight—if you're lucky—you'll beat out fifty-one more. "Crème de la crème"—see?

MC walks off, taking out his pocket mirror to check his hair. BARBARA *stares after him.*

BARBARA Oh my God! That man is—Robert Taylor? ROBERT TAYLOR? My mother's old heart throb of the 1950s? It can't be—can it?

LIZ reappears.

LIZ Miss Utah! Come *on*!
BARBARA Wh-what? Where?

LIZ marches BARBARA *offstage.*

LIZ All you states have to be lined up!

Lights up on MISS ALABAMA *and* MISS ALASKA *in glamorous low-cut evening gowns, staring critically at themselves in a full-length mirror.*

MISS ALABAMA That Miss Utah!—*she's* got guts.
MISS ALASKA Makes me wince seeing my*self* now. "Miss Alaska"—huh!
MISS ALABAMA I was so damn proud being "Miss Alabama"—now, I declare I just don't *know*. (*Shoring up her sizable bosom in both hands*) In the presence of a *natural woman*—
MISS ALASKA (*Adjusting a false eyelash*) —unadorned beauty—
MISS ALABAMA —sincerity—
MISS ALASKA —maturity—
MISS ALABAMA —plus talent, brains—
MISS ALASKA —*true* femininity—
MISS ALABAMA You want to cry out and declare your own true *self*, don't you?
MISS ALASKA (*Grimly*) If you have the guts.

Lights down on MISS ALABAMA, MISS ALASKA.

Lights up on MISS MICHIGAN. *In an equally glamorous evening gown, putting on the final touches of lipstick, powder; brooding into a mirror.*

MISS MICHIGAN Well, girl!—are you proud of yourself for scrambling to the top of the meretricious white bourgeoise slave market?—or are you just plain ashamed? "Miss Michigan"—huh!

Lights down on MISS MICHIGAN.

Lights up on MISS NEW YORK. *In her evening gown, similarly primping and brooding into a mirror.*

MISS NEW YORK   "Miss New York!"—tinsel in the mouth, now you're made to see your hypocrisy—duplicity—mendacity—*falsity*—set beside a true, brave woman. Aren't you ashamed! From nursery school through junior high—from junior high to this very moment—you've played a role in others' eyes—mainly men—your inner worth reflected in *their* vision, and not your *own. (Lifts her long ripply hair, lets fall in a cascade)* Ah, "Miss New York!"—if you had the *guts.*

Lights down on MISS NEW YORK.

Lights to dim. LIZ *runs across the stage.*

LIZ   The call is five minutes. Three minutes. Two minutes. Everybody ready!

A curtain closes on the stage. Lights out. Music: "Here She Is, Miss America" sung by a male vocalist, with unembarrassed passion. Lights up on the curtain as it opens to reveal MC, *striding forward, singing, arms uplifted to the audience. Thunderous (taped) applause.*

MC   Thank you, thank you, ladies and gentlemen! *(Broadly smiling, blowing kisses)* Thank you!

More applause.

MC   Oh, you're a wonnnderfull audience!—some of you regulars have been with us since 1921—God bless your warm, uplifting faces!

MC *wipes at his eyes. More applause.*

MC   Have we got a pageant for you tonight! Ladies and gentlemen, this year's crop of American beauties is the true *crème de la crème!*—the richest most spectacular harvest since our prestigious competition began. But first a word from our—

Theme music comes up. BARBARA, *apparently misreading a cue, enters uncertainly, blinking and squinting in the light. A few scattered handclaps,* BARBARA *is wearing a pink taffeta prom dress, strapless; a shiny banner* MISS UTAH *is draped across her breasts. White gloves, rhinestone earrings. Glasses as before.*

MC *(Rattled)*   B-But first—a word from our sponsor—?

BARBARA *(Petrified with stage fright, wide-eyed)*   I—I'm supposed to introduce myself now? My name is, um, B-Barbara Utah—I mean Miss Utah, and I'm th-th-thrilled to be here tonight . . . *(Hyperventilating)* My h-home state is New York but for s-some reason I'm honored to represent the great state of Utah at this Pageant—so, folks back in Utah, hi! *(Waving, a ghastly smile; then pause, sudden thought)* Oh my God! I came out too soon, didn't I?

MC *(Smoothing over blunder, clapping)*   Miss Utah!—welcome to Atlantic City, New Jersey! You're just in the nick of time, isn't she, folks?—this great-looking gal? Mmmmm, not a nanosecond too soon!

MC leads enthusiastic applause.

BARBARA *(Undertone to MC)*   Sh-Should I go back? I forgot my cue—

BARBARA tries to flee stage in panic; MC restrains her.

MC   No, no, no, Miss Utah! As long as you *are* here— *(Broad wink at audience)* —tell us a little about yourself.

BARBARA   W-What do you want to know? I'm from Katonah, New York, and—

MC *(Cutting her off)*   I bet you sewed that fetching taffeta gown with your own two hands, Miss Utah, didn't you?

BARBARA   No.

MC   No?

BARBARA *(Swallowing, deadly earnest)*   I haven't touched my Singer sewing machine for years. I don't even know where it *is*. That nice woman— *(A vague gesture toward the wings)* —found this for me in a dressing room.

MC   Well, it's very, very pretty—

BARBARA *(Awkwardly cutting him off)*   The funny thing is, it's exactly like my senior prom dress—I wore to my senior prom at Greenwich High—twenty-six years ago next June! *(Caressing the material)* The identical shade of pink!

MC   Did you sew your senior prom gown, Miss Utah?

BARBARA   No. We bought it at Bloomingdale's, in the city.

MC   Well—it's a coincidence anyway, isn't it, folks? *(Leads brief applause, smiling broadly)* A good luck omen, maybe?

BARBARA   Is it time for my tap dance now?

MC *(Forced grin)*   The Talent Performances are a little later in our program, Miss Utah. Right now, we'd like you to tell us about yourself.

BARBARA stares and blinks.

BARBARA *(Awkward laugh)*   My mind just went—blank.

MC *(A wink at audience)*   How could you tell, Miss Utah?

Loud (taped) laughter, a smattering of applause.

BARBARA   I had something to say and—my mind just went blank.

MC   Hmmm, yes. Miss Utah, let's move to the General Questions part of the program. How can the United States most effectively pay off the national debt, combat crime and illiteracy, and remain the world's Number One protector of democracy? Fifteen seconds for your answer!

BARBARA *(Adjusting her glasses, almost crossly)* For God's sake, why ask *me*? What do *I* know? Don't we elect qualified people to public office so that, in turn, they can hire qualified advisors? Isn't that what our taxes are for?

Loud applause.

MC *(Clapping too)* Right on, Miss Utah! You shoot from the hip.

BARBARA All *I* have is a B.A. from Bryn Mawr, Class of '72. I majored in English, I don't *know* anything.

Laughter, applause.

BARBARA Is it time for my tap dance now?

Sudden tap dance music up. BARBARA *begins to dance, with surprising energy and skill.* MC *is drawn into tap dancing with her briefly, as if they're old partners.*

Thunderous applause.

MC *(Wiping face with handkerchief)* Wowee, Miss Utah! *That* was sure some fun!

BARBARA *bows. Tugging up her gown, which is slipping.*

MC But—hmmm!—back to Broader Issues. Tell us, Miss Utah: Do you believe in Life Everlasting?

BARBARA *(An unthinking expression of utter dismay)* Oh, *this* couldn't go on and on forever—could it? *(Hand to mouth, wide-eyed)* Ooops!

Laughter, applause. Isolated cheers.

BARBARA *(Quickly)* Of course, I believe in Life Everlasting. And in God the Father—or whatever He is: people are debating these days maybe He isn't *male*. Whatever—I believe.

Applause comes up.

BARBARA *(Squinting out anxiously into audience)* There *is* a purpose to all this—there's got to be. *(Almost pleading)* Doesn't there?

MC *(Leading audience in applause)* Words of sheer wisdom, Miss Utah! Must be that western air, eh? So fresh, pure—now that nuclear testing is forbidden. *(Pause, salacious smile)* Tell us, Miss Utah—this is crucial—*do you ride a horse?*

BARBARA A horse?

MC *(Gesturing lewdly)*   HORSE. You're on top, he's on the bottom.

Much laughter, applause.

MC *(Sniggering to audience)*   I see we have some HORSE LOVERS out there tonight!

BARBARA   Excuse me, I—I've been trying to explain for hours—I'm *not* from Utah.

MC *(Chuckling)*   Folks, that's code for stage fright—"I'm not from Utah!" *(Wriggles hips, gives a female shriek)* "OOOOHHH I'M NOT FROM UTAH!"

BARBARA *(Pleading)*   But I'm *not.* I wouldn't want anyone to think I'm here under false pretenses—I don't have any connection with Utah at all.

MC *(Humoring her)*   No connection with Utah, Miss Utah?

BARBARA   No connection. *(Pause, hand to mouth)* Ooops!

MC *(A wink at audience)*   What did you just remember, Miss Utah? Can you share it with our studio audience and one hundred million TV viewers?

BARBARA *(Blushing, shakes head)*   I, um—n-no . . .

MC *(Shaking forefinger, chiding)*   Now, Miss Utah! Prime time American TV is truth-telling time, you know that.

BARBARA   I, I—just can't say—I'm so embarrassed—

MC   Can't say—what?

BARBARA   I just remembered, I was— *(She leans to the MC to whisper in his ear)*

MC *(Loudly, gleefully)*   "—conceived in Dinosaur National Park, Utah, July 1950, on my parents' honeymoon!" Wowee!

Wild applause, laughter. BARBARA *tries to smile like a good sport; can't bear it, and hides her face.*

More laughter.

MC *(Leering, winking at audience)*   I'd say that was *some connection,* eh folks?

More laughter.

BARBARA *peers through her fingers, guilty and childlike, as if into a TV camera.*

BARBARA   Mom? Dad? Are you watching? Gee, I'm sorry if I embarrassed you!

MC *(Leaning in, mugging)*   Mmmmm Mom? Dad? *I'd* say you two honeymooners did pretty well. Congratulations! Must be that raunchy Dinosaur air, eh?

BARBARA *lets her hands fall from her face.*

BARBARA *(Staring at MC)* Excuse me, sir—I've got to ask, for Mom's sake: *Are* you Robert Taylor?

MC *continues playing to the audience, unhearing.*

BARBARA You do look like Robert Taylor . . . sort of. He was a big movie star of the 1950s, I guess . . . my mother's old heart throb. In those days, even married women had "heart throbs" and they weren't ashamed to admit it, they were *encouraged*. Except, Mr. Taylor, I thought you were, um, deceased.

MC *(Big smile)* Reports of my demise are GREATLY EXAGGERATED, dear. And nowwwww—

MC *gestures broadly and music comes up. A luridly sweetened and synco- pated version of "America the Beautiful."*

MC Your cue, Miss Utah.
BARBARA My cue—?
MC Your *cue*, Miss Utah.
BARBARA My *cue*—?
MC *(Impatiently, overlapping)* Let's see what Utah's got the rest of the states haven't!

MC *rather forcibly helps* BARBARA *strip off her gown. She is wearing a swimsuit beneath. Her swimsuit is prim and old-fashioned.*

BARBARA, *stiff with terror, ventures out onto the runway. She tries to move with the bouncy music, but can't. She tries what she knows of a model's slinky glide, but can't. A turn, a pirouette, a ghastly smile; her glasses slide down her nose and her strapless suit is slipping.*

Music goes down for BARBARA's *epiphany.*

BARBARA *(Peering at audience)* You . . . aren't really there, are you? And I'm not here, exactly . . . am I? This is a dream . . . isn't it? I'm a forty- four-year-old housewife and mother from Katonah competing in the Miss America Pageant at Atlantic City and it's all a wild, lurid dream . . . isn't it?

Music shifts to "Here She Is, Miss America." MC *sings with unabashed phony passion, gestures.*

MC "Here she is—MISS UTAH! Here she is—OUR IDEAL!"
BARBARA *(More intense, engaging audience)* Mom? This is *your* dream, not mine—is that it? Mom? You can wake up now, Mom—please.

Lights out on BARBARA.

Lights up on MISS ALASKA. *In her evening gown, a shiny banner* MISS ALASKA *across her breasts.*

MISS ALASKA *(Winning smile, seductive, sweet)* Thank you, ladies and gentlemen! I'm just so thrilled to be here tonight to introduce myself! *(Pause)* When I was crowned Miss Alaska a few months ago, on the very eve of my mother's death, it was the happiest day of my life, I tell you. I was THRILLED and DELIGHTED and THRUST ALL PANGS OF CONSCIENCE behind me that Mom was dying of brain cancer in a charity ward in the bush beyond the Arctic Circle—*(Smiling sweetly)* —I figured, what the heck, Mom was an alcoholic, too. *(Pause)* What did *I* care?—I was fiercely pursuing my American dream of becoming, first, MISS ALASKA, and, second, MISS AMERICA—so that I could move out of Alaska as fast as possible, and pursue my career as a model, actress, party girl, top-level executive and maybe go for being the next Mrs. Trump. *(Pause)* Does that surprise you? Why should it? There's more— *(She seductively places an "Eskimo" hood on her head, taking care not to displace her hair)* I AM NOT A U.S. CITIZEN. Does *that* surprise you?

Through MISS ALASKA's *speech the audience has been restive; now we hear isolated boos and catcalls.*

MISS ALASKA *strips provocatively to her glamorous swimsuit.*

MISS ALASKA That's right, folks: I lied. My life is a lie: I lie all the time: I LIKE TO LIE. I am *not* a citizen of your ridiculous country—I forged my birth certificate when I was eight years old, to get into school. My mother was Inuit—the white-racist term for which is "Eskimo." My father is Canadian, and if I'm a citizen of any country it's Canada, where I was born in the Northwest Territory. *(Pause)* Want to know more?—I've been letting my body hairs sprout these last few hours. See? *(Lifts arms to reveal underarm stubble; indicates stubble on legs)*

Outraged response from audience. Lights out.

Lights up on MISS MICHIGAN, *who is already in her swimsuit, the shiny banner* MISS MICHIGAN *across her breasts. She strides out on the runway, very much in control; a sexy-jaunty swagger. Pauses on the runway, arms akimbo in a provocative pose.*

MISS MICHIGAN *(Dazzling smile)* Everything *I* said about myself is true—I'm a straight-A student at Michigan State where I'm studying pre-med 'cause I hope to practice family medicine, I'm captain of the women's swim team, I'm a member of the NAACP and a volunteer Red Cross worker and I'm active in an anti-drug program in East Lansing and I'm a vegetarian and I just love Jane Austen *and* Wynton Marsalis—except—and here I did fib a little: I am not a Sunday School teacher, nor even a member of any church. *(Pause)* Why?—'cause I DON'T BELIEVE IN GOD.

Boos, catcalls.

MISS MICHIGAN *(Taking it all in with satisfaction)* Right! This girl's a born FREE THINKER. Never could swallow that fairy tale shit of a BIG WHITE DADDY in the sky—or any DADDY at all.

Growing angry response.

MISS MICHIGAN *(Taunting)* Uh-huh. There's more. Yo' looking at a RADICAL FEMINIST. *(Pause)* There's more—yo' looking at a RADICAL LESBIAN FEMINIST. And these front teeth— *(Taps them)*—are FALSE.

Lights out to outraged response.

Lights up on MISS NEW YORK *in her glamorous swimsuit, a shiny banner* MISS NEW YORK *across her breasts. Her beautiful hair has been cut and styled as a mohawk and she wears earring clamps and a nose ring.*

MISS NEW YORK *(Beaming)* Plus I vomit thrice daily to gorge *and* keep my figure; *and* I'm actually not a "miss"—I've been married and divorced three times.

Boos, catcalls, whistles.

MISS NEW YORK   To the same woman!

Lights out on MISS NEW YORK.

Lights up on MISS ALABAMA, *in her glamorous swimsuit with a shiny banner* MISS ALABAMA *across her breasts, and the flush-faced* MC *who is trying to prevent her from striding along the runway. They tussle;* MC *loses his balance and sits down, hard;* MISS ALABAMA *strips off false eyelashes, false fingernails, her wig, and reveals that she is wearing a padded bra.*

MISS ALABAMA *(Man's voice)* I'm not a GIRL—I'm a GUY!

Outraged response from audience. Lights out.

Strobe lights. MC, LIZ, *other unidentified figures run about in an emergency state. Cries, shouts of dismay and anger.*

Lights out. Theme music again, as if nothing has gone wrong.

Lights up on BARBARA, *still in her swimsuit, being crowned Miss America with a phonily gleaming "gold" crown. Her shiny banner now reads* MISS

AMERICA. *The dazed, disheveled, grim* MC *lowers the crown on her head as he sings.*

MC *(Flat, forced voice)* "Here she is—MISS AMERICA! Here she is—OUR IDEAL!"

BARBARA *(Wiping at her eyes)* Oh, thank you—oh, I can't believe this—oh, it's a dream come true—

MC *(Waxing more passionate)* "Here she is—MISS AMERRRICAAA! Here she is—OUR IDEEALL!"

BARBARA *(Waving at camera)* Mom? Dad? Charles? Terrill? Ricky? HI! Sorry I didn't get home to make dinner! *(Pause; a thought strikes her)* Ooops! *I'm* not qualified to be Miss America, either—I'm a "Mrs.," not a "Miss."

Boos, catcalls, hisses and instantaneous Lights out.

Lights up. Empty stage.

STAGEHAND 1 *appears, with a broom, moving props around. Loud cheerful whistling.*

STAGEHAND 2 *appears, also with a broom.*

STAGEHAND 1 Hey Bert—wouldja get that crap from over there?
STAGEHAND 2 What crap, where?
STAGEHAND 1 The whadajacallit—
STAGEHAND 2 Flag?

STAGEHAND 2 *lifts the flag on its pedestal to carry backstage.*

STAGEHAND 2 What's this shit?

He has found the MISS MICHIGAN *banner, a high-heeled shoe, and some false red-polished fingernails.*

STAGEHAND 2 *(Sliding the banner across his chest, fitting on a fingernail)* Hey, look: woweee!

In the meantime, STAGEHAND 1 *has found* MISS ALABAMA's *glossy wig, which he fits crookedly on his head; and her padded bra, which he waves high.*

STAGEHAND 1 Woweee! Look at *me!* *(Wriggling hips, etc.)* "Miss America!"

STAGEHAND 2 *whistles, stamps feet.*

STAGEHANDS *return to work. Exit with props.*

A beat. Empty stage.

BARBARA *wanders in, still in her swimsuit and high heels, MISS AMERICA banner across her breasts. She glances about in confusion and worry.*

BARBARA   Why am I . . . still here? *(A beat)* This *is* a dream . . . isn't it? But I should be awake by now. It must be morning by now. *(Strikes heel against floor)* But everything is so *real. (Discovers crown on head, banner across breasts)* Oh, God! I'm starting to get frightened. *(Pause, pleading)* Mom, if this is you, you can wake up now. Mom? *Please?*

Lights slowly out.

THE END

THE SACRIFICE ❧
A Play in One Act

Cast

MURIEL—late twenties
EDDIE—early thirties

These are white Americans of no unusual distinction, though MURIEL is overweight. Both are attractive in the way of smalltown high school attractiveness.

Setting

A bare stage in the foreground, representing a front or side yard of a small bungalow or house trailer. Scattered about are a few children's things—a junior-sized bicycle, a bare, battered doll, a baseball bat, etc.

In the background is the interior of a bungalow or house trailer. The outer wall missing, we see into the rooms, which may be minimally suggested. There must be a refrigerator in the kitchen; and, in the bedroom, an open closet stued with a man's and a woman's clothes. Shoes, in some disorder, on the floor. (If a bed is included, it should be made up, not neatly, but with a look of haste; the covering should be a brightly colored chenille spread. If curtains are included, they should be chintz or floral.)

The time is the present.

Lights up. MURIEL *stands in the foreground, hands on her hips. She wears filmy, loose-fitting summery clothes, a shapeless shift, or smock, with an unbuttoned shirt or jacket over it, as if to disguise her plumpness; her legs are bare, and very pale; her feet dead-white in inexpensive summer sandals. She is prettily made up, despite being a bit disheveled; chipped bright nail polish on both fingernails and toenails. Her permed hair is extremely frizzy, as if to match her mood. Breathless, cheeks flushed and eyes unnaturally shining,* MURIEL *speaks to the audience exactly as if confiding in a woman friend. The expectation is that her outrage is shared.*

MURIEL   Can you imagine?—bragging to my own brother Ray he's gonna do such things! To me! to me, he's married to, has kids with! Not even ashamed or anything! CAN YOU IMAGINE! *(A pause)* Oh sure I got a lawyer—in self-defense. Now *he's* got one too! *(Deep shuddering breath)* And all we *owe*—!

MURIEL *pauses. Moves closer to audience. A sly, hectic, determined smile as she draws a knife out of a pocket—a sharply honed twelve-inch steak knife with a gleaming blade.*

MURIEL *(Whispering, wild-eyed)*   You think I can't do it, huh? You just watch. *(Laughs)*

MURIEL *contemplates the knife, testing possible grips—overhand, underhand.*

MURIEL   The knife-and-scissor sharpener, from Sears—my Christmas present—*that's* gone. But it's done its job.

MURIEL *hides the knife again. In the same pocket, she discovers a brownie, which she nibbles at, as if experimentally; merely tasting.*

MURIEL *(Defensively)*   Didn't have any real breakfast this morning, only coffee. Jesus, who can eat—the world caving in like this! *(Another dainty nibble)* It's stale. *(Another nibble)* I prefer brownies with almonds but the kids spit them out. *(She finds she has finished the brownie, and angrily brushes crumbs off her chin, bosom)* Oh—hell. Sometimes you just want to cry, life's all weak-willedness and giving *in*. *(As if pleading)* I've been Eddie Fitzroy's wife for nine years and—now— what? *(A pause)* Back to—what? My parents' house? My old *room*? Like I never had any kids, never been—loved? *(Fierce)* Well, I sure got kids. And all this, here— *(A wave of her hand, indicating her home, property)* —maybe the bank owns it but I'm sure *here*, and any son of a bitch wants me out is gonna have to *carry* me out.

(Incensed) Had to get a lawyer, to protect myself—*his* lawyer's saying he can file for bankruptcy, so I get—nothing. No place to live no alimony no child support, maybe—can you believe it? *(Wiping face with a tissue)* Eddie Fitzroy, that everybody likes so much. 'Cause he's good-looking and was a quarterback for Ashland High and grins a lot, laughs easy—the bastard. Nine years.

(Grimmer, calmer, "fatalistic" tone) You see it on TV all the time—women rising up against their oppressors. Oh, yes! *(A pause)* This world, you're not loved, y'know what it is?—all broken things. Like—the tops, the shiny surfaces, of things. You turn on the TV, you switch the channels zip zip zip zap everything flying by, that's how I watch TV now, too wired to go slower—except, now, it's broke, it's dead. You walk from here to here and from here to here, you're in the kitchen, you call somebody on the phone to keep from going crazy, then you call somebody else, H'lo it's Muriel! oh hi, h'lo, it's Muriel don't hang up! don't roll your eyes hey please it's just me!—again. Then—the refrigerator door's open—you're eating something in your hand—no taste to it. Then—you get scared—the clock's stuck! If the kids are home you run to find them, you hug them, scare them—Aw Mommy it's O.K. lemme *go*.

MURIEL *picks up the baseball bat, the doll, contemplating them, about to cry. She holds the doll longer, then lets it fall.*

MURIEL *(Distractedly)* Saying he loved me—us—so much. Well—I know for a fact he *did*. All those years he *did*. I started putting on weight when I had Dwayne, he never minded—I'd swear. *I* minded more, going on one diet after another and making myself sick and Eddie would hug me and say, You look real nice to *me*, Muriel. Was he lying? HE WAS NOT LYING. I swear.

(Angry smile) This, what I'm gonna do—strike to the heart!— *(She pats the knife in her pocket)* —is no rash crazy-lady act. No sir it's "premeditated." Oh yes! *(Laughs)* I got my defense all prepared—"PRE-MEN-STRUAL-TEN-SION-SYN-DROME"—you hear about it all the time. Even in the *Pennysaver Shopping News*. *(Laughs)* I read this

article, underlined it, memorized it, threw it out—you bet I'm not that stupid, keeping it on the premises for the police to find.

During this speech, EDDIE has been approaching the refrigerator cautiously. EDDIE wears his longish hair sleekly oiled, and has a perceptible growth of beard. EDDIE wears casual work- or sports-clothes that flatter his hard, muscular physique. He opens the door, reaches for a can of beer—but, without turning, eyes in the back of her head, MURIEL calls out.

MURIEL *(Loudly)*   OUT OF THERE, YOU BASTARD! There's only two beers left, and they're for *me*.

EDDIE quickly withdraws and resumes his task. He casts a disdainful glance at MURIEL.

MURIEL *(Smirking, to audience)*   They're Miller *Lites* anyway—Big Ed likes the "real" thing. *(Pouting, righteous)* Anybody begrudges his wife and children actual groceries, he's got a hell of a nerve going in my refrigerator!

MURIEL finds a broken cracker in one of her pockets and half-consciously nibbles on it during the next speech. She comes forward, to speak with growing sentiment, intimacy. Contradictory feelings during this revelation leave her distracted, blinking, panting, a bit wild-eyed, as if she is truly drawn in warring directions—profound sorrow, and rage. Which is deeper? Which is more real? She caresses the knife in her pocket; also, with equal unconsciousness, her breasts.

MURIEL *(Intensely)*   There's a secret about Eddie Fitzroy nobody knows but me.

At this, EDDIE pauses; glances over, frowning; he seems to have heard this, perhaps not clearly. As he stares at MURIEL his expression is more quizzical than embarrassed, or annoyed. As MURIEL speaks, EDDIE continues putting items of clothing in his receptacles, distractedly, as if he can hear, or almost hear.

MURIEL   Every time we—were together—I mean, made love— *(A pause, for she is embarrassed)* —up till maybe a year ago— *(Pause)* Oh God!—I'm actually *telling* this! Can't believe I'm actually *telling* this when I, I promised—I mean, it went deeper than any promise—that's just words— *(Confused, pats at eyes with tissue)* Oh I've been crying for three weeks my eyes are sore all the time just a big sad cow crying—fearful of looking in a mirror— *(A pause)* Had a nasty dream, after Eddie left, I didn't have any *face*. *(Shudders)* My kids ran screaming from me . . . *(A pause)*
(Groping, intense) Well, the first time him and me were together—like

that—Eddie got so sort of frenzied—afterward—I mean, uh—*(With delicacy)* —after he—came—he was almost crazy like he was fearful of letting me go—saying all kinds of wild things like how he loved me, wouldn't let anything bad ever happen to me, he was crying, actually, can you imagine—Eddie Fitzroy, crying!—that bastard, now!—and he'd be lying on me with all his weight, hot and sweating, like to keep me where I was, and his, uh— *(Word nearly inaudible)* —penis was still inside me, but soft, and slipping out—and he was so—emotional. Hanging on to me so tight I thought my ribs would crack, and I did get bruises— *(Touching herself—breasts, thighs, belly)*—that first year or so till I was pregnant with Dwayne and that changed things, some. *(A pause)* The actual first time, we weren't married yet, but he'd asked me, and I said yes, I was seventeen and didn't know anything, and he was twenty-three which was real mature to me, real grown-up. And he *was,* most of the time. I mean, he acted that way, around people. *(A pause)* That bastard! Could pull the wool over everybody's eyes including my family, including *me,* I was so crazy in love with him and he was crazy in love with me . . . it only happens once, like that. *(A pause)* When we made love, those years, he'd be so—tender—like worried he might get rough and hurt me—then, at the end, he'd lose control and go wild gritting his teeth, grabbing me so hard—I never knew, I mean I guess I still don't—*(Wan laugh)* —is this how a man *is,* or just my husband? *(A pause)* He's the only guy I ever loved—ever been with. Shit!

MURIEL *discovers part of a candy bar in one of her pockets, and this too she nibbles on, unconsciously.*

MURIEL *(Sudden anger)* "Gonna take Muriel to the cleaners"—huh? Can you believe it? Just 'cause he's out of work he don't give a shit for his own kids can you believe it! I'm just so ashamed, what am I s'posed to do, wear a paper bag over my head?—the rest of my life here in Ashland where I was born same as him God damn him! *(A pause)* A man like that, he loved his wife so, he near-about fainted when I was in labor, both times—like, like *he* was in labor. And that was no joke, either. He *was.*

EDDIE *now does seem to be listening, rueful; moved.*

MURIEL *(Softer tone)* He was that way with the kids, too. He'd hug them sometimes squeezing the breath out of them, hurting them so they'd get scared. They'd think Daddy was playing but Daddy wasn't. "I love you honey, I love you"—he'd say to Dwayne, and to Junie. I'd hear him. Like it was some kind of prayer. *(A pause)* I guess you'd have to say he was a good father, sort of a nervous father but a good one, up till maybe a year ago. *(Wistful smile)* Maybe they *all* are—men—fathers—real nice—up to the day when they're *not*.

EDDIE *now lights a cigarette with shaking hands; this time, absorbed in her account,* MURIEL *does not notice.*

MURIEL *speaks passionately, as if the profound mystery at the heart of her experience is something that must be communicated, yet cannot be; she has lost the edge of her aggression and rage, and speaks almost reverently.*

MURIEL So—one day—one night—a few years ago—I'd gained maybe thirty pounds by then—we were in bed and, with Eddie, it was like always, him holding me so tight, all sweaty and scared-like, and groaning, except this time he really *hurt* me— *(She cups one of her breasts tenderly)* —and I panicked and shoved him away, I put on the light and looked at him, "Are you crazy," I said, my teeth were chattering I was so scared, "—what *is* it?" and Eddie's staring at me like he doesn't know me, this look on his face like he's a wild man or something, so now I *was* scared. *(A pause)* "Honey," I said, "—better tell me: what *is* it?" *(A pause, then, breathless)* So he told me. *(A pause)* You won't believe what he told me!

EDDIE *comes forward, hesitantly. He smokes his cigarette distractedly, as* MURIEL *has been eating. As he speaks,* MURIEL *stands to the side, toward the rear, listening; now and then nodding in agreement. At first she tries to remain detached from* EDDIE's *words, but, finally, she begins to cry quietly, wiping at her eyes.* EDDIE *addresses the audience directly, as* MURIEL *has done, except he does not feel that he has the audience's natural sympathy; he must argue for it.*

EDDIE *(Guiltily)* You think I don't feel bad? I do—it makes me sick, having to leave Muriel. And Dwayne, and Junie. Having to. Like, that part of my life's over. Just—over. *(He makes a whistling blowing noise, tantamount to "What can you do?")* Just—letting go. *(A pause)* No shit about filing for bankruptcy—I *am* bankrupt. Your debts outweigh your assets by $23,580—you've borrowed all you can—you're *bankrupt*. *(A pause)* But the hell with that. *(A pause)*
(Trying to be matter-of-fact) This cousin of mine, Bobbie—he was five years old when it happened. I was nine, and he was five. It was an accident, him drowning—that terrible way. But my fault. *(A pause)* We had these sleds—both of us, new sleds—Christmas sleds—playing on the hill at his folks' place—sledding down, and going on the creek—the Yewville Creek—and Bobbie broke through the ice and—
(Breathless, speaking too rapidly, EDDIE *must stop and try again)* My—uh—uncle and aunt, they had a farm up in Schuylersville—and

my dad took us up there a lot, weekends. Bobbie and I played together, he looked up to me I guess, not having a big brother,—we got along real well. Bobbie was . . . a nice kid. *(A pause. Stares at his hands, flexes his fingers)* It's hard to talk. I hate talking. Any kind of serious talk. You can't do it, so why try. Fuck it! *(Tries to control himself)* O.K., there was this big long hill—cow pasture—we'd sled down—to the creek. We took our sleds down the hill but we weren't supposed to go out on the creek even when it was frozen because, in the middle, sometimes, the ice was thin. I'd take my sled out, though, and Bobbie didn't tell on me, *he* was scared, watching me sled out onto the ice— then steer to the side, quick, before the ice cracked. *(Dreamily, as if sledding, steering; a look of rapt, childish concentration)* There was a feeling I'd get if the ice was thin, here— *(He indicates the pit of his belly, scrotum)*—so I'd know. One day I was teasing Bobbie, I guess, and he followed me out onto the ice, but instead of steering to the side like I did he went straight out and right away the ice started cracking and he was screaming and his sled broke through, he was in the water, screaming, this freezing water that's black, and running fast—and I grabbed hold of him by the arm—got down on my stomach on the ice to try to keep it from breaking more—but I couldn't pull him out— he was screaming, "Don't let me go! Don't let me go!"—Jesus, I'll remember it all my life. *(A pause)* He tried to grab onto me too, and pull himself out of the water, but he couldn't, and I couldn't get him out, the ice was breaking, the water was pulling him away, I don't know how long I had hold of him, by the wrist—ten minutes? five?—till my fingers froze and I just . . . had . . . to . . . let . . . him . . . go . . .
(A pause)

(Self-loathing) He was screaming, he didn't want to die. There was nobody but me to save him, nobody in the whole fucking world but me, a nine-year-old kid, and . . . I had to let him go. *(A pause)* So he died, he drowned. *I saw him go. I could see his body go.* *(A pause)*

(Smoking; trying to be matter-of-fact) Well—that was it. Bobbie died, aged five; I was to blame. All the years I was growing up I'd hear him screaming. I hear him now—it's always there. *(A distant look)* And Bobbie's folks, and mine—they'd look at me, and they'd think of him, of *it*. Of what a shit I was, getting him out on the ice, letting him go. Sure, that was what they were thinking—still is. You think I blame them?—I don't. They're right. I'm a shit, I *know.*

MURIEL *has reacted emotionally to this story, as if hearing it for the first time, as a young wife. She approaches* EDDIE *shyly, touches his arm.*

MURIEL *(Sympathetically, tenderly)* Oh hon—oh, my God! That's the saddest thing! I never knew!

EDDIE *(Half-sobbing)*   I let him *go*. I couldn't save him.

MURIEL *(Embracing him)*   It wasn't your fault!

EDDIE *(Holding her, tightly)*   I—I guess it comes over me, sometimes. I sort of black out. I don't know where I am. *(Dazedly, blinking)* Except—there's you. *(Pleading, as if for forgiveness)* Muriel, I love you so much. I love you *so much*. I want to take care of you, you and the kids, forever and ever I'd give my life for you, I love you so. You believe me, don't you? You love me, don't you? Muriel?

MURIEL *(Overlapping with the above)*   I never knew, that poor little boy, but it wasn't your fault, Eddie, hey hon it wasn't your fault, you were such a little boy yourself, try not to think about it, hon—let me hold you.

EDDIE *(Overlapping the above, passionately)*   I swear to God I won't let you go, I won't let *you* go, Muriel, all my life I'll take care of you, I'll show you—you and the kids. Jesus, I love you *so much*.

Light dim briefly as they embrace, to suggest an interlude; a full stop.

Light up. The mood is immediately shattered. MURIEL shoves at EDDIE who sidesteps her, to return to the house and his task of moving out.

MURIEL *(Disbelieving, voice rising)*   What?—*what?* You're moving out?—you want *out?* Eddie— *(Her voice lifts to a fading wail)*

EDDIE *(Stumbling into bicycle)*   FUCK IT! Who left this here! *(Kicking the bicycle)*

MURIEL *(Desperate, flurried, appealing to audience)*   You heard him!—his exact words!—"All my life I'll take care of you!"

EDDIE resumes his task. Moving now hurriedly, carelessly. Grabbing things and stuing them into his receptacle. When one of MURIEL's dresses slips from a hanger he doesn't pick it up. He exhales smoke savagely.

MURIEL *(Furiously, without turning)*   BUTT THAT CIGARETTE, asshole!

EDDIE *(Muttering)*   Fuck you!

EDDIE stubs out the cigarette in a vehement gesture, against any handy surface; tosses the butt to the floor. If a bed is present, he tosses the butt onto the bed.

MURIEL *(To audience, arms out)*   You heard him! You heard him! You heard him! The liar! The bastard! That's the eyes and soul of a bankrupt! *(A pause, dabbing at her warm face with a tissue)* I know we had some hard times together lately. A—cash-flow problem. Buying things on credit—both of us to blame. Then, other things,—"marital problems." *(Embarrassed, tries for brazen cheerfulness)* Well, we all have them, huh?—"marital problems." You're married, that's what you *have*. Don't we? *(Peering at audience; a pause)* We'd been seeing a marriage counsellor, but, hell, you never tell them the truth, so—. *(Laughs)* Eddie'd clip me in the mouth, if I did. *(More somberly, trying to comprehend)* He was cutting down on his drinking, he said—; I was on a new diet, I *am* on it—"Twenty-eight-Day Grapefruit Diet"—so, yeah, I thought things were looking hopeful. Then, one day, instead of sitting down for supper, he looks at me, his face gets all funny, his eyes, and he says he can't do it,—so I say, "Can't do what?" and he says, "Can't eat," and I say, "What? Can't eat?" and he says, "I want out, Muriel, I can't hack it, I want *out*—" Like *out* is some kind of new fucking beer. *(Brays with angry laughter)*

EDDIE *(To* MURIEL's *back, taking up her words)* Muriel, I want out of here. This—that we have—this— *(Stumbling, faltering, with a gesture that takes in their house, household, life together, everything)* —I DON'T BELONG HERE!

MURIEL *(To audience, astounded)* You hear him? You hear him? Like somebody on TV! *(Another wild laugh)*

EDDIE *(Inarticulately)* I'm not the man! This is some other man! Not me!

MURIEL *(To audience, childlike pleading)* Y'know what I wish?—we could go on trial, that's what I wish! Him, and me! "A jury of one's peers!" *(A gesture at the audience)* Then justice would be done!

EDDIE *(Muttering as he holds up an article of clothing, a plaid or checked shirt)* NOT ME!

MURIEL *(Hugging herself tightly)* I read the Bible, now. I'm a sinful woman but I mean to exact justice. This morning, so early! I opened my Bible my grandma gave me—first words I read were— *(MURIEL shuts her eyes, lets her head fall back, an expression of ecstasy on her face)* Psalm 68: "Let God arise, let his enemies be scattered: let them also that hate them flee before him."

In her ecstatic trance, MURIEL *draws the knife out of her pocket. Caresses it against her breasts.* EDDIE *does not see.*

MURIEL "PRE-MED-I-TATED"—"PRE-MEN-STRUAL." *(Laughs)* The jury can decide who's the murderer!

EDDIE *has finished his task, and is eager to leave;* MURIEL, *hiding the knife in the folds of her clothing, or behind her thigh, confronts him.*

MURIEL *(Surprisingly soft, pleading, girlish tone)* Eddie, hon—wait. The school bus will be here in twenty minutes. The kids—

EDDIE *(Guiltily)* I can't.

As EDDIE *tries to ease away,* MURIEL *clutches his shirtsleeve.*

MURIEL *(Pride gone, pleading, close to tears)*   Oh, hon—jeez—!

EDDIE *(Guiltily, sorry for her)*   Muriel, let me go?

MURIEL   Eddie, I love you—how'm I gonna live without you?

EDDIE   Christ, Muriel, you're making it so hard—

MURIEL *(Sobbing)*   Eddie, honey, I'll lose weight—I will! I'll look like I used to! I'll go back to work! I won't bug you about things! Dwayne and Junie, they'll be good—they promised! Wait and see them, they'll tell you themselves—

EDDIE *(Sweating, desperate to escape)*   Muriel, let me go, huh?

MURIEL *(Holding onto his arm)*   "Let me go!"—you promised you'd never let *me* go! Goddamn liar, cruel fucking shameless liar—

EDDIE *(Stumbling away, toward stage right, as MURIEL stumbles with him)*   Muriel, for fuck's sake LET ME GO!

MURIEL *(Raw, unmitigated yearning)*   I LOVE YOU—HOW CAN I "LET YOU GO!"

A brief struggle. EDDIE pushes MURIEL away. Both are panting, hair in their faces. A passionate glisten upon them as of stark, erotic love. But MURIEL crouches, cunning, feet apart, and brings around the knife—gripping it underhand so that, if she swings it, the upward arc will bring its blade into EDDIE's abdomen or groin. EDDIE freezes, staring at the knife.

EDDIE *(Whistling thinly through teeth)*   Hey Muriel—!

MURIEL *(Wildly)*   You think I can't? You think I can't? You think I can't?

MURIEL feints with the knife; EDDIE sidesteps, feints at grabbing her wrist; he misses; MURIEL comes close to stabbing him. EDDIE, scared, crouches, protecting himself with his arms. (He has dropped his things to the floor, and may stumble over them. He may also try to keep them between him and MURIEL.)

EDDIE *(Pleading)*   Oh hell, hon—what's this? Give me the knife.

MURIEL   We're better off dead, both of us.

EDDIE   Muriel, don't talk that way. Hon, listen—

MURIEL swipes at him again with the knife; again, narrowly misses.

EDDIE *(Wild laugh)*   What if the kids see you! Jesus!

MURIEL *(Panting)*   Let them! I want them to! I'll go on trial! I'm not ashamed!

EDDIE   Muriel, this isn't *you.*

MURIEL   Promised you'd take care of us all your life—never let us go like you let your little cousin go—Murderer!

EDDIE *(Pleading, bravely)*   Muriel, hey, hon?—I just can't. I told you—

MURIEL   That little boy you let drown, you liar, stinking hypocrite—

EDDIE *(Angrily)*   Bobbie's got nothing to do with you!

MURIEL   How can you let *me* go, after all that?

A tense pause. They stare at each other, unmoving.

EDDIE *(An outburst)*   Because—I don't love you any more.

There is another tense pause. MURIEL *realizes it is hopeless; she lowers the knife.*

MURIEL *(Sudden flat, ironic tone)*   Then—get the hell out, mister. *(She gestures with the knife, waving him away)*

EDDIE *snatches up his things and backs off. He stares at* MURIEL*—his expression shows guilt, remorse, pity; yet, more than this, simple relief at the prospect of being freed.*

EDDIE *(About to exit)*   I'll call you—first of next week.

MURIEL *(Braying)*   No, call my lawyer! Bankrupt!

EDDIE *exits without looking back.* MURIEL *stares after him.*

Just when we think that MURIEL *is resigned, she loses control; takes up the nude doll, stabs it with the knife, sobbing.*

MURIEL   Ugly thing, Muriel!—poor sad cow, Muriel! Take that, Muriel! Die! *(Throws the doll down, kicks it)*

Lights dim to suggest a brief interlude.

Lights up almost immediately. MURIEL *has gone into the kitchen, is opening the refrigerator door. Pauses midway, to address the audience. (She has tidied her hair somewhat, and straightened her clothing; her demeanor is more composed.)*

MURIEL *(As if confiding in a woman friend)*   So, well—shit! That's that. *(Laughs, embarrassed)* Muriel *tried.* Muriel *sure did.* *(She takes a grapefruit out of the refrigerator, tosses and catches it; then, as she speaks, she cuts it in two with the knife and prepares it to be eaten)* With Sweet-N-Low—plenty of it—these things are real good, actually. I'm getting to like it. *(Laughs)* I lost three pounds this week—that's a start. *(A pause)* I guess my weakness is—I know right from wrong. My parents taught me to be good. *(Shrugs)* Probably couldn't stab Hitler, the bastard's standing in front of me. If that's goodness or just weakness, I don't know. One thing I know—you can't hurt another person to fix up your own life.

MURIEL *eats a grapefruit segment with her fingers, then another, hungrily. Addressing audience, in an appeal, grapefruit in one hand and knife in the other, she speaks "reasonably."*

MURIEL   Except, hell—I'd've liked a jury—"one's own peers." So you could explain it to me. Explain Eddie to me. How a man loves you, and the love wears out. How you love *him*—and that passes too. Like the black water's carrying us all away? Is that it? *(A pause)* Maybe *you* can explain it . . . ? I'm just trying to understand.

MURIEL holds her questioning, appealing pose as lights dim.

THE END

THE REHEARSAL ❦
A Play in One Act

Cast

WOMAN/ACTRESS—approximate age twenty-five to thirty
MAN/ACTOR—several years older than ACTRESS
DIRECTOR—(amplified voice), male, authoritarian

Setting

Center stage is a "stage set" of a living room: sofa, a chair or two, lamp.
A glass-topped coffee table scattered with magazines, newspapers. On one
wall, a handsome framed Metropolitan Museum poster commemorating
a Magritte exhibit. Stage left, a space to be used by the actors for their
break. This space contains a small table with a bottle of Evian water or
coffee-making equipment on it; a few cups, napkins; the "script" for the
play.

Obviously, this rehearsal is not realistic; yet, so far as most audiences
could know, it should seem authentic. The invisible DIRECTOR is off stage,
and might be imagined as sitting in the rear row of the theater.

Lights up, though not fully. Door opens. The WOMAN *enters, accompanied by the* MAN, *who holds her upper arm (In affection? Out of possessiveness? To steady her?); he releases her and she advances haltingly into the room, glancing about. She is a strikingly beautiful young woman with long straight sleek hair; dressed for a party, in a long skirt; she wears a fringed shawl over her shoulders. Conspicuous earrings, rings.* WOMAN *is cold; hugs herself.*

The MAN *shuts, locks, double-bolts the door with an air of finality. When he turns on the light switch the lamp comes on and lights up fully.*

The MAN *is good-looking in a "charismatic" way. He wears a suede or leather jacket, a turtleneck sweater. He is intelligent but ironic; a man of only moderate, thus frustrating, success.*

MAN *(Rubbing hands together briskly, regarding* WOMAN's *back)* Well! *That* was a party! No doubt about it—*that was a party. (Whistles through his teeth)* The champagne!—the flowers!—the view of the river!—the jumbo shrimp, of which I devoured eleven! Those people really know how to get it on. *(Prodding, undercurrent of anger as he regards her)* Is that what you're thinking too, darling?

WOMAN *(Slowly, hesitantly)* You know I—

MAN *(As if unhearing, bemused)* I've been living in New York since the age of nineteen but it's always new to me. Always surprises! Like this party where suddenly *I'm* shaking hands—kissing cheeks!—with the very rich. I'm their *equal*—we're all one another's *equal*—chatting about politics, the arts—all *equal. (Pause, then lightly to conceal bitterness)* While the party lasts.

MAN *waits for* WOMAN's *response, but she withdraws into herself.*

MAN Great for the ego to see yourself perceived by the very rich as an *equal*—while the party lasts. "You've done such wonders with that little theater of yours"— "We do so *admire* you all"—"Such dedication!"

(Executes a graceful softshoe, then in a crafty tone) How casually then I let fall to Mrs. Sol Silverstein that our NEA grant for next year covers only forty-five percent of our budget—those eyes of ferocity and beauty and patrician good taste flashed upon me—she seized my hand— *(Demonstrates)*—and said, "Call me Monday morning, we'll have lunch." *(Pause)* Mmmm—most erotic words in the English language— *(Husky, seductive voice)* "Call me Monday morning, we'll have lunch."

MAN *pats jacket pocket, a surprised, sly expression on his face.*

MAN *(Drawing a jumbo shrimp out of the pocket and holding it aloft)* Ooops!—one last shrimp. *(Eats it, sensuously)* Crustaceans are delicious once their antennae are removed. *(Pats the other pocket, discovers another shrimp)* Uh-oh: *this* is the last. *(Holds the shrimp out to the* WOMAN, *who shakes her head, no; he eats it, as before)*

MAN *removes his jacket and tosses it onto the sofa. Approaches the* WOMAN *slowly and deliberately. She takes a step or two backward. A tense moment—yet the* MAN *chooses to behave as if there is nothing wrong.*

MAN You did want to come back— *(Pause, as if he's about to say "home")* —here with me, didn't you. Or did you have other plans?

WOMAN *(Defiantly)* I was ready to leave the party an hour ago. You know that.

The MAN *removes the* WOMAN's *shawl from her shoulders; in so doing, he embraces her impulsively from behind and buries his face in her neck. The* WOMAN *shudders, pushes away. She has reacted instinctively.*

MAN *(Ironically)* Well! Sorry.

WOMAN No, no—I'm sorry. *(Hands through hair, nervously)* I don't know what's wrong with me.

The MAN *crumples the shawl in his fists; after a beat or two he realizes what he's doing, and lays it carefully across the back of a chair. Smooths it with his fingers.*

MAN *(Meaning the shawl)* Pretty.

WOMAN I didn't even want to go to the party. You were the one.

MAN But, once there, as always, in others' admiring eyes—you generated quite an aura.

WOMAN *(Speaking precisely)* Because, look, you wanted to go—I wanted to do what *you* wanted. But— *(Laughs at this absurdity)* I didn't *want* to do it.

MAN Like hell. You said you wanted to go. Right here— *(Checks watch)* —three hours and eight minutes ago.

WOMAN   Because you'd have been angry otherwise.

MAN   Angry? Me? Don't tell me my own fucking emotions.

WOMAN *(A sudden wild laugh)*   Why not? why not? You're always telling me mine.

MAN   Someone has to. You're so blind, yourself.

The WOMAN *moves as if to leave the room, and the* MAN *seizes her arm to stop her.*

WOMAN *(Slapping at him, voice rising)*   Don't! don't! don't! don't! leave me alone!

They struggle together; the MAN *manages to fold the* WOMAN *in his embrace, as in a straitjacket. But the* WOMAN *reacts desperately, sobbing, hyperventilating—and the* MAN *releases her. The* WOMAN *loses her balance, falls to her hands and knees.*

The rehearsal sequence is abruptly terminated.

As if someone has snapped his fingers, the WOMAN *becomes the* ACTRESS *and the* MAN, *the* ACTOR.

DIRECTOR'S VOICE *(Impatient, perplexed)*   ("Mary"), what is it?—you've done the same damned thing again.

The ACTRESS *and the* ACTOR *should be addressed by the names, or the near-names, of the actual actress and actor who are performing the roles. If the exact name isn't desired, the name chosen should sound very like it: "Mary" for Marie," "Jake" for "Jack," "Carol Ann" for "Carolyn," and so forth.*

ACTRESS, ACTOR *look toward the* DIRECTOR.

ACTRESS *(Upset, apologetic)*   I'm sorry! Let me try it again.

DIRECTOR'S VOICE   You're frightened of this man, ("Mary"), he's hurt you in the past and he will probably hurt you again. But you love him.

ACTRESS   I know!

ACTOR *(Joking)*   You adore me, I'm irresistible. It says so in the script.

ACTRESS *laughs heartily, as if to demonstrate how she is not the* WOMAN.

ACTRESS *(In an undertone)*   I'm dying for a cigarette, that's what's wrong.

DIRECTOR'S VOICE   You love him, you're hypnotized by him. You don't *fight* him.

ACTRESS   I realize that. I got confused. With that, that later scene. I'm sorry.

The ACTRESS *and the* ACTOR *recompose themselves. They shift into their respective roles again but, from this point onward, we are aware of them as* ACTORS.

ACTRESS *(A little too forcibly)* "Because, look, you wanted to go—"
(Pause) No, sorry. Let me, uh—try again. *(Pause)* "Because, look, you
wanted to go—I wanted to do what you wanted me to do. But—"
(Has forgotten lines)

DIRECTOR'S VOICE *(Exuding patience)* "Because, look, you wanted to
go—I wanted to do what *you* wanted. But—"

ACTRESS *(Quickly)* "—I didn't *want* to do it." O.K. *(Prepares to begin
again, brushes hair out of face, composes herself)* "Because, look, you
wanted to go—I wanted to do what *you* wanted. But— *(Laughs, not
convincingly; laughs again)* —I didn't *want* to do it."

ACTOR "Like hell. You said you wanted to go. Right here— *(checks
watch)* —three hours and eight minutes ago."

ACTRESS "Because you'd have been angry otherwise."

ACTOR "Angry? Me? Don't tell me my own emotions." *(Correcting himself)* "—fucking emotions."

ACTRESS *(Overlapping, with a nervous, wild laugh)* "Why not? why
not? You're always telling me mine."

ACTOR "Someone has to, you're so blind, yourself."

*The ACTRESS misses her cue and begins to move belatedly. The ACTOR
moves to seize her arm. The action is uncoordinated.*

ACTRESS *(Dissolving in laughter)* Oh! Oh shit! This isn't my morning,
is it!

ACTOR *("Mary")*, come on. It was terrific at the beginning.

DIRECTOR'S VOICE Take a few deep breaths, and you're fine. C'mon.

*ACTRESS, ACTOR take several deep restorative breaths. They visibly recom-
pose themselves.*

DIRECTOR'S VOICE Let's go back to the beginning, all right? The pacing's
a little slow anyway. Exit!

ACTRESS, ACTOR, snatching up their shawl and jacket, exit.

Lights down.

*Lights up, dimly, as before. Door opens; ACTRESS enters; ACTOR close be-
hind her, gripping her upper arm; ACTRESS advances into the room, as before. ACTOR locks door, flicks light switch. (A re-staging of the opening of
this play. However it was played originally, it is now played differently.
The pacing is certainly faster—though some of the pauses may be longer.
Both the ACTRESS and the ACTOR are now self-conscious and trying too
hard: we may be aware of their technique. This time through the dramatic
focus is not on the "story" but on the performers.)*

ACTOR *(Rubbing hands together briskly, regarding* ACTRESS's *back)*
"Well! *That* was a party! No doubt about it—*that was a party. (Whistles through his teeth)* The champagne!—the flowers!—the view of the river!—the jumbo shrimp, of which I devoured eleven! Those people really know how to get it on. *(Prodding, as before)* Is that what you're thinking too, darling?"

ACTRESS *(Slowly, hesitantly)* "You k-know I—"

ACTOR *(Cutting her off)* "I've been living in New York since the age of nineteen but it's always new to me. Always surprises. Like this party where suddenly *I'm* shaking hands—kissing cheeks!—with the very rich. I'm their *equal*—we're all one another's *equal*—chatting about politics, the arts—all *equal. (Pause, then lightly, to conceal bitterness)* While the party lasts."

ACTOR *waits for* ACTRESS's *response, but she has turned away. Nervous mannerisms, brushes hair out of face, etc.*

ACTOR "Great for the ego to see yourself perceived by the very rich as an *equal*—while the party lasts. 'You've done such wonders with that little theater of yours'—'We do so *admire* you all'—'Such dedication!' *(Executes a graceful softshoe, then in a crafty tone)* How casually then I let fall to Mrs. Sol Silverstein that our NEA grant for next year covers only forty-five percent of our budget—those eyes of ferocity and beauty and patrician good taste flashed upon me—she seized my hand— *(Demonstrates)*—and said, 'Call me Monday morning, we'll have lunch.' *(Pause)* Mmmm—most erotic words in the English language— *(Husky, seductive voice)* 'Call me Monday morning, we'll have lunch.'"

ACTOR *pats jacket pocket as before, sly expression on his face.*

ACTOR *(Drawing an invisible shrimp out of his pocket)* "Ooops!—one last shrimp. *(Pretends to eat)* Crustaceans are delicious once their antennae are removed. *(Discovers the second shrimp in his pocket, etc.)* Uh-oh: *this* is the last one." *(Offers the invisible shrimp to* ACTRESS, *who, staring at him, fails to respond)*

ACTOR *removes jacket, tosses at the sofa; it slips to the floor.* ACTOR *approaches* ACTRESS *who moves awkwardly backward colliding with a chair.*

ACTOR "You *did* want to come back—here—with me—didn't you? Or did you have other plans?"

ACTRESS *(A little too emphatically)* "I was ready to leave the party an hour ago. You know that."

ACTOR *comes to remove the shawl from* ACTRESS's *shoulders; in so doing,*

he embraces her from behind, presses his mouth against her throat. The
ACTRESS *responds with a little cry, clutching at him.*

This is not in the script. The ACTRESS *immediately acknowledges it, with
a snap of her fingers, a repentant gesture.*

ACTRESS   No! Wrong. Sorry.

DIRECTOR'S VOICE *(Overlapping)*   Wrong move. You *shudder,* and—

ACTRESS *(Overlapping, quickly)*   Right! Right! I know! I shudder and
step away.

DIRECTOR'S VOICE *(Overbearing)*   The playwright says it's like she has
this sexual rush—this orgasm—when he touches her. Right?

ACTRESS, ACTOR *exchange glances; roll eyes.*

ACTRESS *(Undertone)*   Orgasm —what a lot of shit! *(To* DIRECTOR*)*
Right! That's right. I *know* that.

DIRECTOR'S VOICE   The playwright has the entire play choreographed. It's
like a ballet. It *is* a ballet. If it's performed right, it will be beautiful.

ACTRESS, ACTOR *(Animatedly)*   That's right! Beautiful.

ACTRESS, ACTOR *take several deep breaths to recompose themselves. They
begin again, where they'd left off.*

ACTOR *removes the shawl from* ACTRESS's *shoulders; embraces her from
behind, presses his mouth against her throat. This time she shudders and
pushes away. But the moment is spoiled by her sudden coughing.*

There is a pause while the ACTRESS *searches for a tissue, to wipe her
mouth and eyes; and, in a quick gesture, her throat, where the* ACTOR *has
pressed his mouth.* ACTOR *waits patiently.*

They resume the rehearsal.

ACTOR *(Ironically, loudly)*   "Well! *Sorry.*"

ACTRESS   "N-No, no—I'm sorry. I don't know what's—what's wrong
with me."

ACTOR *crumples the shawl in his fists but this time holds it against his
torso for a beat or two; then, realizing what he's doing, he smooths it
across the back of a chair.*

ACTOR *(Resuming rehearsal)*   "Pretty."

ACTRESS *(Wavering, speaking sharply)*   "I didn't even want to go to the
party! You were the one."

ACTOR   "But, once there, as always, in others' admiring eyes—you generated quite an aura."

ACTRESS *(Determined not to stumble, enunciating words)*   "Because,
look, *you* wanted to go—I wanted to do what you wanted. But—*(A
peal of wild laughter)* —I didn't *want* to do it."

ACTOR *laughs, too, As if about to lose control.*

ACTOR "Like hell! You said you, you wanted to go. Right here— *(A gesture meaning the space about them)* —three hours and eight minutes ago."

ACTRESS "Because you'd have been angry otherwise."

ACTOR "Angry? Me? Don't tell me my own fucking emotions!"

ACTRESS *(Angry laughter)* "Why not? why not? You're always telling me mine!"

ACTRESS has forgotten to move, to leave the room; ACTOR advances upon her.

ACTOR *(Reaching for her arm)* "Someone has to. You're so blind, yourself."

This time when they struggle together, and the ACTOR folds the ACTRESS in his tight embrace, the ACTRESS goes limp and does not resist.

A beat or two.

ACTOR "The first glimpse I had of you, seeing how others, not just men but women, too, were watching you, I thought, 'A woman like that is blind. She is seen, but cannot see.'"

ACTRESS sinks to the floor beside ACTOR, placatingly; clutching at his hands, his knees.

ACTRESS *(Desperate, yet "feminine," seductive)* "Don't be angry with me. I *am* blind without you—I see, but I don't understand what I see. Please forgive me . . . "

ACTOR *(As if barely retaining control)* "You did lie, then? About tonight?—the party? And last week—being with your mother, those nights?—was that a lie, too?"

ACTRESS "No. No."

ACTOR *(Shuts his fist in ACTRESS's hair, draws her head back painfully)* "Tonight, the party, you *did* want to go, yes you wanted to go, didn't you?"

ACTRESS "Yes."

ACTOR "Because I wanted you to, or because you wanted to—?"

ACTRESS "Because, because—what you want me to do, *I* want to do—"

ACTOR *(Still gripping her hair)* "And what happened?—since I saw, you might as well tell the truth."

ACTRESS "I—I—"

ACTOR *(Overlapping)* "Who was it, what did he say to you?—don't lie."

ACTRESS "—nothing—"

ACTOR *(Overlapping)* "Don't lie."

ACTOR continues to grip ACTRESS's *hair, twisting her head back; she tries to defend herself, but ineffectually, using no force of her own.*

ACTOR *(Baring teeth)* "I saw him, the big man, Silverstein, was it?—or one of his friends?—I saw, I didn't need to hear, I got the picture—I wasn't going to interrupt."

ACTRESS "No, it wasn't— Don't hurt me—"

ACTOR "Where'd you go with him? Where'd he take you? I looked around, and you were gone."

ACTRESS "I wasn't gone, I—"

ACTOR *(Overlapping)* "I looked around, there were maybe one hundred people in that fucking living room but not you, not you and not him, where'd he take you?—you think *I'm* blind?"

ACTRESS *(Overlapping)* "No, don't, please—"

ACTOR *(As he jerks* ACTRESS's *head rhythmically)* "Out on the fucking balcony to see the East River by moonlight?—into the fucking hothouse to see the tropical flowers?—in the fucking "master" bedroom to see the Van Gogh over the bed?" *(*ACTRESS *sobs,* ACTOR *releases her and pushes her away, as if in disgust, yet with an air of bemusement, too)* "No, you'll tell me, like the last time: you didn't mean for any of it to happen, it just *happened*."

ACTRESS *is sobbing. Hides her face.* ACTOR *crouches over her, an arm slung across her shoulders, against her breasts; he peers over her head, toward the audience.*

ACTOR "Not that I want to control you. Not that I will cease to love you. There *is* only you and me. None of our friends—" *(A gesture as if to include the audience)* —knows, or can guess, how it *is* between us. *(Gripping her tight, in a voice of strange, tender anguish)* How. It. Is. Between. Us."

A pause.

DIRECTOR'S VOICE *(Loud, jarring)* O.K. Not bad. Not terrific, but not bad. Let's go back to where he takes hold of her hair. *(As* ACTRESS, ACTOR *rise, reposition themselves)* ("Jack"), a little more force this time, passion, not like you're afraid to hurt her, hurting her's the bond, she *loves* it, right? ("Mary"), I don't want to push but I'm frankly not one hundred percent convinced you're *in* this role yet.

ACTRESS *(Defensive, nervous)* I have to move at my own pace.

ACTOR *(To* DIRECTOR*)* Why don't we do the lines, and smooth out the physical stuff later?

DIRECTOR'S VOICE *(Pedantic)* "In theatre of such visceral intensity, language and action, voice and body, are *one*."

ACTRESS *(Rubbing her neck, a wry tone)* That figures!

DIRECTOR'S VOICE *(A bit sharply)* You've got a question of interpretation, ("Mary")?

ACTRESS *(A sharp reply, disguised by a smile)* Oh no, no!—*you* do the interpretation for me.

ACTOR *(To DIRECTOR)* Where do we start, her on the floor and me, "You did lie, then?" or—

DIRECTOR "The first glimpse I had of you."

ACTOR *embraces* ACTRESS, *awkwardly; taking a beat or two to get into position. (Whispering to each other, "Like this—?" "Where was my hand?" "No, like this—" "Like this," etc.)*

However the scene was previously played, it is played differently this time.

ACTOR "The first glimpse I had of you . . . seeing how others, not just men but women, too, were watching you . . . I thought, 'A woman like that is blind. She is *seen,* but cannot *see.*' "

On "blind," ACTRESS *sinks to her knees beside* ACTOR, *clutching placatingly at him.*

ACTRESS "Don't be angry with me. I—I *am* b-blind—"

ACTRESS *seems to panic; loses control; wrenches herself away from* ACTOR; *hides her face in hands.*

A startled beat or two of silence.

DIRECTOR'S VOICE *(Exuding patience)* O.K., ("Mary")—we'll break now.

ACTRESS *gets to her feet breathless, apologetic; tears in her eyes. She seems to have been pushed to the limit of her endurance but is unwilling to accept the fact, or even to comprehend it.*

ACTOR, *however, understands: his expression is hurt, guilty, resolved.*

ACTRESS God, I'm so sorry! I don't know what's wrong with me. It's like I'm not myself. *(Appealing)* I love this play, it means so much to me to be in it—

DIRECTOR'S VOICE *(Dryly)* So you've said. *(Pause)* O.K., ("Mary"), ("Jack"), we'll resume at 11:15 prompt.

ACTRESS *(Calling after DIRECTOR)* I'm crazy about this playwright's work, it's a profound challenge, like nothing I've ever done before— *(As DIRECTOR passes out of earshot; with increasing frustration, fury)* —also I need work.

ACTOR *(Starting after DIRECTOR)* I need to talk to him.

ACTRESS *(Pulling at ACTOR's arm, stopping him)* No, ("Jack"), you don't. Stay here.

ACTOR ("Mary"), this isn't fair to you. I can't do this to you.

ACTRESS   What the hell are you saying?

ACTOR   You know.

ACTRESS   I don't! I don't know. It's my nerves, it's *my* problem.

ACTOR *(Looks at her searchingly)*   ("Mary"), come on. You're scared to death of me. It's in your eyes right now. You can't help it, it *is*.

ACTRESS *(Frightened)*   What is? What is? What's in my eyes I can't help?

ACTOR   I shouldn't have accepted the role. I shouldn't be working.

ACTRESS *(Forefinger to lips)*   Not so loud!

ACTOR   It isn't fair to you.

ACTRESS *(Taking his hand, appealing)*   ("Jack"), we talked it over, I made my decision. I want to work with you. My God, I'm honored to work with you. You're a hero to me—now more than ever.

ACTOR   There's too much—physical contact in this Goddamned play. I don't like hurting you, and I sure as hell don't like scaring you.

ACTRESS   Look, I'm a professional. I've been acting since the age of sixteen. I'm pretty good—usually. I've just got to get into this. It isn't you, ("Jack"), it's me.

ACTOR *(Dubiously)*   Your eyes say something different.

ACTRESS   Oh, the hell with my eyes! It's my contact lenses you see.

ACTOR   You're scared. Of me. *(Pause)* I don't blame you, ("Mary"), *I'm* scared of me.

A pause.

ACTRESS *(Fumbling for cigarettes in bag)*   I'm not scared of you, ("Jack"), I'm scared for you. There's a difference. *(Offering him a cigarette)*

ACTOR *(Declining)*   Are you kidding? Never again!

ACTRESS *(Embarrassed)*   Oh! of course. The medication—

ACTOR *(Gently correcting)*   What the medication's *for.*

ACTRESS, ACTOR *have their break on the set. Evian water, or coffee;* ACTOR *may take some pills, eat a quick lunch from a deli container; or may do aerobics movements intermittently.* ACTRESS *smokes, may remove her high-heeled shoes, refashions her hair, paces nervously about.*

ACTOR *(Disapproving)*   That, too—smoking. You'd stopped for, how long?—two, three years? Now you've started again.

ACTRESS   But not because of you! Christ, you're paranoid.

ACTOR *(Quickly)*   Don't say that.

ACTRESS *(Placating)*   I just meant, no, it has nothing to do with you, ("Jack").

ACTOR   All right. So why say it—"paranoid."

ACTRESS   It's just a, an expression—"paranoid." It doesn't mean—

ACTOR   Because I really don't think I'm—like that. I really think I'm handling it O.K.

ACTRESS   Everybody's paranoid these days. *(Realizes this, too, is a mistake to say, too late.)* Oh, am *I* crazy! *(Emphatically stubbing out cigarette)*

ACTRESS *may light up another cigarette later in this scene, and again fairly quickly stub it out.*

ACTRESS *(Quickly)*   The main thing is, ("Jack"), you're a—well person. You look terrific. You've never looked better. I mean really. *(Pause)* No one would know.

ACTOR *(Not wanting to seem too hopeful)*   D'you really think so?

ACTRESS   Yes. Definitely. *(Pause)* This play, working with you, it's a, an honor for me, y'know?—I mean, we've worked together before, but this is special. Only two roles. And *this* playwright—Mr. Macho-"Sensitive." Oh I want so badly to do well! I'm *not* afraid of you.

ACTOR   Then what?

ACTRESS   Of—well—maybe—failure.

ACTOR *(Shrugs)*   Well! *(Meaning, "That's the case with us all")*

ACTRESS *(Quickly)*   So much—for me—is riding on this— It's my—I guess you could say—"big chance." I'm like *her*—an actress who's been "promising" for too long. *(Pause)* I'm *not* afraid of—you.

ACTOR   Sure you are. I mean—after all. Friendship can only go so far, self-survival's got to be a stronger instinct. *(Tentative air)*

ACTRESS   No! *(Pause)* How many people . . . know?

ACTOR *(Counting on fingers)*   —Six, seven— No, he died. Six.

ACTRESS *(With dread)*   Who was that?

ACTOR *makes a gesture meaning, "Please don't ask."*

ACTRESS   Well, please don't tell *him*— *(A gesture to indicate the* DIRECTOR*)* That'd be a mistake, to tell *him*.

ACTOR   I've considered—maybe it's a matter of conscience.

ACTRESS   Whose conscience?

ACTOR   Mine, of course.

ACTRESS *(Incensed)*   What about other people's consciences!

ACTOR   You think he'd fire me?

ACTRESS   He can't fire you—can he?

ACTOR   I've always sort of wondered, is he homophobic. The way he goes on about his "gay" friends.

ACTRESS   Oh, I don't think so, I think he means well . . . Christ, I don't know. *(Pause)* He's misogynous, that's for damned sure.

ACTOR *(Laughing)*   So what's new?—every heterosexual male above the age of twelve is misogynous. Goes with the territory.

ACTRESS   Oh, no!

ACTOR   Well, maybe just the ones I know.

ACTRESS *(Mimicking DIRECTOR, an undercurrent of ange.)* "The play-wright says—it's like she has this SEXUAL RUSH—this OR-GASM—when he TOUCHES her." Oh, wow.

ACTOR *(Falling in zestfully)* "Hurting her's the bond, she *loves* it." *(Pause)* "It's a BALLET. It's BEAUTIFUL."

ACTRESS The sons of bitches! *(Pause, then suddenly)* I hate this play!

ACTOR *(Shocked)* Not so loud, ("Mary")!

ACTRESS I hate it! I hate *her*, and I hate *him*, I hate this sick sado-macho crap! And I hate *me* in it, trying so hard! Every day I read in the pa-per about the famine in Africa, I see these starving children on televi-sion, there's the homeless right outside the theater here on the street, there's drugs, poverty— *(Slight hesitation)*—AIDS. A universe of true, profound suffering and we're trapped in this fevered little world, it's just a, a—*set. (Looking wildly around)* A *set*. I'm living out my adult life on a *set*.

ACTOR *(Cautioning)* He's going to hear you.

ACTRESS *(Voice rising recklessly)* Let him! I hate *him*! Nothing I do is ever good enough for him! The last time I worked with him, he reduced me to a quivering mass of hysteria, I am *not* a quivering mass of hysteria— *(Excitedly, "quivering")* —I am a human being, an adult woman. The last time, I vowed it would be the last time, he broke me down to *this*, and just watched me, and d'you know what the bastard said?

ACTOR Sure. He said, "Now put that emotion into your role, and you'll be terrific."

ACTRESS *(A bit crestfallen)* How did you know?

ACTOR He did the same thing with me, the first time we worked together.

ACTRESS *You?*

ACTOR Me.

ACTRESS *(After a pause)* I did put the emotion into the role, and I *was* terrific. People said. *(Pause)* Actually, ("Jack"), this play isn't too far from, from my own life, that's one of the reasons I'm having trouble. Some of this sick-hypnosis stuff, him saying how their friends could never guess the way it is between them—

ACTOR *(Mock-passionate)* "How. It. Is. Between. Us."

ACTRESS —and she doesn't exist without him—I've been there. I know.

ACTOR *(With delicacy)* You and—Alec?

ACTRESS *(In a rush of confiding)* I can hardly believe it now, the way I depended upon him, needed him—even when I was working, and working well, getting good reviews, I was desperate I'd lose him, and there wouldn't be any point to my work, no one to share it with, just—nothing. Then I got pregnant, a purposeful accident Alec said, and, well— *(A gesture as if to say, "You know the story.")*

ACTOR *(Sympathetically, tactfully)* That was a while back, wasn't it?

ACTRESS *(Quickly)* Oh, I'm not like that, now: I'm much stronger now. *(Pause)* It's just I remember, my God, on my knees, too, like her, my actual knees, on bare floorboards! in this loft! on Varick! and I'm begging a man not to stop loving me—

ACTOR You! That's hard to believe . . .

ACTRESS I'd never tell anyone—except you. It's like you and your private life—not telling your family, even—about your, your condition—you *can't.*

ACTOR "Once said, never unsaid." My Irish grandmother was always warning me. Like she knew I'd be the one who'd have secrets and disgrace the family—

ACTRESS ("Jack"), come on! Your family must be damned proud of you.

ACTOR Must they? *(A pause)* ("Mary"), you said that the "main thing"is I'm a well person right now, I look "terrific"—but you know, and I know, that isn't true. The "main thing" is I'm HIV-positive, I'm a carrier and I'm infectious and what's wrong with me is invisible and potentially fatal—and no known cure. That's the "main thing."

ACTRESS *(Rattled)* But they, they could find a cure—we could pick up the *Times* tomorrow, and—a big front-page headline—

ACTOR *(Laughs)* I've actually dreamt that headline, I've seen it. Then I tried to read the story, and the newsprint was too small. *(Pause)* My sister's husband, he's a high school principal in Carbondale, not a bad guy at all—one Christmas a few years ago I'm back home, it's a family gathering, he tells this joke—"A 'gay' calls home and announces to his parents, 'I have some news for you: bad news, and good news.' And they ask, 'What is it, son?' and the son says, 'The bad news is, I'm queer; the good news is, I've got AIDS' " *(Laughs)*

A pause.

ACTRESS I can't believe that. You're making that up.

ACTOR My sister'd never gotten around to telling her husband she had— has—a gay younger brother.

ACTRESS It's just so . . . hard to believe.

ACTOR Honey, no, nothing's hard to believe.

ACTRESS *stares blankly at* ACTOR; *succumbs to a quick spasm of sobbing; immediately checks herself.*

ACTRESS You're so . . . courageous. In your place, I . . . Oh God, I'm not—handling this right.

ACTOR *(As if to comfort her)* ("Mary"), look: it isn't what they call a life-threatening condition, at least not now. And it might never be. I just tested—"positive." But no symptoms. No—*(Pause)* —symptoms.

ACTRESS *(Rattled)* No symptoms. Yes. *No.* I can s-see that.

ACTOR *(Flexing muscles)*   Actually, I've gained a little. I've been working out . . .

ACTRESS   This medication—it helps?

ACTOR *(Regarding her closely)*   You know, ("Mary"), I think I'd better . . . don't you?

ACTRESS   Better—what?

ACTOR   Talk to him. Explain.

ACTRESS   Explain—?

ACTOR   Why you're having such a hard time, and why I'm going to drop out.

ACTRESS   My God, no! You can't. I mean, you *can't.*

ACTOR   You're stressed out, look at you. I've never seen you like this.

ACTRESS   I had a bad night last night, that's all—

ACTOR   I could feel you trembling when I held you, like your heartbeat was everywhere in your body. I can't put you through it.

ACTRESS   Goddamn it, I'm a professional. Since the age of sixteen. The day after my miscarriage I got out of bed and worked. You *know* me.

ACTOR   This is something else.

ACTRESS   No. I can control it. I promise.

ACTOR   If you keep blowing it the way you've been, he'll have to, you know, talk to you—

ACTRESS *(Overlapping)*   —Fire me—

ACTOR *(Overlapping)*   I won't let that happen.

ACTRESS   *I* won't let that happen. *(Pause)* I know I wasn't his first choice for this role, I was at least his third—yes? *(ACTOR makes gesture of innocence, as if not knowing)* Well, I wouldn't have auditioned at all, I figured I didn't have a chance, they'd want some bigger name, like you, but—*he* called *me.*

ACTOR *(Protesting)*   Hey look, ("Mary"), he thinks you're terrific. He called *me* up, he said, "You won't believe who I've cast for the play."

ACTRESS *(Pathetically hopeful)*   He—did?

ACTOR   He did.

ACTRESS   I still don't trust him. If you talked to him, if you—explained— you'd never get work again. I just know.

ACTOR *(Irritated)*   That's a lot of shit. I don't buy that.

ACTRESS *(Backing down)*   Well, maybe—it depends.

ACTOR   There's a network of sympathetic people in the theatre, for God's sake. I trust them, they're my friends.

ACTRESS   That—that's right.

ACTOR   It's not like Hollywood, Hollywood's pure shit. There's a rumor about you, you're dead meat.

ACTRESS   I—I've heard that. I don't know.

ACTOR   Here, you can rely on your friends.

ACTRESS   You said you told—six people?

ACTOR   Yes, counting you.

ACTRESS   But, with those six people, it's a secret. It's better to keep it— secret. As long as you can.

ACTOR *(Pacing about, exasperated)*   Oh for Christ's sake—we'll give it another try. Through today's rehearsal. If, y'know, you keep blowing it—I'll tell him I'm out.

ACTRESS   Who can he cast, so late? Who's as good as you?

ACTOR *(Resolved)*   I'm out.

ACTRESS   *I'm* out. Why should you be sacrificed?

ACTOR *(Bluntly)*   I *am* a carrier. *(Pause)*

ACTRESS *(Quickly)*   Yes, but that—doesn't mean—it isn't like, like T.B., that new strain of T.B., that's—really lethal.

ACTOR *(Wonderingly)*   It's a mystery . . . so, so strange: to be lethal, yet not sick yourself; to carry death in your loins, where you believe there's love. It's a . . . metaphysical paradox. To wake up one day, and learn you're a "carrier." Like, what are you carrying? *(Pause)* Who *are* you? *(ACTOR has been moving restlessly about; now pauses, recites in a sonorous, contemplative tone)*

> Whereto answering, the sea,
> Delaying not, hurrying not,
> Whisper'd me through the night, and very plainly before
>   daybreak,
> Lisp'd to me the low and delicious word *death*,
> And again *death, death, death, death* . . .

A pause.

ACTRESS *(Spooked, backing off)*   Oh God! What *is* that?

ACTOR   Walt Whitman, "Out of the Cradle Endlessly Rocking."

ACTRESS   The *cradle*?

ACTOR   Well. That's how I feel sometimes. *(Pause)* Much of the time. *(Pause) All* of the time.

ACTRESS   God, ("Jack"), I wish I could . . . help you.

ACTOR   Nah, I'm fine, really: me, my "self," the one you see, and know, I'm fine. As long as I'm working, I'm—transcendent.

ACTRESS   But, ("Jack")—

ACTOR   My only problem with this play is, I wish I liked shrimp better. I have to eat two damned shrimp each performance, and I think I'm allergic to shellfish.

ACTRESS *(Blankly at first)*   Maybe it could be changed to—cocktail sausage?

ACTOR   I asked. It's got to be fucking "jumbo shrimp."

ACTRESS   You mean the playwright insists? It's got to be *shrimp*?

ACTOR   Jumbo shrimp.

ACTRESS   Is that petty! *(Picks up script, leafs through it)* It's funny how, when you're in it, a role's your life, almost—realer than real. Afterward, you forget.

ACTOR   You have to forget. You couldn't be all those people at once.

ACTRESS   But they're still there, inside. Like past lives. Buried selves. But where's the actual core? When he says to her— *(She indicates lines in the script)* —"You know you can't do—"

ACTOR *(Taking over, reciting, most convincingly)*   "You know you can't do "life," you can only do scripts. Without your technique you're nothing."

ACTRESS *(Shivering)*   —It just goes through me like a knife blade. This woman, this actress, like me, with a career like mine —he's got her down cold. That's really how it is. Without a script, I get scared. Like now. Anything can happen. *(Glancing around)* Doesn't it scare you, too?

ACTOR *(Shrugs)*   I try not to think about it. I think about my work.

ACTRESS   I almost can't remember what it's like, without "technique" between myself and other people. I suppose, when I was a little girl, I must have been real.

ACTOR *(Laughing)*   ("Mary"), c'mon, you're real right now.

ACTRESS *(As if baffled)*   Am I? My body maybe . . . my clothes. *(Looking down at herself)* When I was pregnant, that part of me was real . . . I think.

ACTOR *(A confession)*   I feel I'm always acting, it's just a matter of degree. How badly I'm trying for applause.

ACTRESS   With me it's "good" acting and "not-so-good" acting. But it's *acting.*

ACTOR   When you're . . . making love?

ACTRESS   Are you kidding? *Especially* when I'm making love.

ACTOR   Me, too. I mean—when I did. *(Pause)* Except, right now, talking with you, I'm actually not acting.

ACTRESS   I guess I'm not . . . actually . . . acting . . . either. *(Pause; a shiver)* It's like the outermost layer of my skin's been peeled away, just the air hurts.

A pause.

ACTOR   This, uh, what we've been saying—what I said about being a "carrier"—I haven't talked like that to anybody much, in fact nobody, so I'd appreciate it if—

ACTRESS *(Quickly, understanding)* Of course!—

ACTOR *(Earnestly)* —you didn't say anything to anybody, because if it got back to Jeff—if he knew how I felt—

ACTRESS —No, no, of course— *(Pause)* How is—?

ACTOR *(A bit stiffly)* Jeff is fine.

ACTRESS I guess I haven't seen him in a—

ACTOR We don't go out of the house much anymore.

ACTRESS *(Awkwardly)* Well—I miss him. *(A pause; ACTRESS returns to an easier subject, the play, lifting the script in her hand)* ("Jack"), I wanted to ask you, why do you think there's this business in the play about her mother?—her father's death, and the fact he'd been an astronomer? *(Locates the lines in the script, but recites rather than reads them)* "I did go to Mother's. I have to go when she calls me. Since Daddy died she can't sleep . . . she hears him calling her name . . . at night . . . he's in the night sky . . . his voice is disembodied . . . everywhere." *(Pause)* "But what I hear is . . . silence. The night sky doesn't talk to *me*."

ACTOR *(Reciting, in a jocular tone)* "The night sky sure as hell doesn't talk to *me*."

ACTRESS What's it mean?

ACTOR Means what it says. "The night sky sure as hell doesn't talk to *us*."

ACTRESS I kept hoping, when I first read the script, her mother would show up, though I saw the cast is just two people. *(A sudden rising of ACTRESS's voice)* She misses her mother! Her mother could save her from *him*.

ACTOR But she doesn't want to be saved. That's why, when the phone rings, she won't answer it.

ACTRESS *I'd* answer it.

ACTOR *(Playful threat)* Not if I forbade you to.

ACTRESS The producer was saying, when it was workshopped at Long Wharf, it had a different ending. Wonder what it was!

ACTOR He strangles her. With her "pretty" shawl.

ACTRESS No!

ACTOR Just joking.

ACTRESS I've never been killed yet. Unless you count Hedda Gabler and Miss Julie—but that's off-stage.

ACTOR I've been killed, but only on TV. That doesn't count, somehow.

ACTRESS Right on screen?

ACTOR Yes. But the screen's so *small*. You can't take it seriously.

ACTRESS *(Dubiously)* D'you think the ending here is going to work?— looping back on itself?

ACTOR I think it's a great ending. Given this hell they're in together, it's the perfect ending.

ACTRESS   But a lot has changed. She's changed. You get the idea she's maybe going to leave him—"survive" him. There's that hope.

ACTOR *(Dubiously)*   That's how you interpret it . . . ?

ACTRESS   And that part, too, I love, this Silverstein character she did go off with— *(Reciting, defiantly)* "All right Goddamn you yes he did, we did, and it isn't a Van Gogh over the bed it's only a Warhol." Revenge! *(Laughs)*

ACTOR *(Objecting)*   Revenge? That's what *he* wants, it's his fantasy.

ACTRESS *(Incensed)*   His? Like hell, ("Jack")! It's hers, but it isn't fantasy.

ACTOR   Yes, he's willing her to confess. There isn't any "Silverstein" really.

ACTRESS   What? Are you kidding? If there's a "Mrs. Silverstein" why isn't there a "Mr.?"

ACTOR   But the man is *his* agent. He possesses her by way of "Silverstein"—and other men she's had one-shot affairs with. He's a voyeur, he's Prospero. He's the playwright—see?

ACTRESS   But the painting over the bed—she saw it.

ACTOR   Maybe.

ACTRESS   I SAW IT! *(Trying to remain calm)* These people, these rich patrons of the arts—they can buy artists—us—like consumer goods—some of us, at least—but they don't know true art, they can't recognize it. "It isn't a Van Gogh"—a surpassingly great artist—"it's only a Warhol"—a flat-out spiritually bankrupt late twentieth-century phony. That cinches it, for me. *I love it.*

ACTOR *(Entering into the spirit of it, speaking as his character in the play, pitying, derisive, "hypnotic")*   "No, no! What a fantasy! Did you think you could exist without me?—imagine yourself for a single hour, without me? You poor—"

ACTRESS *(Interrupting)*   —Don't say it, Goddamn you!

ACTOR   "—cunt." *(Since he's been interrupted, he repeats, cruelly)* "You poor cunt."

ACTRESS *(A cry)*   I told you *don't*!

ACTRESS slaps ACTOR as a child might; flailing out; dropping her cigarette, spilling some of the contents of his cup onto him.

ACTRESS *(Immediately appalled, contrite)*   Oh Christ—I'm sorry.

ACTOR *(Annoyed but laughing)*   *I'm* sorry.

Both ACTRESS and ACTOR brush at his clothes.

ACTRESS *(Apologetic yet still aggressive, even defiant)*   I just can't tolerate that—epithet.

ACTOR *(Making light of it)*   ("Mary"), it's O.K. Forget it.

ACTRESS   Every play by a male playwright I've been in for the past five years—except *A Christmas Carol*—I get called a cunt. I just freaked.

ACTOR   O.K., I don't blame you. I get freaked, too, when I'm called a cunt.

ACTRESS   *(Earnestly)*   It's like men hate women so much, and women don't know why. I mean, *why?* Why do they hate us?

ACTOR   Don't ask *me.*

ACTRESS   Is it because we're—just—different—from men? Our bodies are—soft? Or—we can have babies? And *they're* the babies, and resent it?

ACTOR   Honey, how would *I* know? I'm just a bystander.

ACTRESS   *(In her sudden emotion, speaking unpremeditatedly)*   I love you.

A stunned pause. ACTOR *may fumble something he's holding.*

ACTOR   Well, I—love you.

ACTRESS   *(Quickly)*   Oh no, no—you don't have to. *(Laughs girlishly)* The first time I ever saw you—you were Solyony, at the Yale Rep— remember? In your uniform, so handsome! God, I was in love with you, I didn't know it was hopeless.

ACTOR   Solyony! That long ago! But it's like yesterday . . . *(To deflect his embarrassment he clowns a bit, making handwashing motions)* Poor Solyony!—can't get his hands to smell like anything but a corpse—

ACTRESS   *(Simply)*   Now it isn't that I'm *in* love with you, I just . . . love you.

ACTOR   Eight, nine years ago . . . Like yesterday.

ACTRESS *is about to speak when* DIRECTOR'S VOICE *interrupts. Both* ACTRESS *and* ACTOR *are startled.*

DIRECTOR'S VOICE   *(Jarring, brisk)*   ("Mary"), ("Jack"), ready to begin?

ACTRESS, ACTOR   *(Staring out, like frightened children)*   Yes . . . ready . . .

DIRECTOR'S VOICE   You're O.K., ("Mary")? Back on keel?

ACTRESS   *(With resolution)*   Yes.

DIRECTOR'S VOICE   ("Jack")?

ACTOR *has been staring out at* DIRECTOR, *eyes intense.*

ACTOR   *(With resolution)*   Sure thing.

DIRECTOR'S VOICE   Back to the beginning. Only three more rehearsals before the first preview.

ACTRESS, ACTOR *return to set as lights dim.*

Lights up. Door opens, ACTRESS *appears, wearing her shawl,* ACTOR *close behind her. Action as before.*

ACTOR *(As he'd opened the play originally)*   "Well! *That* was a party! No doubt about it—*that was a party. (Whistles through his teeth)* The champagne!—the flowers!—the view of the river!—the jumbo shrimp, of which I devoured eleven! Those people really know how to get it on. *(Pause)* Is that what you're thinking too, darling?"

ACTRESS stands erect, defiantly smiling.

During ACTOR's speech lights dim slowly.

THE END

ONTOLOGICAL PROOF OF MY EXISTENCE ❧

A Play in One Act

Cast

SHELLEY—a girl of about sixteen
PETER V.—a man of indeterminate age
SHELLEY'S FATHER—a man in his forties
MARTIN RAVEN—a man in his thirties

What are the proofs of God?
—a question frequently posed in past centuries: but no longer.
What are the proofs of man?
—a question more reasonably posed for our time.

Setting

A room with a high ceiling; unpainted brick walls; unfurnished and yet cluttered; desolate; inhuman; on the edge of nowhere. Yet comfortable, lived-in. A curiously domestic hovel. A window, stage right. A door, stage left. A mattress on the floor stage right.

Lights up, slowly. SHELLEY *is lying immobile on the mattress, beneath a filthy blanket. The lights continue to come up: cold, impersonal, dream-like. There is something unreal about the lighting as well as the setting, as if the play were taking place at the lowest level of human vitality, at the point at which the human passes subtly and unprotestingly into the unhuman.*

SHELLEY *wakes. She comes gradually to life—to consciousness. One must feel the difficulty, the struggle. To come back! To come back—again! She is exhausted, drugged, groggy: she shakes her head, trying to clear her thoughts. At first it isn't clear whether she is a boy or a girl—she is extremely thin, with very short clipped hair, a face that is neuter, innocent, blank, raw.* (SHELLEY's *face is important, as we shall see. She must possess, beneath her apparent face, one of a curious stubborn strength, hardboned, even defiant. For—from a certain angle—*SHELLEY *is the strongest personality in this drama.)*

SHELLEY *gets to her feet with difficulty. She is wearing jeans and a boy's T-shirt with nothing beneath it. She is barefoot, or in dirty socks. At first her manner is groggy and whining; then she becomes excited, manic. There is an unfocused, restless, jerky quality to her movements.*

SHELLEY   In the next hour they are going to prove that I exist. . . . *(In a clearer voice)* In the next hour they are going to prove that I exist! The proof will be shown to me! Demonstrated here on this stage! For I am a laboratory experiment. . . . I submit, I don't resist. *(Approaching the stage apron, slightly mocking)* I am the girl whose body is found in a vacant lot, beneath a pile of rubble . . . or in a jail cell . . . where I've hanged myself, out of spite for the matron who wouldn't give me cigarettes. Sometimes I am found in condemned buildings like this one: in rooms with high ceilings, bare floors, exposed pipes, a single stained mattress on the floor. You give me a single column on page seventeen of the newspaper and then you turn the page . . . for . . . after all. . . . *(Yawning)* After all there is page eighteen to be read. *(A pause, then briskly)* This is an era of proofs! Scientists have proven a great deal! The sun has been proven to be a perfectly ordinary star with a diameter of one million three hundred and ninety-two thousand kilometers lying at an average distance of one hundred and forty-nine million, six hundred thousand kilometers from the earth . . . it will continue to shine so brightly and cheerily for another five thousand million years before exploding and swallowing us all up. Solar systems have been discovered in the cavities of our back molars . . . great kingdoms in our chromosomes . . . of which we know nothing. Television proves that many people exist: you switch them on, you switch them off: it's electricity: it's—*easy.* God exists—God can be found in the dictionary and in the old chronicles. Slaps, kicks, love-maulings, a fistful of your hair pulled from your head—these are proofs that other people exist. You'll see them. You'll feel them. Do they hurt? Oh yes! Yes. *(Pause)* My head was banged on the floor over there *(Pointing to a corner of the stage)* and it made me understand that the floor exists. One day I got very tall and the ceiling up there *(Pointing to the ceiling)* brushed against the top of my head, so I knew that the ceiling existed also. I'm hungry.

SHELLEY *walks slowly about the stage, in a daze, looking for something to eat.*

SHELLEY   There's food in here somewhere. Where did he put it? I think I smell food. Is it under here? *(Lifting some junk)* My head aches. I think it's because I haven't eaten. I ate the day before yesterday, but what about yesterday? I made my husband, Martin, something to eat yesterday, or maybe it was the day before yesterday. I wonder if he ate all of it, or did he leave some? Where is it? My head aches but I'm not really hungry. My stomach is very tight and probably food couldn't squeeze into it. I don't like the smell in here. Too many people have lived in here. Now the building is condemned, I overheard Peter telling Martin that, I think I overheard him saying that. . . . Where is Peter? He hasn't been up here for three days. I need Peter. He should return in the next hour. Peter can hold back all this crowd, all these people. He understands. I need him, I need medicine from him, help from him, I am in love with him and he gives me love. Sometimes he presses me flat against the floor, right against the floor, so that I can't move. Then he breathes into me. . . . My head aches. I can't see right. Are the corners of this room fixed right? *(Pause)* The people who will come in this room are: Peter V., my lover; my Father, who is hurrying here now; and another man who is a mystery, Martin Raven, my new husband. Three men, and myself. There is a crowd of men around me. *(She brushes at her hair with her hands, quickly, coquettishly)* I wonder if I'm still pretty? Peter forgot to bring a mirror up. He said he would, then he forgot. I have been in this room for a long time now; I don't go out. They don't let me out. I would hurt myself outside on the street, anyway . . . someone would find me. I don't think the door there is locked, but Peter V. told me never to leave and so I can't leave. He gave me absolute instructions ten days ago, or a month ago. I don't remember. If he hadn't forbidden me to leave I think I would leave . . . I'm hungry, I think I would leave . . . I would walk over to the door, *(She walks to the door)* I would see if I could open it . . . *(She opens the door, which is not locked)* and if it was unlocked I would leave. But it's locked. It's been locked for a month now. I can't get out.

SHELLEY *stands at the door, gazing out abstractedly. She speaks in a sing-song, monotonous voice, which gradually becomes more animated, more excited.*

SHELLEY   Outside this door there is a corridor. The plaster is falling down. I can see the top of a stairway. There are doors along the corridor—some of them are open. Some are closed. Listen!—is that someone crying? *(She listens; no sound)* I think there are many people in this building besides myself. I heard some girls giggling last night. Little girls. There are thuds, screams, long monotonous arguments, radios, televisions, footsteps. . . . This is Peter's building and he can populate it the way he wants. He loves many girls, not just me. I know this. I'm not jealous. I'm not certain of my body *(She touches herself vaguely)* so how can I be jealous? How can I be jealous of what he does to other bodies in this building? I wish Peter would come back. I need him. And my father, I know that my father is on his way, yes, he's on his way, and my new husband Martin is on his way, they are all drawing together, coming together in this room, in me, a crowd of men coming together inside me. . . . I wish Peter would get here first! I wish everything would speed up, my life speed up, the beating in my head get faster, faster, so that I could be shown how I exist the way you are all certain that you exist. . . .

SHELLEY *walks slowly to the left of the stage.* PETER V. *appears in the doorway and enters, silently. He is anywhere from twenty-five to forty years old. His clothes are rakish and jaunty, expensive. An ascot, white shoes. Friendly, sinsiter. He wll contend with* SHELLEY *for the audience's sympathy.*

SHELLEY *(At the window)*   I wish you could see out this window! Streets converge . . . crowds . . . listen to that traffic! This must be the center of the world where all the winds rush together. *(Softly)* There is a building across the street exactly like this building. Perhaps it is a mirror-image? And I see a mirror-Shelley at one of the windows, looking out. Most of the windows are boarded up . . . that building is condemned too, like this one . . . another Peter owns it . . . or maybe it is my Peter, my lover. *(She waves, hesitantly)* Oh but she isn't waving back! Just a face . . . a very pale face . . . big eyes . . . eyes set deep in their sockets. . . . She isn't cute, like me. He wouldn't love *her.*

PETER *(Fondly, contemptuously)*   The very first night I brought her here, she acted exactly like that! Always posing . . . showing off . . . primping and preening . . . as if before an audience . . . an audience of *very interested* and *sympathetic* people. The way girls do . . . it's so American . . . so cute . . . a curse, so cute. Girls are—well, so cute! You can shake them until their eyes roll back in their skulls, you can hug them until their ribs crack, you can knock their pretty front teeth out . . . and still they're posing for you, anxious and hopeful, sweet little things, their underarms shaved hairless and innocent—a sign of great virtue. Right? Cute as cheerleaders. In fact, many of them have been cheerleaders—several, among my wide acquaintance. And Shelley too. Is Shelley her name? Shelley. Yes. My Shelley. Observe her: after forty-five days of this she's still ready to break into a cheer, to jump up and stretch her shapely little body, leading our team to victory . . . and all that. *(PETER is speaking zestfully, as if promoting goods; but SHELLEY slouches wearily)*

SHELLEY   That first night I ran to the window here, I pushed at the glass. . . . Did I want to jump out the window? It's five stories to the sidewalk. Or did I want to scare him? *(Giggling)* My new boy friend! . . . I wonder how I looked. My hair was long then, my skin was clear, I know I was pretty. All girls my age are pretty, more or less. We can't help it. I can remember pushing at the window . . . standing here . . . my long hair . . . people out on the street . . . late Saturday afternoon and lots of people . . . the smells of food from the street . . . I wanted to push the window apart so that people could see me up here. I wanted to cry out to them, "Look, it's me, it's Shelley, I've come to live here with you, I'm going to be one of you! I'm in love!" Peter V. came up behind me and put his arms around me. Oh, he loved me then, he loved me for a week or more . . . he told me it was the longest he'd ever loved anyone. . . .

PETER   A girl of sixteen or seventeen, like that girl, is irresistible. Even if you've been out on business for three days, as I have . . . three days straight with only a few hours sleep, collecting fees, paying people off, making telephone calls, in and out of taxis and in and out of buildings—what a life! I know too many people. Too many girls like this one. Still, she's irresistible, isn't she? Look at her healthy gleaming hair, look at her healthy body! The very heartland of America is between her ribs, I promise you. Her legs are pearly and long and lovely. About her there is only the odor of talcolm powder and corn flakes—nothing more, I promise you! The Girl Scout insignia is tattooed on her breast. I promise all that, and more.

SHELLEY   I thought I was calling out for people down there to see me so that they would be jealous. After all, Peter had picked me! But now I think I was calling for help. He had the door locked already. I couldn't get out. He locked the door first, then pressed me flat on the floor—

not on the mattress, it wasn't in here yet. He kept banging my head against the floor, making love to me. He convinced me that I didn't exist. My body broke up into pieces, in his hands. It's all different pieces.

PETER *(Enthusiastically)* Is she trying to break the window? Trying to jump out? I'm not going to let her, not yet. Look at the spirit she has! What muscles! What a lovely girl, eh? How much is she worth to you? She has held up very well, it must have been her excellent family life back home, the good dental care and the fortified cereal and the fuzzy lined boots; she is from an excellent suburb of one of our great American cities. Great care went into her making, centuries of care. She's a Midwestern beauty. Look, she's preening, she's posing for us out of sheer exuberance! *(SHELLEY stands without moving, staring down into the street)*

SHELLEY *(Turning blindly, not seeing PETER)* He broke my body up into pieces. I am like a jigsaw puzzle. It was right here, on the floor . . . this spot here. . . . But there's no mark. There's no blood. People get nailed to the floor and bleed to death and there is no mark to show what they went through, no evidence, no proof of their existence. . . . The world is crowded with invisible people who can't prove that they exist. *(Lightly, lyrically)* Anyway, he loved me! He might love me again! Peter, you did love me!

She runs to PETER and extends her arms, still without quite seeing him. PETER eludes her, like a dancer. He makes a gesture to the audience, grinning, as if exhibiting the girl, a possession of his.

SHELLEY I got on a bus and got off a bus, and there I was outside, a few yards away from here, on a Saturday afternoon. What a crowd! All those happy people! I could smell food—hotdogs, mustard, pizza—I ran along the sidewalk with my coat flapping open around me, my skirt very short, my legs very pretty in bright blue stockings, like legs seen flashing through water—And you came up behind me, Peter, and put your arms around me—

PETER I stood on the sidewalk and watched you run up to me. What a lovely little girl! If I closed my eyes slightly you turned into a herd of lovely little girls!—a herd, and all so cute! Your hair was very long then, in the style of your suburb, well-brushed and healthy, a golden brown. Your yellow coat flapped open to show your cute little body and your busy little legs, in blue stockings. I was like a light-house, I stood in the crowd and you saw me.

SHELLEY You took my arm. . . .

PETER You grabbed my arm.

SHELLEY My fingers closed about your arm by themselves . . . I clutched at you, I was falling, drowning, I couldn't keep my balance. . . . I felt so weak . . . I didn't know where I was. . . . I grabbed your arm and everything seemed to fall toward you. The sidewalk tilted toward you. Gravity began. *(She poses prettily)* I got off the bus and there you were! You were what I had been promised. I dreamt about you or someone like you. Two times before I had run away from home, but I never found you. . . . Never. Only police matrons, women with coarse tired skin, cigarette breath, sour and ironic from years of doing good deeds. . . .

PETER   What was I wearing?

SHELLEY   Something white—with green stripes—a green necktie—a straw hat—sunglasses—white shoes— You were so handsome! Your teeth were so white! Your hair was curly, like wood-shavings, stiff and curly and bunched up around your hat! My hand went out to you and my fingers closed about your arm, grasping your arm—

PETER   I saw that you were five foot four inches, that you weighed a hundred and fifteen pounds, that you were sixteen years old, out for a holiday and needing someone to protect you. Your eyes were hazy even then—such pretty blue eyes!—tiny circles radiated out from the iris, looking so blind, so trusting, so much in love. You wanted me to explain to you that you didn't exist, that it wasn't your fault and you were not to blame and nobody would punish you—so I took you home.

SHELLEY   *(Turning away suddenly)*   You kept bumping my head against the floor. It was the first time for me. You didn't listen. I had to come all those miles on the bus to get away from home, to find someone to love, it was the first time for me, but you didn't listen. Oh, everything entered me! It came into me! The pavement outside—the crowds—the traffic—the buildings—the windows—the doors—the roofs— Everything entered my body, flooding into me. You were like a light-house —the beacon on a light-house! That light! That beam of light! My body broke. It flowed out into the city. It came apart into pieces. *(She touches her body, as if in a daze; she looks down at herself)* There is a body here. I know that. And I am thinking, I am speaking, out of a skull that is on top of this body, covered with flesh, a living skull, the bone hidden from sight. I know this. But there is no connection between myself and this body. I could go on talking and my voice could float away, into the clouds . . . I am the size of an angel, the size of a fingernail . . . I could be borne into the sky on a piece of soot, a piece of charred paper flying in the air. . . . *(Suddenly, frightened)* Peter is coming! I can hear him coming!

SHELLEY throws herself down on the mattress. PETER leaves the doorway and returns again, rapping on the door. He claps his hands. His tone is louder, even more hearty, slightly scolding.

PETER *(Playfully)* What the hell? What? Wake up, little girl! Get up! Don't you know it's five o'clock in the afternoon, it's time for you to be fixing the house, cleaning and polishing and cooking, don't you know your husband will be home in half an hour?

SHELLEY *(Pretends to be waking)* My head aches . . . what happened . . . ? I don't feel right. . . .

PETER You were lying in that same position when I left three days ago. Shame on you, how lazy you are! For shame! What will your husband say? Do you want to anger him again? Why isn't supper on the stove?

SHELLEY I can't make myself sit up . . . my head aches . . . I feel sick. . . .

PETER Up, up! *(Clapping his hands)* For shame! Have you been hoarding those little white pills? Has someone rolled pills under the door to you? Have you made friends with another little girl, are you rapping on the walls in a secret code? You know you're forbidden to communicate with anyone.

SHELLEY Yes. . . .

PETER Then wake up, get going! *(Pulls her to her feet in a parody of a dance routine—lightly, musically)* First make the bed. Yes, like that. Yes. Tidy up the house. Yes. This is fine. *(Looking about at the mess)* This is what he's paying for, after all. Domestic life. But you'd better start supper right away so that he can smell it when he climbs the stairs. That's important. He needs to smell supper cooking when he climbs the stairs. He works all day and thinks of this time—smelling supper as he climbs the stairs, dreaming of you, his head filled with you— *(Seizing her and walking her back to the cupboard and sink, the "kitchen" area, barking out commands)* Open the cupboard door! Take out that can of soup! Chicken noodle soup, fine! Open it up!

SHELLEY How do I open it. . . .

PETER Where is the can-opener? You need a can-opener.

SHELLEY *(Turning the can around helplessly in her hands)* There is no place to get a hole started, no place that is indented . . . my fingernails are breaking. . . .

PETER No, you need a can-opener. What did you do with the can-opener?

SHELLEY *(Looking around feverishly)* The can-opener. . . .

PETER It must be here someplace. Where did you put it? How could you lose it? Your brain must be like a sieve! *(A pause)* I wonder what you think about when I'm not with you. Do you think at all? Do you think of opening yourself up with the can-opener and escaping me?

SHELLEY No, I love you. . . .

PETER What?

SHELLEY I love you, only you. . . .

PETER *(Discovering the can-opener on the floor; kicking it over to her)* Here it is! The mysterious goddam can-opener!

SHELLEY *picks it up. Awkwardly, dreamily, she mimes opening the can, and pours its contents into a pan. She turns on the hot plate, etc., moving sluggishly.*

PETER   What's that, the faucet dripping? It's more than a drip, it's a constant trickle. No wonder you can't wake up, you're hypnotized by that sound. Good. Water—waves—the ocean. It reminds us of our first home, the ocean. We can sleep better, awash in that sound. It's good for us. It calms our nerves. *(Shouting)* Don't stand there staring at me! Get to work! He'll be home in a few minutes, you've got to look good to him—why are you trying to embarrass me?

SHELLEY   *(Pressing her hands against her chest, as if out of breath, exhausted)*   What is his name again . . . ? Gordon?

PETER   No.

SHELLEY   Is it Arthur?

PETER   Arthur belongs to the past. An extreme personality, but charming—not that I blame him for what he did to you. He had every right. I don't defend him because I am a man, defending another man; I defend him because his taste turned out to be better than I had suspected. No, Arthur is gone.

SHELLEY   Then it's . . . Brockwood? Brockway? What was his name again . . . ?

PETER   Brockway disappeared, the bastard. Forget about him and fix yourself up for your new husband Martin. Martin Raven. Now do you remember?

SHELLEY   *(Slowly)*   I remember him. I think I remember him. You took me to your place, and to the bathroom there . . . you ran hot water in the sink . . . you washed my hair. . . . You were so loving, your hands, the smell of the shampoo . . . did you love me then?

PETER *is looking through a small notebook he has taken out of his pocket; he pays no attention to* SHELLEY.

SHELLEY   Yes, you loved me. My knees kept buckling and you held me steady with your own knees, your legs, your thighs . . . you loved me . . . you washed my hair, you shampooed it with green shampoo that burst into lovely white bubbles, sliding through your fingers, like blossoms . . . you were whistling under your breath. . . . The soap ran into my eye and I screamed because it stung so. You had to hold me still. I was crazy that day, so strung-out . . . I don't blame you. . . . You had to press my face down in the water to make me stop screaming. . . . And then you rinsed my hair out and dried it in a big white towel. You, yourself, drying my hair! Peter himself! With so much work and so many people hanging on you, needing you . . . you took the time to wash my hair and then you dried it for me and then you put my dress on me and zipped it up the back, and helped me walk . . . and we met this man, this new man . . . what is his name again . . . ?

PETER   You aren't as stupid as you pretend! Wake up!

SHELLEY   I can almost remember him. . . . We were sitting in a parked car? Was that it?

PETER *(Shaking her)*   Martin Raven is his name!

SHELLEY   Martin Raven. Martin. Yes. Martin Raven. Martin Raven. Martin Raven.

PETER   You could do a little more with yourself. Perfume behind the ears, a little more bounce to your walk, fluff out your hair—You aren't really old yet, you know. You have years left. Here, let me straighten your eyebrows a little. *(Wets his finger, "fixes" her up, etc.)* You look as if you've been sleeping on your face for three days! Let's see. Your skin is still good. A few pimples on the forehead, but we can fix that—cover it up with your bangs. Like this. Cute. How is your breath? Eh, it isn't very fresh! It smells dried, parched, stale, it smells like this room—and what's this, scum on your teeth? A film of scum on your teeth? *(He rubs at her teeth with his forefinger)* Who is going to want to kiss you, when your breath is stale and there's scum on your teeth! You will lose your popularity if you're not careful!

SHELLEY *embraces him;* PETER *is annoyed but tries not to show it.*

PETER   What's wrong? Are you sniffling? Are you catching a cold?

SHELLEY   I'm sorry.

PETER   You're not wiping your nose on my shirt, are you? Are you sick?

SHELLEY   My mind is not right. I can't wake up. I can't see the corners of the room.

PETER   Are you catching a cold, that's what I asked.

SHELLEY   I don't know.

PETER   A little girl started out like this—sniffling—then her throat got sore. I looked in her mouth and it was all white with red spots. She started coughing, she couldn't breathe, she kept spitting up mucous. That wasn't so cute, all that mucous! Her cuteness came to an end. I said goodbye and started her walking down the sidewalk to where the patrol car is usually parked, and that was the end of that. I don't want that to happen to you. First the sniffling—then the sore throat—then the pneumonia or whatever it was—then they disappear. I don't want that to happen to you.

SHELLEY   No—please—

PETER   Make yourself look pretty. Hurry up. It never used to take you this long. Smile. Come on, smile.

SHELLEY   I need some of those white things—

PETER   First smile.

SHELLEY *(Confused)*   Smile. How do I smile? How does it go again . . . ?

PETER *(Putting his hands around her head and shaking it)*   Is your brain turning to mucous? Are you dissolving? Wake up!

SHELLEY   Tell me what to do—

PETER   Smile! Like this! *(With his fingers he forces her mouth into a smile, which she holds, frozen)* That's better.

SHELLEY   Tell me what else to do. I can't remember. Should I move my hands around when I talk? Should I toss my hair? Where is the ceiling? Is it a low ceiling or a high ceiling? I'm sort of afraid of bumping my head. . . . How far down are my feet from my head? I'm afraid I might knock my chin against my knees. Tell me what to do.

PETER   Go to the stove. See how supper is progressing. Fast! *(Clapping his hands)* You are in the center of the city and in the center of America. Between your legs is the center of the world. You possess everything. You're as old as Buddha. You're immortal because you're a female. You mustn't let Peter V. down. You mustn't drag him down with you.

SHELLEY *(Puppet-like)*   If I reach out with my hand I can touch things. I see this hand; I see it reaching out. It's my own hand. I'm sure of that. Here is something that is not my hand. . . . *(Picking up a knife, turning it in the air)* It wasn't in my hand a second ago. It's something different from myself. . . . It's dazzling. The light hurts my eyes. It has something to do with the parts of my brain that are always going on and off, winking on and off, like lights. They're lighting up now. It's like sparks, all that activity in my head! *(Turning, laughing; PETER is looking through his notebook again)* It's like electricity, or bubbles in soda pop. . . . Peter explained to me that he loved me. He said it was fate. He did love me. He told me that I did not exist. He told me not to worry. He told me he would take care of me. He told me I was light as smoke, lovely in his arms, he entered me and the whole world entered me with him, flowing along my veins, making my veins bulge so that I thought they would burst. . . . And is that true, Peter, that I don't exist?

PETER *(Absent-mindedly)*   Absolutely. You do not exist.

SHELLEY   That I have no name?

PETER   I designate the spot you occupy by the word "Shelley." After all, we found that name in your billfold. It seemed a convenient word. You identified yourself in bright blue ink as "Shelley," on the card called "Identification," and on your driver's license there was another name, "Michele." So I could call you one name or the other. I could call you "S" or "M." Also "Shell." Or "Michael," or "Mitch" or "Mitya." Or "X." You would be obliged to answer. Or any one of a cascade of names here, if one opened up for your use. Some of these names are adorable! *(Flips through notebook; addresses audience)* Listen to this—lovely names, lovely American sounds—Debby, Rose Ann, Ruthie, Dora Lee, Suzy, Bitsy, Dolly, Blondie, Annie, Kitsie, Kitty—

As he speaks SHELLEY *approaches him with the knife raised, as if hypnotized.*

SHELLEY   You love them and not me. . . .
PETER   Franny, Barbie, Sylvie, Laurie, Trixie, Shelley, Nancy, Kathy. . . .
SHELLEY *(Screaming)*   You love them and not me!

SHELLEY *runs at him with the knife.* PETER *backs up, alarmed.*

PETER   Of course I love them! I love all of them and I love you. They are your sisters. You should love them yourself!
SHELLEY   You love them and not me!
PETER   You are only names in my book, why are you upset? You know what your place is among them! You are lovely little girls, you are lovely little names. None of you exist. You are only names in my book, don't worry, you are all loved equally, I will take care of you, you would all have died years ago except for lovers like me—
SHELLEY *(Shaking her head)*   You love them and not me!
PETER   I love them and I love you. I love all of you. It's all the same girl. What would you do without me? I tunnel inside you, I put you to sleep, I liberate you, I take you gently apart in handfuls, I put you back together again, I take you apart, I put you back together, I take you apart, I put you back together—
SHELLEY   I want to be the only one you love! Only me!
PETER   But there isn't any you. What do you mean?
SHELLEY *(About to rush at him)*   I can see you. I know you. I can see my hand. I can see this knife. I am going to kill you, *I* am going to kill you. . . . *I am going* to kill you. . . . I know that I am going to do something after all these weeks, it's myself that will do it, *I* am going to do it. . . .
PETER *(With his arms outspread, smiling)*   Yes, but why?
SHELLEY   Why . . . ?
PETER   Why are you going to do it?
SHELLEY *(Confused)*   Why . . . ? I don't know. . . .
PETER   It isn't you, but an evil spirit in you. Who is it? Who is poisoning you against me?
SHELLEY   I don't understand. . . .
PETER   Is it another man? Your father, maybe? You mentioned your father . . . you thought he was following you? Is he following you? Is his spirit inside you right now?

SHELLEY I don't know . . . I can't remember. . . . Why am I standing here, what am I going to do?

PETER That dripping faucet is what you should listen to! Listen to it—learn from it—concentrate upon it—make it your meditation! Do you understand? Your meditation—your rosary. The cords in your neck, dear girl, are standing out; you make yourself ugly; I see tiny white lines beginning in your face—at the corners of your eyes, bracketing your mouth. Remember that silly little girl from—where was it—Arkansas—and what happened to her—screaming at one of her husbands—coming at poor Peter with a paring knife that wouldn't have pared a *carrot*—

SHELLEY Arkansas? It was—West Virginia—We talked—we whispered together—she told me—*(Pausing)* She told me lies—

PETER Love me. Relax. Forget your father. He won't find you. He's evil: forget him. If he finds you he'll lose you again: it has happened before. Do you understand? Do you know what Peter is saying? He's evil—he's *inconsequential*. Nothing is transmitted with the genes. Why are you looking at me so strangely, Shelley? *I'm* not your father! You *love* me! It's proper that there should be love between us because I am *not* your father. Why should you want to kill me, dear, when you love me? . . . When you love me?

SHELLEY *(Vaguely)* I was going to . . . going to do something. . . .

PETER You know you love me.

SHELLEY I love you, yes. . . .

PETER Of course. Now finish supper.

SHELLEY *(Turning, baffled)* It must be my father. You're right. His spirit is inside me, poisoning me. I know he's going to find me. He won't give up until he finds me. *(She lets the knife fall to the floor)* The other time I left home he found me in three days. He notified the police everywhere in the state. Everyone knew about me. I couldn't get away. *Runaway,* they called me, they wrote that down. But they were very nice to me. That was years ago, I was only a child then . . . my father came and took me in his arms and we wept together. . . . Last year I left home again but I got sick. My insides ached. I got the flu from something I ate in a restaurant in the bus station . . . I was very sick . . . so I went to the police myself, I turned myself in. My father was only a few hours behind me. He drove down and picked me up. This time I've been away for weeks, I can hardly remember my home, it seems that I've been away for years and that I'm a different person, that everything has changed . . . when I think back *(In an attitude of painful thought)* I can't really remember that home . . . it's like a glacier has come down over it . . . everything is frozen back there, the people frozen, and there is a girl who used to be myself who is frozen there, a child. . . . What if my father finds me here?

PETER Don't worry, he won't find you.

SHELLEY He'll find me, he'll make me go back home with him. . . .

PETER He can't make you do anything. I'll protect you.

SHELLEY I don't want to be that girl again, I don't want to be Shelley. He'll try to take me in his arms and he'll cry over me, he'll make me cry again . . . I want to forget him, I want to forget Shelley. . . . I cut off her hair to spite her and I went without eating to spite her, to make her thin, very thin, to make her dizzy from not eating, to kill her!

PETER You did right. You got her weight down to ninety-five pounds; you're very chic now, like a model! I prefer girls as thin as possible, so thin I can fit their delicate little wrists between my teeth, I prefer skin transparent like yours, it's the latest style! And your hair is long enough like that. I'll cut it a little with a razor in a few days. There are some men who like girls that are boys, and some men who like boys that are really girls; the market must be accommodated. How else can we make contact with other people except by accommodating them . . . ? We need our bodies for that. We need our bodies for communion with others. The age craves communion! We can't deny our deepest impulses! Why did you want to be Shelley, then, why did you want to kill me? Did you want to return to your old self, to that particular body and that particular name, did you want to forget me, did you want to belong again to your father and a woman said to be your mother, why did you want all that again when it never pleased you . . . did it? You hated it!

SHELLEY *(Dully)* Yes, I hated it. . . .

PETER You hated your father and your mother. Your father especially.

SHELLEY *(More emphatically)* Yes, I hated them! Him especially . . . because he loved me more than she did. . . . He kept after me with his love, he wanted to own me, he wants to take me back with him. . . . My father is a doctor. He wants to cure everyone. He wants to clean them up, he wants to fix things, he wants to put bandages on everything, sterilize everything, he wanted me always to wash my hands after I went to the bathroom, he was always spying on me! He wouldn't let me alone! He loved me too much! He wouldn't let me be like the water coming out of that faucet, trickling away, emptying itself out. . . .

PETER *(To the audience)* I had no father, myself. I named myself. I gave birth to myself. I read a certain novel, I came across the character of Peter Verkhovansky, he leapt back into the vacancy that was myself, and I gave birth to myself at the age of twenty-five! I introduced myself to everyone as Peter V., because they would not understand that I am really Peter Verkhovansky of Dostoyevsky's great novel *The Possessed*. Peter came to America; he lost his political fervor; he became an American, a capitalist. He became me. I became him. But no one can understand that, not even this sympathetic young lady here, not even you, really there is no one who can appreciate me, and so I don't explain myself. I had no father. I was born at the age of twenty-five. Therefore I have no Oedipal complex, I have no superego, in fact I have no unconscious at all. I am pure consciousness. I am pure ego.

SHELLEY   My father is coming to get me—I'm afraid—

PETER   He can't bring the police. They need a warrant. You're untouchable, you have every right to live here, in this room, for the rest of your life. Remember that!

SHELLEY   If he comes here and calls me by name—

PETER   I'll protect you.

SHELLEY   Listen! I hear someone coming.

PETER   There's nothing.

They listen; there is no sound.

SHELLEY *(Panicked)*   Yes, he's coming! I can hear his footsteps! He's on the stairs . . . he must have found out about this room . . . he must have had a detective looking for me. . . . There's nowhere I can go that he can't find me. . . .

PETER   I don't hear anyone. . . .

SHELLEY   Listen! He's on the stairs!

PETER   Don't be frightened, what's wrong with you? I said I'd protect you. It might be Martin Raven coming home. . . .

SHELLEY   Footsteps. . . .

PETER *(Watching the door)*   Remember that you belong to me. Relax. You belong here. With me. None of this is your fault. You belong to me and to no one else, not even yourself. You're in love. You are sometimes high as the ceiling, bouncing around against the ceiling, you are sometimes flat against the floor, your nostrils pressed to a crack in the floor, you are mine, you are not to blame, you're in love. . . .

There is a knock at the door. PETER *and* SHELLEY *do not respond. The door is opened and* SHELLEY'S FATHER *appears. He is a well-dressed, distraught man in his forties; he carries a small suitcase. He enters and he and* SHELLEY *stare at each other.*

PETER *(Amiably)*   How do you do? Have we met? Are you looking for someone? Why have you entered our apartment without knocking? Are you a stranger here? This is my building, didn't you see the sign downstairs—*condemned by order of the fire department*? *(He laughs)* Not looking for a place to hide out, are you? What is your business with Mrs. Raven and myself?

FATHER   . . .Mrs. Raven . . . ?

SHELLEY *shakes her head, no, as if answering her father against her will.*

FATHER *(Quietly)* What's happened to you?

SHELLEY stares at him and does not reply. FATHER is stunned, baffled. He keeps passing his fingers through his hair.

PETER If you have any questions, address them to me. Why don't you introduce yourself? My name is Peter V., a friend of the young lady's, a businessman, a kind of Ariel—

FATHER *(To SHELLEY)* My God, you've lost weight. . . . What's happened to you? Are you sick? Your hair has been cut so short. . . .

PETER *(Trying to shake hands with him)* I said my name is Peter V., I am a businessman and a friend of the young lady's. You'd better shake hands with me. I'll call the police and have you thrown out. I don't think you're a gentleman, to walk in here like this. . . . I have friends among the police. I have friends everywhere. You'd better explain yourself.

FATHER You know who I am.

PETER What do you want with us?

FATHER I want to take her back with me. . . .

SHELLEY turns away: she laughs contemptuously. PETER joins in her laughter and manages to force FATHER to shake hands with him.

PETER But what is your claim? Who are you?

FATHER You know who I am, I'm Shelley's father. . . .

PETER The girl in this room with us is not necessarily Shelley. She is not necessarily your daughter. Are you making a claim?

FATHER What did you do to her? She's sick, isn't she?

PETER I saved her life.

FATHER Can she—can she hear us? Can she understand what we're saying?

PETER She can hear us if I give her permission.

FATHER Shelley. . . .

PETER Shelley, come here! Look at her! She's playful as a kitten, as a puppy! There's something so innocent about her. . . . She's a piece of matter the spirit has left, it's drained out and left her very innocent. Her soul drained out through the cracks of her darling little body, through its various delicate clefts and holes!—isn't that right, Shelley? Come here and stand by me. You can listen to us if you want to. Isn't she beautiful? She pretends to be sicker than she is. They all do. They want to be pitied and cuddled and then they change their minds, they get afraid, they run away, and then they change their minds again and weep because they have no one to hold them, they can't determine the limitations of their bodies unless someone is always with them, embracing them. Oh, they change their minds twenty times a day! They slip in and out of their minds like clothing! All of them want to die in a man's embrace, the life squeezed out of them, a big bear hug, a cosmic bear hug? Look at her. Between her legs the universe opens up—that darkness, that lovely dark machinery!—but she doesn't know it, she's too far gone.

FATHER   What's wrong with her . . . ?

PETER   We must talk man to man. Of course you're not her father. You've looked me up to make a deal with me; you want the girl for yourself. Right?

FATHER   Shelley, are you ready to come home with me?

SHELLEY *laughs wildly, waving him away. She "poses," arching her back, moving coquettishly.* PETER *rubs his hands.*

PETER   If I seriously thought you were this girl's father, barging in here to ruin her life, to take her back to that prison, I would call the police and have them beat you up. After all, this building is mine! I bought it for ten thousand dollars on a land contract last May and only three years ago it was worth a hundred and ten thousand dollars—think of that! Everything in this city is falling—the tax base, the sidewalks, the streets, everything! It's a time when people like myself have only to stoop to pick up prizes; all we have to do is bend over. Our talent thrives in such troubled times! Ah, we are the truest Americans, the truest talents!—Are you listening to me? I don't believe you're this girl's father. Tell us who you are.

SHELLEY *stands beside* PETER, *her head against his shoulder; he "cuddles" her.*

FATHER   *(Rubbing his eyes, very confused)*   What are you talking about . . . ? I can't understand you. . . .

PETER   You understand me well enough!

FATHER   I haven't slept for two days. . . . I've been calling home to see if Shelley is back yet, but every time I call it's the same, nothing ever changes. . . . Your mother says you died and you should be forgotten. But I can't forget.

PETER   *(Cheerfully)*   You're telling us lies! You're making all this up!

FATHER   Once I saw a girl on the street, in Toledo, and I ran after her thinking it was you. . . .

PETER   What's in that suitcase?

FATHER   A projector—

PETER   What?

FATHER   A projector—for slides and films—

PETER   Home movies?

FATHER   Let me explain. Please. You are always interrupting me—

PETER   But we're listening, we're fascinated!

FATHER   I put together some things to show her—if I found her—I wanted to explain myself to her—

PETER   Explain what?

FATHER   I want to be logical and objective. I don't want to force her to do anything.

PETER   What have you got, home movies?

FATHER   Some slides made from snapshots. A few things. I put it together before I left home . . . a few things to show her. . . . There is something I must prove to her.

SHELLEY   *(Violently)*   He saved my life, not you! Peter saved my life!

FATHER   Shelley. . . .

SHELLEY   He made me into the dark side of the world. Most of the world is water. I bet you didn't know that! You can sink in it forever, that dark water, it's always moving, pulsating, ebbing, flowing, streaming, draining away, flowing back, flooding, rising, crashing. . . . Try to stop it! You can't! He made me into that water, he made me the dark side of the world, he saved my life by kissing me, it was a kiss that lasted for hours, for days. . . . He breathed into my mouth, he breathed himself into me.

FATHER   You're not well. You're—

SHELLEY   I can't hear you. I'm not even listening. I'm not your daughter or anyone's daughter. I don't remember anything. I am not convinced that anything ever happened to me. I don't remember. If Peter exists then I exist, but only when he's in the same room with me. He's gone most of the time. I wait for him and when he returns I come alive again. There is nothing that anyone else can say to me. *(A sudden gesture of anger, embarrassment)* Oh, that stupid thing! That projector of yours! You were always embarrassing us, taking pictures all the time—birthdays, Christmas, Easter Sunday, graduation!—how I hated that, being herded around and made to smile, to look pretty, you with your camera trying to put us all on film!

FATHER   You wanted me to take pictures of you—

SHELLEY   I did not!

FATHER   And you loved to watch the movies we made—the whole family loved them!

SHELLEY   I was lying to you.

FATHER   What do you mean? You weren't lying. . . . Now your voice is so strange. . . . It's as if someone else were speaking for you.

SHELLEY *waves him away.*

FATHER   Who is this man, Shelley? What did he do to you?

PETER *(Courteously)* I have already introduced myself. . . .

SHELLEY *(To FATHER)* To you I lied, I was a lie myself—my body was rotten with lies. To him I tell the truth. I tell Peter everything.

FATHER Who is he?

SHELLEY A man who saved my life!

PETER *(To FATHER)* Why don't you open up your suitcase? I'm anxious to see what you have. Is it an expensive outfit? I'm thinking of getting a movie camera myself, but I'm careful about buying things, I go slowly, I consider a purchase like that quite an investment. I think I'd wait for sales in January.

SHELLEY *(Her hands to her face)* I don't want to look at anything he has. Nothing of his. Nothing he has to show me.

FATHER *(Opening the suitcase, moving slowly and apologetically)* Shelley, please . . . I put together a few things to show you. . . . You don't have to do anything. I won't force you to do anything.

SHELLEY I won't look!

PETER *(Examining the projector)* This looks like a good piece of equipment. Where did you get it?

SHELLEY Make him leave! There's nothing of my life I want to look at—it's finished—

PETER Photographs show us the flatness of our bodies. They're really two-dimensional, our bodies. They would be one-dimensional if they could be, but unfortunately one-dimensional things are invisible. The soul is one-dimensional, if it exists. That's why I like photographs and the apparatus that makes photographs possible. I'm grateful to you for coming here this afternoon!

FATHER *(Abruptly)* Get away from there?

PETER *(Cringing, fawning, mocking)* Are you afraid I'll contaminate your machine?

FATHER I don't want you touching it.

PETER My fingers are absolutely clean. I'm sterile inside and out. You're a doctor and you think people must be crawling with germs, and only you can save them. But I'm absolutely clean.

FATHER *(Confused)* I'm sorry . . . for losing my temper. . . . I haven't slept for a while. . . . And what is that, that noise? I keep hearing a noise. . . .

PETER Just a faucet. Does it make you nervous?

FATHER A faucet . . . ?

SHELLEY *runs to the sink. She tries to stop the water by sticking her finger up the faucet.*

SHELLEY *(Laughing)* Nothing can stop this! We need a plumber up here. It's been dripping for weeks, it's made the sink rusty, there's a rust-colored ring in the sink. . . . In a few more weeks it will wear the sink away and leak out onto the floor.

FATHER I'm a little nervous, my hands are shaky. . . .

PETER It's too bad you haven't slept. Would you like to sleep here, on our mattress? We'd be very quiet—we'd tip-toe around and speak only in whispers.

FATHER No . . . no. . . . I want to . . . I want to show Shelley these things, and then I'll leave if she wants me to. . . .

FATHER sets up the apparatus, moving clumsily.

PETER (*Goes briskly to the right to turn off the lights, so that the stage is dim but not dark; he returns to center stage, rubbing his hands*) I'll turn off the lights! Excellent! So you want to interfere with our souls, eh? You want to display yourself to us? You know, in antiquity the gods did not interfere with souls; they were content to maim bodies. You might be walking out in ordinary sunlight and a hand would grab your hair and lift you up into the sky—no surprise! You had to expect such things. Or, because two gods loved you, you might be gored to death by an animal with fabulous tusks, perhaps an animal invented right at that moment. . . . But you fathers want to be newer gods; you want to interfere with our souls, your children's souls. But you won't succeed. We no longer have any souls.

FATHER (*As the first slide flashes on the wall—a snapshot of a man and a woman, black and white*) Shelley, this is my mother and father. The year is 1922.

SHELLEY (*Angrily*) What do I care about your mother and father?

FATHER Your grandparents. . . .

SHELLEY I don't have any grandparents! Anyway I've seen that picture before. I don't know those people, I have nothing to do with them! They're dead.

PETER They're strangely ugly people, aren't they?

SHELLEY They're dead!

FATHER My father was about twenty-five when this was taken. He was a very energetic man, a wonderful man . . . he liked to hunt . . . he bought a gas station and worked very hard, but he lost money . . . everything went wrong. . . . He lost everything in the thirties. He lost his will to live.

SHELLEY (*Hysterically*) I don't want to hear this! It's all dead, all finished! It's like breathing into me, opening me up the way Peter did. They want to pump love into you. Everyone wants to pump love into everyone else.

PETER It's inconclusive, however. Everyone—nearly everyone—has grandparents.

FATHER *(As another slide comes on)* My family. My parents, and my two sisters and my brother. . . .

PETER   And yourself. I would recognize you anywhere.

FATHER   This was taken in 1935.

PETER   You were a skinny kid. Look at those eyes! Christ, you're staring at us—everything is in those eyes! *(Walks up to the wall, peering at the picture)*

FATHER *(As another slide appears)* Your mother and I. . . .

SHELLEY   I don't want to see this!

FATHER   . . .before we were married. I was twenty-four then. Wasn't your mother pretty? She was such a pretty woman.

PETER   Is she dead now?

FATHER   Of course not. She's waiting for us back home.

PETER   I thought all those people were dead.

FATHER   They're living, they're not dead. . . . *(As another slide appears)* And this—this is Shelley—only a few weeks old—

Silence.

FATHER *(To SHELLEY)* What are you thinking?

SHELLEY *turns away.*

FATHER   Are you—are you well enough to understand what I'm showing you?

PETER   She's afraid of crowds. You brought a crowd into the room.

FATHER   I don't understand you.

PETER   She came running out of a crowd and into my arms, this girl you claim as your daughter. It's the same protoplasm as the infant up on the wall, I suppose, but you can't prove it. Really, you can't prove anything. The crowd opened up and a girl ran toward me, I could see she was terrified, she needed love, she needed me to mythologize her. So I took her in my arms. I saved her from the crowd. You're bringing the crowd back, you're confusing her.

FATHER   Shelley? Come here.

When she does not immediately respond, PETER snaps his fingers. SHELLEY approaches him as if against her will. Her hands are pressed against her face.

SHELLEY   I can't see anything.

FATHER   More pictures of Shelley . . . eight months old . . . a year old . . . eighteen months . . . two years . . . three years . . . this was taken on Christmas Day 1957. . . .

SHELLEY   Stop it!

FATHER   Your sister Jeanne. . . .

SHELLEY   I don't have any sister!

FATHER   Easter Sunday—

PETER   The sister is quite pretty!

FATHER   Shelley in high school, fourteen years old. . . .

SHELLEY   It isn't me! Go to hell!

FATHER   Another picture of Shelley. Her mother took it; that's me in the background. Do you recognize this, Shelley? Cape Cod. Do you recognize that bathing suit, Shelley? That tiger kitten that belonged to the neighbors' children. . . .

SHELLEY   My head is being blown up like a balloon. You're killing me. If my head gets much bigger I'll float up against the ceiling . . . you'll have to pull me down by grabbing hold of my ankles. . . .

FATHER   This was taken the same day. Look at her beautiful long hair!

PETER   Did you love her?

FATHER   Why—why do you speak in the past tense?

PETER   Do you love her?

FATHER   Yes, I love her. I only followed her here to talk with her, quietly. To show her these things. I don't want to force her into anything, I want to prove something to her, I won't make demands upon her . . . I want to prove something to her. . . .

SHELLEY   He wants to prove that I exist!

PETER   *(Motioning her away)*   Calm down, please. There's an odor released from you when you're excited. It isn't very cute. Men don't smell like that.

SHELLEY   I'm not a man but I'm not a girl either. I'm not male and I'm not female. Look at that ugly body in the picture! That body! Breasts and hips and legs and long hair and that smile, that stupid smile! I could hack that girl into pieces with a knife! I could tear her into pieces with my teeth!

FATHER   This one was taken in the fall . . . the light was a little dim. . . .

PETER   The three women in your family, eh? Your wife and your two daughters. . . . Why did you take all these pictures?

FATHER   Because. . . .

PETER   Why do Americans take so many pictures?

FATHER   Because . . . because. . . .

SHELLEY   They want to prove that they exist!

PETER   Don't stand so near me. You smell like that mattress, you smell like blood. . . .

SHELLEY   I don't smell of blood!

PETER   Your underwear was stained when I first met you.

FATHER   *(As if not hearing)*   And this is your mother on her birthday last year. Remember those flowers? Your mother was saying, just as I took this picture, "It won't turn out, it's too dark in here. . . . "

SHELLEY   He's bringing everyone in this room!

FATHER   Another of Shelley. Look at that smile! She knows she's much prettier than her sister . . . she seems to offer her face up to the camera like a flower, a lovely flower. . . .

SHELLEY   They are all coming in this room, all of them. . . .

SHELLEY rushes at FATHER and tries to knock the projector over. FATHER takes hold of her and they struggle.

SHELLEY   He's touching me! I can feel him touching me!

In the struggle the apparatus is knocked over. PETER tries to pull SHELLEY away.

SHELLEY   It doesn't prove anything—

FATHER   Shelley, what's wrong with you? Stop—

SHELLEY *(Screaming)*   There's nothing there! Pictures! I didn't see them— they're not real—You failed! You failed to convince me!

PETER turns the lights on, hurrying. Then he crosses to SHELLEY and tries to calm her.

PETER   You're hysterical. Be quiet.

FATHER   I'm taking you home with me—

SHELLEY *(Screaming)*   You failed! Failed!

PETER *(Righting the projector, gathering the slides together)*   It was an interesting interlude, but now we must return to real life. All this emotion is embarrassing. The girl's husband will be home at any minute. She has certain duties she must perform for him. Everything in the past is buried, nobody cares about the past, shovelfuls of time have buried it. Leave us. Go away.

FATHER   No, she's coming back with me—

PETER   What do you want with a girl like that? She's too far gone. She's not much good, believe me.

FATHER *(Shoving PETER)*   I'll kill you—

PETER jumps to his feet and pushes FATHER away.

PETER *(Scornfully)*   An old god! Old mythology! Go to hell!

FATHER   I'll call the police—

PETER   I'll have the police kick your teeth out, you old bastard!

FATHER   I—I'll—

SHELLEY *(Her hands to her face)*   Make him leave!

PETER   Now you must leave, really. Everything is over. The lights are on and it's embarrassing now.

FATHER   But I had more pictures yet. . . . And I didn't explain the ones I showed, I had more to say, much more . . . everything went so quickly, it was so confused. . . . I had more to say. I should have written it down. . . .

SHELLEY   Make him leave!

PETER   This is my building and you must leave. I don't like to speak harshly to a man your age, but. . . .

The door opens suddenly and MARTIN RAVEN *enters. He is a heavy-set man of ordinary appearance, rather pale. He is startled at seeing the* FATHER.

PETER *(Cheerfully)*   Hello, Martin!

MARTIN   What's all this?

PETER   He's just leaving.

MARTIN   He looks like trouble. He looks like a detective. . . .

PETER   No, that isn't it. He's a friend of the girl's but he's leaving.

FATHER   Who is this?

PETER   Her young husband has just come home; their domestic life must begin; there is no room for you. Private life is sacred.

FATHER   Shelley—

SHELLEY   Don't make me look at you!

FATHER *hesitates, then puts his things together slowly and prepares to leave.* SHELLEY *stands with her back to him, her hands pressed against her face.*

PETER *(To* FATHER)   You don't exist to her. You're just a beak and claw fluttering around her head; she's always dreaming about that kind of thing; she dreams of crowds. Up here, we take care of her. We love her.

FATHER   But I can't leave her here. . . .

MARTIN   Who the hell is this guy?

PETER *(Briskly)*   Sit down and relax! You've had a hard day at the post office, right? You want some supper, right? You want some loving, right? This gentleman is on his way out.

FATHER   But if I leave. . . . *(Appealing to her)* If I leave, Shelley, I won't return. . . .

MARTIN *(Frightened and insolent)*   Look, you, get the hell out of here! I don't like the looks of things!

FATHER   Shelley . . . ?

SHELLEY *(Sinking to the floor; weakly yet stubbornly)*   I don't hear anything! Anyone's voice! There is no Shelley—you can't claim me—I don't *hear* you—go away, leave me—go away—

FATHER   Shelley . . . ?

Silence; FATHER *picks up the suitcases and leaves.*

PETER *(After applauding her performance, mockingly yet robustly)*   Very good! Very . . . very good. Now, my girl, let's set you going

again. . . . *(He heaves her to her feet. She begins to fall again; roughly, he holds her up; steadies her)* Come on, come on. We've been extremely patient. . . . *(Her knees threaten to buckle again; but finally he
manages to steady her. He releases her, experimentally)* All right? Fine?
He's gone and he won't return and you're safe: right?

SHELLEY *mutely acquiesces.*

PETER *(Playfully)* All right? Yes? Forever and ever and ever? 'Till death—?
Right? *(A pause)* 'Till death.

*A long pause; then an abrupt change in the mood and pacing of the play:
a sort of bawdy fast-moving humor.*

MARTIN   What the hell was that all about? I thought nobody knew about
her up here. What if the cops come? Who's been talking?
PETER   Relax, take off your shoes. Take off your coat. Did you smell supper as you came up the stairs?
MARTIN   The hell with supper. I'm not eating here.

MARTIN *crosses to* SHELLEY *and takes hold of her by the back of the neck
and shakes her.*

MARTIN   You! I don't trust you—you're sweating like a pig! You smell
like a pig!

SHELLEY *is passive in his hands; she submits to being shaken, mauled.*

PETER   I guarantee you that she has not been unfaithful. I was here all
along.
MARTIN *(Flat, rapid voice)*   I can't stay all night this time. My mother is
suspicious. She asks about me—worries about me—I'm only thirty-
two—my health isn't good. I'm susceptible to colds, sore throats. . . .
What if I catch a disease from this little maniac, how could I tell my
mother? I'd be so ashamed!
PETER *(At the sink; washing his face)*   She's absolutely clean, I swear it.
You worried excessively about the one from Arkansas, don't you re-
member, and it came to nothing.
MARTIN *(Suspiciously)*   But she wasn't—she wasn't very strong. She did-
n't last.
PETER *(Chuckling)*   You were a little rough with her.
MARTIN   The one Freddy had, from West Virginia—
PETER   Never mind about Freddy: that doesn't concern you.
MARTIN   She lasted a lot longer. She put up a real *fight. (Turning to*
SHELLEY*)* Who are you gaping at? Whose face are you memorizing?
What are you, anyway? Beneath these things? A little boy, a skinny lit-
tle girl? —Don't you resist *me!*

Joyce Carol Oates

MARTIN and SHELLEY struggle together. SHELLEY cries out; MARTIN claps his hand over her mouth; throws her down. The lights fade on them, and concentrate upon PETER, now shaving at the sink.

PETER   There are risks, and there are rewards. One has doubts—naturally! But one continues. I don't at all mind the competition—it's healthy, it's American—it's in our great tradition—I thrive on it, in fact—I find it exhilarating. I am a vigorous young man standing at a sink in a condemned building—but it's *my* building—and I have controlled the scenario. I take pride in my existence—pride enough to shave. *My* face is very real, and has never been photographed. You can't catch and make permanent my—essence. Not mine. My face is real, I am said to be quite handsome, that's neither here nor there, I control the definitions, I control the terms of commerce, I navigate the seven seas, I do a great deal of smiling. . . . Now *that* worries me, upon occasion. For what if all this smiling wears my face out? *My* face? The way water wears out porcelain? *(A pause)* Will we all wear out, then? *Must we?* Like Shelley . . . last year's Shelley . . . whatever her name. . . . Must our existences be so cruelly questioned? *(He pauses, contemplating the audience. Sincere, forthright, man-to-man)* These are all legitimate, indeed profound issues, which we may take up at another time, in more congenial surroundings. Unfortunately I'm rather rushed: and I find this setting rather depressing, as I'm sure you do. Another time—? I'm *really* in rather a hurry.

Lights fade to blackout.

THE END

HOMESICK 🌿
A Play in Two Scenes

Cast

WOMAN/PINKTOES—a young woman
MAN/MR. AMERICA—a man in his mid-thirties

SCENE 1: PINKTOES

Lights up. A young woman wrapped loosely in a coarse stained blanket, bare-legged, wearing only bloodstained pink wool socks on her feet, speaks.

(With childlike hurt, reproach, staring out into audience) Momma—! *(Pause)* You see what happened to me . . . it's your fault. *(Pause)* Wouldn't never of left home if . . . *you* know . . . you needed to love me better. *(Angrily wipes at eyes)* Now, happens nobody even knows my name where I am. Where I ended up. A long way from home . . . *(Pause)* JANE DOE "PINKTOES" is my name—'cause all I was wearing, the Texas cops found me, was these socks Gramma knitted for me. All filthy by then, yanked down my ankles and half off my feet. Like whoever it was undressing me—after he'd raped me, and strangled me, and battered my head till blood leaked out my ears, nose, mouth like a burst tomato—was too rushed to finish the job, or scared off too soon. *(Pause)*

(Her voice rises to a faint scream) I DON'T REMEMBER HIS FACE I COULDN'T IDENTIFY HIM! Just these tattoos up and down his arms . . .

(Pause; regains composure; ironically matter-of-fact) They judged me between eighteen and twenty. So I'll always be that age. Sprawled face down in the weeds in a drainage ditch. Ten yards from the highway. I was dying maybe three, four hours hearing traffic go by . . . like thunder . . . God telling me how bad I was . . . runaway from home O.K. now see what happens! what you deserve . . . *(Pause)* Texas Interstate I-35 two miles east of Roscommon. Where I'd never been, and had no connection with. I-35 runs from Salina, Kansas to Laredo, Texas on the Mexican border, seven hundred and fifty miles. Long stretches just empty, desolate like the moon. Where you find us, off I-35, it's never where we're from—only where we're dumped.

(Defensive) No I never knew any of them other girls that was killed along here. If it was the same guy or somebody else killed them. *(Bitter satisfaction)* *Their* Mommas feeling like shit, too, I bet! *(Pause)*

She walks about wrapped in the blanket; almost preening; an arrogant, adolescent tone to her voice; no self-pity.

Happened to be Hallowe'en morning they found me, cops out patrolling "Devil's Night" damage. This naked dead girl a truck driver saw and pulled over to the side but didn't come too close. *(Pause)* JANE DOE "PINKTOES"—TEXAS INTERSTATE 35—ROSCOMMON—10/31/94/ Dead only about forty-eight hours, decomposition just beginning. *(Waves away flies, vehement, ironic)* Goddamn, GET!

(Pause; chagrined) Holey old handknit socks yanked half off my feet, and the feet filthy, not washed in weeks. *(Remembering)* Yeah I asked him could I take a bath . . . wanted to wash my hair . . . he said . . . he'd get a motel room . . . *(Pause; goes blank, reverts to earlier continuation, glancing down at herself)* Flecks of old grape-colored nailpolish on my toenails and dirt lodged solid beneath. Except for the missing teeth—swelling and discoloration—I was still "good-looking"— *(Laughs scornfully)* That's what the cops said. Or maybe always say. Out of pity. Like they got their own daughters and sisters. *(Pause)*

Funny how you're *in* your body so you know it's just this kind of vehicle God gave you to use. Where the spirit abides. *(Sings)* "This little light of mine, I'm gonna let it shine . . . " *(Voice trails off)* Gramma taught me that. *(Pause)* Once you're dead, though, in folks' eyes, the body is all you *are*. All that's left for folks to deal with. *(Glances at herself inside the blanket, wincing)* Jesus!—all these scars—scabs—bruises— bites—and so skinny, my damn ribs showing, my collarbone—ninety pounds at the end. Some of the injuries fresh and some of them years old. Like this weird rip like a zipper, purplish-brown, here— *(Indicates her left thigh)* Cut myself up running from a cop—behind a 7-Eleven store in Tulsa—ran into some barbed wire—bleeding like a stuck pig in the back of the squad car and the cops disgusted with me . . . *(Pause)*

Been pregnant one time, and lost it. The coroner picked up on that. Can't hide nothing from them . . . bastards.

V.D., too, it says on the record—"herpes." *(Mispronounces)*

The only jewelry on the "cadaver" was this little jade cross on a gold chain around my neck. *(Indicates necklace, on a thin chain)* Except it wasn't real jade some guy gave me, and it sure wasn't real gold. Anybody'd guess that, seeing me dumped there dead in the weeds like a tossed-away beer bottle. Dirty pink socks is all I'm wearing.

Well, I been gone from home for a long time. Four years in December. Except I ain't gonna get to December this year. Momma, you listening? *(Stares into audience)* Naw, you ain't. I know.

(Continues with the assessment of her body) My stomach was empty mostly. Just Coke he'd bought me at the reststop. Said he'd get us some Kentucky Fried Chicken and some beer and . . . *(Goes blank again; pause)*

In my hurt vagina, jammed up into my uterus by whatever he'd used, which the coroner speculated was some kind of a stick, or rod, and the dried semen on my belly, were blood-soaked shreds of paper towels used as as a tampon. *(Pause)* I'd make my own in the women's restrooms, truck stop highway places down through Kansas, Oklahoma, north Texas . . . Yeah I'd hate it—those restrooms with fucking hot-air driers. Like the bastards'd caught on, so I'd have to wad up toilet paper to use and it's the cheap scratchy kind not absorbant like the towels so if my period was heavy which sometimes it was, pretty bad, it'd leak down my leg . . . *shit*! *(Agitated)* Say I'm riding in a truck cab next to this guy how the hell am I going to deal with it? So ashamed, sometimes I'd just start crying. He'd look at me, and Jesus I'm crying! Or if I was high I'd maybe burst out laughing and the guy'd grin and laugh too—"What's the joke, baby?"

First time I heard this I sure did laugh—"A blow job is better'n no job." *(Laughs)* Now *that's* funny, and it's sure true. *(Pause)*

(Dreamy) Gramma picked me her favorite to spite the rest of them. She'd say, "You're my girl, ain't you?" Because I was a little slow through grammar school. Because I was the one to help Gramma wash her long hair, that she was proud she never cut all her life. "Your Grampa made me promise I'd never cut my hair, so I never did. Isn't that something!—sixty years back. And him dead since 1941."

(Pause) And I'd wash Gramma's feet for her where she was too stout to bend. And clip her toenails, and bunions all grown over like scabs. Could be Gramma's dead now, I don't know. *(Pause)* Momma said I sure didn't take after *her*. Yeah I hated my sisters—so *pretty-pretty*! You get your way if you're *pretty-pretty* on TV or in the movies so if you're not, learn to take your own way. When I threw my plate on the floor I'd go hungry, but they caught on to respect me. When I shouted, I didn't stammer.

Reflective, winding herself tighter in the blanket, backing away as lights dim elsewhere on stage.

So, O.K.—JANE DOE "PINKTOES" is the one I came to be. There's twenty-two of us since 1988. Nobody ever named *me*—no "missing persons" in my home state. Momma took it, *I* ran away from home, I'm *out*. She washed her hands of me, can't say I blame her. *(Pause)*

So—where Pinktoes is from, who my folks were, or are, who I was or was intended to be—anybody's guess. All they know is I was found Hallowe'en morning in a ditch. Scabby legs open to the air, wide Texas sky. Stinging black flies. High circling hawks, crows. *(Sudden cry, despairing, as the realization washes over her)* NO! I'm too young to die! . . . *(Pause; forces herself to regain composure)* No. I accept my fate. "PINKTOES" . . . *(Pause)*

They're thinking maybe I'm from the Laredo stretch of I-35, or maybe east around Gainsville. Maybe one of the big cities—Houston, or Dallas—where it's easy to get lost. Or maybe out of state. *(Nodding)* Yeah—one of those sad little shrinking towns in Kansas, or Nebraska, or Iowa nobody knows the names of except the folks who live in them, and, for a while, till they forget, guys who pass through.

Lights down.

SCENE 2: MR. AMERICA

Lights up. A man in his mid-thirties, husky, in cheaply stylish but not new clothes, hair slickly oiled, a two- or three-days' growth of beard, addresses the audience.

(Proudly, an air of reverence) The first time, I was five years old. Ashland, West Virginia where I was born. My momma run me out of the trailer 'cause she was entertaining a guest so I was down by the creek bank and it was dark and I looked and saw this . . . fire . . . this Burning Bush . . . except it was going along the ground like a wheel. I wasn't scared. I knew it was God giving me a sign. I ran after it trying to catch it in my hands but it wouldn't stop . . . rolling *whoosh!* along the ground. *(Demonstrates)* Oh my fingers was burnt and blistered but I didn't feel no pain, I was struck down where I stood. And Momma next morning she finds me sleeping under the trailer my hands so hurt like they was *she* was repentant like a sinner called to judgment. *(Pause)* Her hair like corn tassels and her face like a shining light . . . *(Pause)*

(Self-condemning) There is a ministry of Love, and there is a ministry of Hurt. I know I was born to preach the one not practice the other and how this came to be *I* don't comprehend.

(Defensive) I tell you truly I don't recall. There's so many of them. And the pictures of them where they don't look like who they were exactly but like others of them—females. *(Pause)* Who I blame is the police and

the thr'pists always letting me go I'd tell them "No sir, no ma'am, naw not me, I'm a good boy washed in the Blood of the Lamb, not me." *(Wide innocent mock-smile, quickly fading)*

(Matter-of-fact) Picked this one, in the pink socks, 'cause she was there, and I was there. Truck-stop on I-35, Oklahoma. The sky all afire where the sun was going down, a long long time setting so my eyes was seared, I took that for a sign. All my life there's these signs . . . *(Shakes his head as if to clear it)* She was by herself at one of them picnic tables in the dark, she'd been crying and her face all puffy and eyes red so I was drawn to her as to a sister. Saw this poor child was a lost soul needing help. And that was so. *(Pause, gestures as if taking hold of the girl's shoulders, lifting her)* Told her I'd buy us some fried chicken and a six-pack but not right here so I got her to the car and we drove off how many hours I don't know. She was asleep going into Texas, her head on my shoulder . . . *(Pause)* I accept my fate, it's no choice for a reasonable man. I know there is God but He is far away.

(As if a profound insight) On I-35 where I make my journeys there are long stretches just empty like the moon would be empty. There's no words to put to them . . .

(Righteous, angry) These "court-appointed" thr'pists as they call themselves, and the l'wyers—nothing but a game with them, they don't give a shit. And the "doctors"—hoo, *that's* a laugh!—these jerk-offs at Plainfield couldn't speak English *nor* comprehend it. Dark enough to be niggers but *not*—one of 'em wearing a fucking turban. *(Indicating his own head with a winding motion; derisive)* *Them* saying I suffer from "temporal lobe trauma"—"lead and cadmium toxins"—from when I was a kid. Momma banged me around some, and Momma's men friends—O.K. But that's a long time ago. *(Pause, reminiscing)* This one time my mother was gone . . . went off with somebody . . . I hid out in the woods . . . getting stuff to eat out of garbage cans, dumpsters . . . one night, a guy took a shot at me with a twenty-two, told me to get the hell out what'd I think I was, a fucking raccoon? *(Laughs, ironic)* Yes, and Jesus saying, "Light is come into the world—!"

(Urgent, matter-of-fact) There was this woman turned up in Blacksburg. Where we was then with one of Momma's man friends. She was slow-witted you could see. Said she would have sex with me then changed her mind seeing something in my face. She was a dirty whore. She was cross-eyed. She was the one I blame. *(Pause)* In a field beyond the old train yard there's oil drums, freight cars . . . she started fighting me, screaming so I got pissed— *(Strangling motions with hands)*—shut her up good! Whore! Then I fucked her—good! Two, three times! Dragged some tarpaulin over her so nobody'd see then I went home to Mr. Cady's where Momma was "housekeeper" . . . I was fifteen years

old. He was going to send me to Bible College, said he detected the fire of the Lord in my eye. *He* was in a wheelchair, poor old bastard. Momma'd get drunk and laugh saying all he had was a— *(Gesturing at his crotch)* —old limp rubbery carrot. *(Laughs sadly)* They was going to get married but some folks of his fucked up the plans. *(Pause)* There was school there but I didn't go. I'd make myself wait then go back to the train yard and every time I'd think there's nothing there, naw—and every time *she was still there* under the tarpaulin. And nobody knew! And nobody was going to know! *(Pause, breathing swiftly)* I'd get excited . . . I'd . . . yeah I'd screw her . . . couldn't stop myself. *(A moment's anguish; pause)* They don't judge you in that state. *(Pause)*

A beat. MR. AMERICA hides his face, sways.

(Abrupt anger, dropping his hands) Huh! I know you're thinking you are SUPERIOR to me. BETTER EDUCATED and BETTER BACKGROUND, huh! BETTER NOURISHED in your mother's womb and your mother wasn't no PROSTITUTE. *(Spitting gesture)* Well, fuck that! *(Evangelical voice)* "For unto every one that hath shall be given, and he shall have abundance: but from him that hath not shall be taken away *even that which he hath*." *(Pause)* Think I don't know that? A man like me don't know that? God give me His sign, I am of the ministry of hurt. *(Rolls up his left sleeve to reveal a lewd crimson flame tattooed on his bicep)* Take heed: all through this United States of America there's those of us recognize each other by His sign. No matter how far from home we are—we are home.

(Righteous, incensed) She was a Christian girl she pretended. Wearing a little cross around her neck. Poor sad child in the pink socks. So far from home, she said, she'd about forgot where was her home. I asked her was she lost and she said she ain't ever been lost. I asked her were her folks missing her at that very moment and she said No! nobody was missing her! ever! but she started crying . . . poor sad child. *(Pause; now reflective)* Oh God how she was hoping to get a bath, she said. Wash out some of her dirty clothes. Her pink socks—been wearing them so long. At first she seemed kind of scared of me, but interested like they are. Saying, Mister, I'm so tired, I'm by myself, I'm hungry—you got anything to eat? I sure took pity on her from the first sight. That's the tender kind can break your heart—if you let them.

(Sadly) I miss my home, too. My momma that was always moving around. But where she *was*, that *was* home. If I could get there . . . I could be washed in the Blood of the Lamb. Momma hoped to make amends, her cousin was Reverend Willy Robbins baptized me and her together . . . we were happy, then. For how long I don't know but we

were happy and nobody came between us . . . *(Pause, shakes head)* At Plainfield they said it was "delusions"—these things I told them they didn't want to believe. "Frontal lobe epilepsy"—so they give me these hot-stinging shots in the ass. Thorazine—that'll make you into a walking zombie. How I escaped?—I *walked right out.* Work duty in the laundry and the laundry truck comes in, and the gates are open, and—*I walk right out.* Hoo!

(Continuing, matter-of-fact) I was driving down to Galveston where there was the promise of a job. Oil rig. I'm a good worker, I keep my nose clean I don't cause trouble. Any man knows he can trust me. Long as I'm not drinking. So any judge I come before, there's these "character references" and they're impressed. Never yet had a jury trial, nor wanted one. I told the police all I could remember but it was like a shadow—you can say, sure this is a "human being" but it don't *seem so.* There isn't the weight, or the—what you call it— *(Rubs thumb and forefinger together)* —the thickness—*texture.* The actual killing, when it happens, it's like the shadow is there and a flame flies up over it and that is the flame of Death. *(Pause)* I have been a witness from, say, twenty feet away. This last time, they were in a drainage ditch, and I was up on a bridge. I saw—but if I blinked, or shut my eyes, it wasn't there. It ceased to exist.

(Contemplative) You learn to accept your fate. You bow your head. *(Sings, a tentative, flat, yet yearning voice)* "Jesus meek and Jesus mild, Jesus became a little child . . . " Amen! *(Pause)* Couple years ago in Blacksburg in the psych'ric hospital I visited momma at last. This fat bald bulldog-woman I wouldna known! Momma, I said, I was near to crying, oh Momma you used to be so pretty! and she said, So did you, and laughed. She said, Yeah, my yellow hair fell out one day I wasn't looking. *(Laughs)* Momma always had a sense of humor. These guys beating on her, and stealing from her and she could take it long as there was food to eat and clothes for me, I was her baby she nursed me at her breast. In the visitors' room right on that filthy floor we prayed together on our knees. I could see she would die soon, they had pumped her so full of poison she was like a waterlogged corpse, and one of her eyes filmed over. She says, May God forgive me, son, that night I got drunk and burnt your hands, held your baby hands in the kerosene stove, and I was crying no matter who was watching me, I said, Oh Momma, that never happened, there's no need to be forgiven. She said, Son, that did happen, not once but many times, see these scars— *(He lifts his hands to contemplate the palms, turns them outward to the audience)* I said NO MOMMA THESE ARE FROM GOD. These are a sign from God to me, and He has sent others. *(Pause, bitter)* Damn ol' senile woman! Bitch! WHORE!

(Regaining control, an air of regret) This girl last week, in the pink socks—that was the one I saw, I whispered, "Sweet Jesus, let me love her." You want to offer your soul to somebody. You want to do some fucking GOOD in the world. We drove all night and the morning sky was like fire inside the clouds where there was God's face if you had eyes to see. *(Hiding his eyes)* A sheet of fire washed over the car, the hood all blinding . . . I was *hurt* all over my skin like . . . like lye . . . like a time I hoped to purify myself rubbing myself with lye . . . and there was a bridge we drove over exiting from the interstate, and a drainage ditch all dry . . . big cracks in the earth, and the earth so red . . . like Mars. That far away!

(Shift in tone) Never counted but my thirty-seven years I have been in-car-cer-ated fifteen. Going back to Boys' Home when Momma had to give me up for a while. It's O.K. inside. It's what you know. Six A.M. the bell goes and you get up and wash. Six-fifteen a bell goes and you step out of your cell and march off to mess hall and eat and you're *hungry*—say it's cereal, it's toast, it's canned peaches or something—it tastes real good. And coffee! O.K. then you march out of mess hall dropping your spoon, knife, fork in a bucket a guard's holding. You march to your work duty say it's custodian, or grounds, or tag shop where you dip license plates in paint. O.K., nine-thirty A.M. the bell goes and you can smoke. A bell goes and you get back to work. Eleven-thirty, bell goes again you stop work, wash up, march back to your cellhouse. Twelve noon, bell rings and you march to mess hall where you eat, and Jesus you're hungry—it might be meat loaf, fried potatoes, cornbread. *(Smacks lips)* Twelve-thirty a bell goes and you march out dropping your spoon, knife, fork in a bucket a guard's holding. You return to work duty. At three P.M. a bell goes and you can smoke. A bell goes and you get back to work. Four-thirty a bell goes and you can wash and march back to your cellhouse. Five o'clock a bell goes and you march to supper. Five-thirty a bell goes and you march to your cellhouse for the night. *(Pause)* You can pray on your knees long hours. You can read if your eyes don't upset you. There's noise in the cellhouse like in the world but in your cell there's peace. In Boys' Home they beat me and fucked me up the ass, made me their slave, O.K. but that ain't now, now I am my own man, and nobody fucks with me. *(Pause)* You can make of your body a vessel of strength. *(He does several quick push-ups, then rises, flushed and triumphant, flexing biceps)* You can prepare for your day of release hoping it won't come too soon. *(Pause, as he rolls up his other sleeve, to reveal a tattoo of an American eagle clutching a flag)* Which is why they call me "Mister America"—NOBODY FUCKS WITH ME.

(Reflective) There was others—lots of 'em—never knew their names. Nor even faces. It's like the weather, the wind blowing the clouds overhead . . . clouds' shadows you see flying along before you. *(Pause)* I told the Texas cops, confessed all I could recall, like puking it up . . . the years of it. Sixteen hours I talked to them! I was real eager to cooperate!—but the judge tossed it out, on account of I didn't have "proper counsel." I told the cops I didn't want no fucking lawyer and I didn't—*don't*. O.K. but the court assigned me one anyway. You need thr'py he said. Got me to plead guilty—"second-degree manslaughter"—and all that prior stuff was dropped. That's "delusion"—"confab-u-lation" they call it. They got to prove it and they got no proof my lawyer said so O.K., man! Hooo! *(Shakes head, bemused)* There's a deal with the court seven-to-thirty years. Up for parole in four years and I will be only forty-one then, not old. Not old, at all.

Lights out.

THE END

BLACK 🌿

A Play in Two Acts

Cast

JONATHAN BOYD—white, thirty-five years old
DEBRA O'DONNELL—white, early thirties
LLEWELLYN CLAYBROOK—black, mid- or late thirties

Setting

The living room/dining room of DEBRA O'DONNELL's house. If furnished
more than minimally, it should contain attractive "modern" furniture: a
sofa and chairs in neutral, subdued colors; bookshelves (containing both
books and CD's); a stereo; a coffee table; an end table with a stained-glass
lamp; a dining room table and matching chairs; perhaps a large potted
plant in the background. On the floor, near the door, are several cardboard boxes (containing BOYD's things).

NOTE: *though* JONATHAN BOYD *has come to visit his former wife* DEBRA O'DONNELL *with a secret agenda, one should have the sense that he is improvising at times, too—following the drift of his own, and others' emotions. He must not seem overbearing, or he will lose the audience's sympathy; one should see why* DEBRA *was once in love with him—and why she is no longer in love with him.*

*The relationship between the men, too, should be fluid and inventive. Though guarded with each other, they are naturally drawn to each other—*BOYD *is especially drawn to* CLAYBROOK. *Perhaps* BOYD *seeks a "brother" as desperately as he seeks his "wife."*

Ultimately, the crux of the action turns upon DEBRA's *new-found self-definition and her courage in the face of possible death. The play's climax is her refusal to acquiesce to* BOYD's *demand that she tell the "truth"—a "truth" she denies. The director should create a dramatic space for* DEBRA's *act of courage. She must not seem to be subordinate to the ostensibly stronger-willed men.*

BOYD *is both defeated by the events of this evening and liberated by them. He should be accorded one final moment—looking at his former wife, gazing out into his former house, and by extension into the future.*

ACT 1

SCENE 1

Darkness. Several bars of a classic blues number, "Cry Me a River." Then the music fades, to continue in the background through the telephone conversation.

Lights up extreme stage right. JONATHAN BOYD *is making a telephone call at a pay phone in a café. Cigarette in mouth.*

As the phone rings in DEBRA O'DONNELL's *living room, lights up there.*

DEBRA *hurriedly enters from stage left and picks up the receiver on the fourth ring.* DEBRA *is a very attractive, though rather guarded, woman in her early thirties; in a cream-colored outfit (a dress, or a skirt and matched sweater); wearing expensive-looking high-heeled shoes.* DEBRA *is nervous, but* BOYD's *more agitated state has the effect of calming her.*

DEBRA   Yes? Hello? *(A pause, as* BOYD *stands unspeaking; café noises in the background)* Hello—?

BOYD *(Guiltily, yet eagerly)*   Debra? Is that you?

DEBRA   Boyd? Where are you?

BOYD   It's—you?

DEBRA   Where are you?—are you all right?

BOYD   Your voice is—different.

DEBRA   I'm sorry—what? I can't hear you very—

BOYD   This *is* Debra?

DEBRA *(Concerned, impatient)*   Boyd, we've been waiting for you— we've been worried. Where *are* you?

BOYD   I wasn't sure—when you wanted me. I mean—exactly.

DEBRA   Come as soon as you can. Are you still on the Turnpike?

BOYD *(Anxiously)*   When did you say you wanted me there?—

DEBRA   I thought we said seven—

BOYD   Oh Christ, I *am* late.

DEBRA   Boyd, just come. We've been waiting.

BOYD   Look, I'm sorry—I'm in Passaic. At the Anchor Inn.

DEBRA *(Puzzled, alarmed)*   You're *there?* Ten minutes away? Why?

BOYD   I wasn't sure when you—wanted me.

DEBRA   Oh, Boyd! Don't do this. *(Pause)* You haven't been drinking, have you?

BOYD *(Mutters)* "Sorry!" *(As café noises increase.)*

DEBRA I can't hear you—what's going on there? Boyd?

LLEWELLYN CLAYBROOK enters, from stage left. He approaches DEBRA deliberately; graceful on his feet; slides his arms around her, from behind; she is startled, then responds with affection, even passion. CLAYBROOK is a black man in his early thirties; intelligent; well-groomed; casually but tastefully dressed (in a sport coat of a conservative color and texture, a good sport shirt or turtleneck sweater); he may wear a beard or a goatee. He need not be handsome, but he should carry himself with a certain measure of dignity—which, we sense, is sometimes willed, self-conscious.

DEBRA *(More assertive now)* Boyd, just *come.* We'll be expecting you in a few minutes.

BOYD But—is it all right?

DEBRA I can't hear you—. For God's sake please just *come!*

DEBRA hangs up the phone, with an exclamation of exasperation and amusement. She turns to CLAYBROOK's embrace and embraces him; hides her face in his neck. They freeze as lights go down and out, center stage.

BOYD *(Still on telephone, angry, despairing)* You don't want me there— I'm out, I'm dead—you know it—you and—*him.*

BOYD hangs up the phone so hard that the receiver slips from the hook and he has to replace it.

Lights out. Blues number ends.

SCENE 2

Lights up. As doorbell rings, DEBRA and CLAYBROOK open the door to BOYD, who is carrying a duffel bag (slung over his shoulder) and a long-stemmed red rose and a bottle of wine. Surprisingly, he appears calm; smiling; charming; keyed-up, but seemingly in control. For the briefest moment, he stares at DEBRA and CLAYBROOK—then takes DEBRA's hand, murmuring "Hello" as DEBRA in turn murmurs a near-inaudible greeting; and, after a moment's hesitation, leans forward and kisses him on the cheek. One should sense that BOYD and DEBRA have not seen each other for some time; their feelings are powerful but inchoate and undefined.

BOYD God, I'm sorry—I guess I'm late?—it's snowing, the Turnpike traffic is—slow.

DEBRA *(Just slightly edgy, but seemingly warm, sincere)* We're so happy to see you, Boyd—we were worried. *(She turns to* CLAYBROOK*)* Boyd, this is Llewellyn Claybrook—Lew—my friend; Lew, this is Jonathan Boyd—his friends all call him *Boyd.*

BOYD *and* CLAYBROOK *energetically shake hands, each trying to outdo the other in affability, self-composure, man-to-man equanimity.*

BOYD   Hey! Great to meet you!

CLAYBROOK   Great to meet *you!*

BOYD   Yes I'm— *(Merest pause, staring at* CLAYBROOK*, as if confused)* — so glad to meet you—Lew. Your name is—?

CLAYBROOK   Some friends call me Lew, some call me Clay.

BOYD *(Staring, nonplussed)*   Uh— Lew? *Clay?*

DEBRA *(An arm through* CLAYBROOK'*s arm)*   Llewellyn's *Lew.*

BOYD   Well, I—I'm—so relieved to be here, to be off that Turnpike. For you, Debra— *(Hands her the rose),* and, uh, Lew— *(Hands him the bottle of wine)*

DEBRA   Thank you, Boyd.

CLAYBROOK   Thanks!

DEBRA   You aren't wearing a coat, Boyd?

BOYD *shrugs, smiling. As* DEBRA *closes the door,* BOYD *comes forward, in a manner that is both shy and aggressive; his eyes dart quickly about, taking in the scene. He flicks snowflakes off his hair. Behind him,* DEBRA *and* CLAYBROOK *exchange a significant look;* CLAYBROOK *shows* DEBRA *the label on the wine bottle, eyebrows raised (to indicate that the wine is expensive).*

BOYD *is an attractive man of thirty-five; but many appear subtly fatigued, ravaged; with a just perceptible growth of beard, and hair, disheveled, a little too long and uneven. We sense that* BOYD *is but precariously in control of himself and that, often, he does not know his own motives, though, being intelligent and verbal, he can readily invent and assign motives. His smile—an American boy's quick, sunny smile—is sometimes strained, and sometimes genuine. He is wearing a once-good sport coat; a dark shirt with a carelessly knotted tie; chino trousers; well-worn jogging shoes. He is tall and well-built, vain of his physical prowess and presence.*

BOYD *swings his duffel bag down and sets it onto the floor. As* DEBRA *and* CLAYBROOK *approach, in the manner of hosts welcoming a guest,* BOYD *paws through the duffel bag (his back to them), takes up an object in his hand, rises, perhaps leaps to his feet, to face them. His behavior is threatening, as, no doubt, he means it to be, even as, with his boyish smile, he pretends otherwise.*

BOYD   Freeze! Like that! Great! *Perfect!*

BOYD *takes a flash photograph of* DEBRA *and* CLAYBROOK *who, caught off guard, look very startled and confused.*

With the flash, lights out.

SCENE 3

Lights up, immediately.

As DEBRA *and* CLAYBROOK *manage to compose themselves, exchanging looks,* BOYD *walks about the living room, rubbing his hands together (and blowing on them, as if to warm them), smiling, as if in a mild daze.*

BOYD   So warm here—so *nice.* I'd forgotten how—*nice. (He touches the sofa, kneels to touch the rug, drawing his fingers sensuously across the fabric)* No sign of—damage. So *nice.*

DEBRA *(Nervous laugh)*   Things aren't much changed.

BOYD   No, the room is larger—the space. The walls back there *(Pointing outward, toward rear of theater)* are farther away than they used to be. It's definitely—larger.

DEBRA   A few things are new—

CLAYBROOK *(Not certain if* BOYD *was joking)*   What kind of damage—?

BOYD   Yes it's changed. It's the same but definitely changed. *(At bookshelves, examines CD's)* Mmmm—Ellington, Tatum, Coltrane—the best. *(Pause, as he looks through CD's, of which there are perhaps two dozen)*

DEBRA *(Hesitantly touching* BOYD'S *arm)*   Boyd, would you—

BOYD *(Boyishly, addresses* CLAYBROOK*)*   Could we hear one of these? Would you mind?

CLAYBROOK   I surely wouldn't *mind,* what's your preference?

BOYD *(Handing him a CD)*   This—this is fine. *(As* CLAYBROOK *inserts CD, music starts)* Last month, can't remember where, had a fever of one hundred and four degrees, I started hearing *this*—kept me calm and pulled me back to life—like, you pull a sagging-heavy boat in the water with just a rope.

Jazz, which should be cool, mellow, subtly erotic, any familiar piece (or sequence of pieces), continues through the scene, gradually decreasing in volume.

BOYD *(Staring at stained-glass lamp on table)*   This—this is new. *(As he touches it,* DEBRA *makes an involuntary protective gesture, as if she's afraid he might knock it over)*

DEBRA   Lew's father made it. He's—

BOYD *(Not hearing, smiling; has sighted boxes on floor)*   I guess these are my left-over things?—ready to go?

DEBRA   Well—eventually. Right now, would you—like a drink?

BOYD *(Squatting on heels beside boxes, looking through them)*   God, this!—I'd forgotten all about *this*! *(Lifts tennis racquet)* And these shoes— *(Lifts a pair of shoes)* And, what's this— *(A notebook, through which he glances hastily)*—handwriting I don't recognize but I guess it's mine. *(He takes up a tape recorder, a single glove, a hat, some paperback books, etc., in turn)* It's so kind of you, Debra, to have packed all this. Another woman, in your place, might have— *(As he lets one of the items fall)* —tossed all this crap out with the trash.

DEBRA and CLAYBROOK speak simultaneously:

DEBRA   Yes but I *didn't*, Boyd—

CLAYBROOK   Debra isn't "another woman"—

BOYD *(Lifting camera)*   My old Sunpack. So it wasn't lost after all. *(Examines the camera almost tenderly, lifts it to sight areas of the room in the viewfinder, including DEBRA, who tries not to appear tense or apprehensive)*

DEBRA   Boyd, why don't you sit down, relax— You've come a long way, you must be—

BOYD *(Continuing to stare at DEBRA)*   —So it wasn't lost after all. It was here all the time.

DEBRA *(Patiently)*   I'm sure I told you that, Boyd. You just never took the time to— *(Pause, tries to smile)* Why don't I get you something to drink?

BOYD replaces the camera, gets to his feet; he's unsteady, as if he has been drinking already.

CLAYBROOK *(Hospitably)*   There's beer, wine, scotch—whatever. Good Kentucky bourbon. *(Raises wine bottle)* Not quite this quality, Boyd, but almost.

BOYD sits heavily on the sofa; has surprised himself by the way in which his legs give out. He runs a hand swiftly and nervously through his hair— an unconscious mannerism that recurs, yet should not be allowed to become predictable or obtrusive. We sense that BOYD does this when he is quite literally trying to think or position himself.

CLAYBROOK *(Admiring wine)*   This, we'll have with dinner.

BOYD *(Staring up at him, blinking, as if the light is too strong)*   I'll have a, a—club soda.

CLAYBROOK *(As if doubtfully)*   Club soda? Un—with lemon, lime—?

BOYD *(Suddenly grinning, pointing to* CLAYBROOK *as he tugs at his neck-tie)* Right, man, that's a good sign—no tie. *(Pulls tie off roughly and stuffs in his pocket)*

DEBRA *(Another involuntary gesture)* Oh Boyd—that *tie.*

BOYD Eh?

DEBRA That's that—expensive tie—isn't it?—silk, Italian?—your mother gave you.

BOYD *(Bemused, to* CLAYBROOK*)* Yes. Well. My mother isn't *here.*

CLAYBROOK, *moving toward kitchen, off stage-left, takes the rose from* DEBRA *in passing.* BOYD, *not noticing, calls after him, awkwardly joking.*

BOYD My mother has been dead for six years, that's one of the reasons why— *(Clumsy, now embarrassed)* —why she *isn't.*

CLAYBROOK *has exited.*

Except for the jazz, there is silence. We expect DEBRA *and* BOYD *to speak but they do not. They appear suddenly stricken and can barely look at each other.*

DEBRA *remains standing beside the sofa; not quite in* BOYD's *line of vision, as if reluctant to sit down.* BOYD, *on the sofa, stretches his arms wide; sighs; makes sounds meant to suggest both fatigue and relief.*

BOYD *(As if making decision)* Yes. This is it.

DEBRA *remains motionless; uncertain how to approach* BOYD.

BOYD *turns to look at* DEBRA, *squinting as if, again, the light is blinding.*

BOYD *(Softly)* . . . beautiful.

DEBRA *(As if not hearing)* How hard *is* it snowing out?

BOYD *(As before)* You. Like always. Beautiful.

DEBRA, *after a pause, takes a seat in one of the chairs; smiles faintly; clasps hands on lap. It is clear that she is very agitated, but shows little.*

BOYD *(Indicating the room)* All like a dream—but not *my* dream.

DEBRA You were sick, you said?—a fever? When?

We hear CLAYBROOK *whistling off-stage.*

BOYD Is that—him? Sounds so happy. *(Pause)* He isn't what I'd been— led to expect. *(Pause, as* DEBRA *resists the implications of this)* Oh, I caught malaria—in Africa. Second time, actually. I'm fine, now.

DEBRA You've lost weight.

BOYD *(Trying not to stare)* And you—you've gained. *(Pause)* You've come back to life.

DEBRA *(Simply)* Yes. I have.

BOYD *(Passionately)* God, when I drove up here just now, the look of the, the house—the lighted windows—the light around the blinds—it went through me like a knife blade. I see that you're *here*; and I'm *not*. *(laughs)* That's it.

DEBRA You're back in the country, now? Living in D.C.?

BOYD *(Evasively)* I'm looking around.

DEBRA *(Lightly ironic)* How's the Anchor Inn?

BOYD Benny's still bartending, he asked after you. He—was wondering why he hadn't seen us. *(Pause)* In so long.

DEBRA And what did you tell him?

BOYD The truth. *(Pause)*

DEBRA And tonight you're staying—?

BOYD A motel on the Turnpike. I'm fine. *(Pause)* You're so kind to do this. *(Pause)* You and—him. Both. *(Pause, then, boyish-sly)* For a moment, he didn't want to shake my hand. *(Laughs)* At the door. *(Runs hand through hair)* Once, I did that piece on Roberto Durán, the boxer, remember?—for *Sports Illustrated?*—*(As DEBRA doesn't seem to remember)*—well, Durán was being introduced to a boxer he was going to fight, and the other man put out his hand to be shaken, and Durán jumped away, and screamed at him, "Get away! get away! I'm not your friend!" *(Laughs, demonstrating some of this, then more earnestly)* You let me in that door—you must have—forgiven me? *(Pause)* Maybe—you shouldn't have.

DEBRA *(Trying to shift to a lighter tone)* Shouldn't have forgiven you?— or let you in the door?

BOYD *stares at* DEBRA, *not replying. His eyes are hooded; his manner intense, erotic. It is clear that he is very strongly attached to* DEBRA; *or to something she represents.*

CLAYBROOK's *whistling grows louder.* CLAYBROOK *reappears, in the doorway to the kitchen.*

CLAYBROOK *(Smiling, genial)* Uh, say, Jonathan—I mean, Boyd—you're *sure* you want just a club soda? I'm having a Heineken.

BOYD *(As if needing to be tempted)* Uh—Heineken dark?

CLAYBROOK *(With pleasure)* Real dark.

BOYD *(Hesitantly)* Well—O.K.—make that two. Thanks!

CLAYBROOK *signals O.K. with thumb and forefinger; disappears back into kitchen.*

DEBRA *laughs; then presses fingers to lips.*

BOYD *(Wide smile)* Something funny, Debra?

DEBRA *(Quickly)* No.

BOYD   You're laughing.

DEBRA   I'm—smiling.

BOYD   *(Soberly)*   I stick to beer, now. This will be my first of the day. *(Pause)* First in *two* days.

DEBRA   It's fine, Boyd. It's all right.

BOYD   It *is* fine, I promise. *(Pause)* I am not the way I—the way you remember—me.

DEBRA   *(Almost tenderly)*   I know that, Boyd.

BOYD   *(Flaring up)*   You don't *know* it, I'm telling you.

DEBRA stiffens.

CLAYBROOK returns, cheerful, hospitable. He is carrying a tray containing two bottles of beer, two tall glasses, a glass of wine for DEBRA, a bowl of nuts, and the long-stemmed rose in a slender vase. He serves DEBRA and BOYD, takes a bottle of beer and a glass for himself.

BOYD   *(Lifting glass)*   Chilled. That's real class! Thanks, Lew.

DEBRA   *(Sipping wine)*   Thanks, Lew. How is the veal?

CLAYBROOK   Everything's under control. *(Checks watch)* I'll start the pasta at nine. *(As DEBRA seems about to rise)* No, sit *still;* I'm in charge.

BOYD is drinking thirstily; scooping nuts out of the bowl to devour.

BOYD   Driving on the Turnpike—after dark—it's mesmerizing. And the snow falling. And the oncoming headlights. You start to float free— don't know where the hell you *are.*

CLAYBROOK   It can be dangerous, at night. Driving alone.

BOYD   *(With a smile)*   Driving alone is always dangerous.

CLAYBROOK   So! *(Slight pause)* Debra was telling me, you've been traveling?

BOYD   I'm back for good, now. For now.

DEBRA   *That* isn't very likely.

BOYD   My bones ache. *(As if amused)* I'm thirty-five years old.

DEBRA   You were treated for the malaria, I hope?

BOYD   *(Laughs)*   If I wasn't, I wouldn't be here now. *(Drinks)* I *am* here— I guess?

CLAYBROOK   *(Looking through a pile of magazines on a table, but not finding the one he wants)*   Debra showed me—I mean, I read—the article you did on Northern Ireland.

BOYD   *(Surprised and touched)*   You read it?

CLAYBROOK   —thought it was here, somewhere.

DEBRA   It's around somewhere.

BOYD   In *The New York Times Magazine.* But that was last year.

CLAYBROOK   It was very powerful, I thought—first-rate. Man!—you were taking chances, eh? Interviewing the IRA?

BOYD   That was a while back.

DEBRA   This time you were in—? Ethiopia?

BOYD *(Flattered by the attention)*   In Addis Abbabe mainly. It didn't work out too well. I got sick, and I came back, to Europe I mean, I was supposed to go to East Germany, for *Newsweek,* and— *(Vaguely, drinking)* —Poland— But— Traveling, crossing time zones, you can really displace who you *are. (Pause)* One of my cameras was stolen in Budapest. In the Hilton of all places.

CLAYBROOK   I've been there—the Budapest Hilton. Pretty swanky.

BOYD *(Surprised)*   *You've* been there?

CLAYBROOK *(Ignoring BOYD's condescension)*   Well—not recently. Back before all hell broke loose in East Europe.

DEBRA *(Defensively)*   Lew travels too, or did. To professional conferences.

CLAYBROOK *(Wryly)*   Yeah—*did.* When I was, like, more a theorist—a teacher.

DEBRA *(Proudly)*   At Rutgers-New Brunswick, The School of Social Work. That's where we met—Lew was my professor.

CLAYBROOK   Now, I'm in the real world, trying to practice what I preach. *(Shakes head)* No more *theory.*

BOYD *(As if puzzled)*   I guess I've been told some—inaccurate things about you.

CLAYBROOK *(Coolly, not responding to this remark)*   Well. People *will* talk. *(Smoothly)* Yes, I surely do envy you, Boyd. I'd always wanted to visit the Iron Curtain countries, and never got there, and now it's totally changed. The Berlin Wall—I'd've liked to see that.

BOYD *(Shuddering)*   The Wall!—that was a, a hard fact to deal with. If your mind's susceptible to—things.

DEBRA   Well, the Wall's down now.

BOYD *(Smiling)*   Debra doesn't want me to talk about the Berlin Wall, there're bad personal memories associated with the Wall, so, O.K., I won't. *(Pause)* Just ten days we spent there, once—in West Berlin—I was on assignment for *Life. (Searching in pockets for cigarettes, without success)*

CLAYBROOK *(To change subject)*   Well, we're living in boom times. For history, I mean. Almost too many surprises, these last few years.

BOYD *(Goes to his duffel bag, to rifle through it)*   The thing about West Berlin people won't realize, and lots of Americans didn't know at the time—the Wall *surrounded* the city. It wasn't just some division of West and East. *(Gesturing)* Some people freaked, if they stayed there too long. It could really get to you, if you were susceptible. *(Locates a pack of cigarettes, rises, starts to light cigarette)*

DEBRA   Excuse me, Boyd—

BOYD   Yes?

DEBRA   I'd rather you didn't smoke, if it's all right with you.

BOYD *(Glancing about for ashtrays)*   You've quit?

DEBRA   I'm trying to. I'm about eighty-five percent successful. Lew doesn't smoke— *(She squeezes LEW's hand)*—he gives me moral support.

BOYD *(Awkward with his cigarettes, puts them in pocket)*   Well. I hope it lasts, Debra. *(Pause; laughs)* Remember that time?—that Christmas, we both gave up.

DEBRA *(Ruefully)*   For forty-eight hours.

BOYD   No! It was longer than that.

DEBRA   For you, not me. Women get more addicted to nicotine than men, I think. It's a terrible thing.

BOYD *(Coughing)*   God! I just think of smoking, and—I start coughing.

CLAYBROOK   Why don't you have a seat, Boyd—make yourself at home.

At this, BOYD laughs; and again coughs.

DEBRA   Sit down, please, Boyd—don't hover.

BOYD *(To CLAYBROOK)*   She used to say that all the time—Boyd, don't hover. *(Flapping arms)* I used to be a bat.

CLAYBROOK laughs, DEBRA smiles faintly.

BOYD *(Sitting, as before; brushes against stained-glass lamp in passing, but doesn't knock it over)*   You did miss something historic, Lew—I mean Clay—no Lew—by not seeing the Berlin Wall. Nothing like it. Weird fucking symbol but, y'know, *real*.

DEBRA *(Laughing impatiently)*   Boyd, the Wall's *down*.

BOYD   It's the ones you can't see that kill you. Walls, I mean. *(A significant glance at DEBRA)* You told him about it, eh?—that time?

DEBRA *(Incensed)*   I did not tell Lew about that—that sorry episode. Or any other.

BOYD *(Regarding her quizzically)*   Didn't?

DEBRA   The past is *past*.

BOYD *(Looking from CLAYBROOK to DEBRA, and back)*   Yes but you have to share the past, don't you?—good times, bad times?—misfortunes?—happy memories? That's love, right?

DEBRA *(As BOYD utters the word "love")*   I've told Lew very *little*. *(She has become a bit shrill, as if the wine has gone to her head; takes CLAYBROOK's hand and squeezes it)* We have plenty of other things to talk about.

BOYD   And to *do*. Uh-huhhhh. *(Slightly mocking-suggestive tone; BOYD has drained his glass of beer and now drinks from the bottle, emptying it in an extravagant gesture)*

CLAYBROOK *(Restless)*   You about ready for another, Boyd?—I'm on my way.

DEBRA *(Not wanting to be alone with BOYD)*   Oh no, Honey, wait—I'll go.

CLAYBROOK *(Warmly, but also accustomed to having his own way)*   No no *no,* Debra. You stay with your—guest. *(His hand on her shoulder, gently but decisively)* Boyd—another beer?

BOYD   Well—if you are.

CLAYBROOK   Sure thing!

CLAYBROOK removes the empty bottles; exits stage left. In his wake there is a brief silence. Then, startling her, BOYD reaches over to squeeze DEBRA's hand.

BOYD   He's—nice. I like him, Debra.

DEBRA *(Almost shyly)*   I thought you might. *(Pause)* I mean, I thought you might like each other.

BOYD   You think he likes—*me?*

DEBRA *(Withdrawing her hand)*   Oh, Lew likes *everyone.*

BOYD *(A bit deflated)*   What's he, a Christian or something?

DEBRA *(Pleased to be talking about her lover)*   In fact, Lew's father *is* a preacher—in the African Methodist Episcopal Church. In Philadelphia.

BOYD *(Running a hand through his hair, bemused)*   Well—I was certainly misled about all this.

DEBRA *(Coolly)*   What's "all this"—?

BOYD *(Shrugging)*   You, here. And him.

DEBRA *(Voice rising)*   Who's been talking about me?—our mutual friends? Whose business is my life but my own?

BOYD *(Portentously)*   I bear a certain—responsibility. We were together eleven years.

DEBRA   We were married nine years.

BOYD   We were *together* eleven years—that can't be changed. *(Pause)* Almost a third of my lifetime.

DEBRA   Don't think about it, that's all. I've stopped.

BOYD   You've—stopped?

DEBRA   I've *stopped.*

BOYD sets his glass down carelessly, nearly spills his drink.

BOYD   Sorry! My hands are—sort of—shaky.

DEBRA   How long were you drinking before you came here?

BOYD *(Ignoring this)*   He's so sharp, isn't he—just now, he left at the right moment, knowing he can trust me with you.

DEBRA *(Laughing, incensed)*   Of course he can trust you with me.

BOYD   He can trust *you* with *me.*

DEBRA   What is that supposed to mean?

BOYD *(In an undertone)* Is he—moved *in*? Here?

DEBRA *(Implacably)* To a degree.

BOYD I mean—is it serious, permanent?

DEBRA On my side, it is.

BOYD *(Shrewdly)* He isn't married, or anything?

DEBRA *(After a moment's hesitation)* Ask him.

BOYD I wouldn't want you to be hurt, Debra—that's all.

DEBRA *(Laughing)* From *you*—that's funny.

BOYD He *has* been married, right?—his age, he must have children.

DEBRA *(Irritably)* Llewellyn Claybrook is a very special person, but he's a very private person. He isn't, in some ways, like *us*.

BOYD Not like white people, or not like *us*?

DEBRA With him, I don't think in terms of *white*, or *black*. *(As BOYD makes a gesture of disbelief)* I'm in love.

A long painful pause.

BOYD *(Stiffly)* I see.

DEBRA There's no reason why you can't be friends with Lew—with us. You and he are both men of—integrity.

BOYD Are we. *(BOYD tugs at his shirt collar, suddenly warm)*

DEBRA Your idealism just got in the way of, of *you*—for a while. You had some rough times but they're over.

BOYD *(Mirthless joke)* Yeah, like thirty years. *(Pause, glancing toward kitchen)* You think he's hiding in there?—from me?

DEBRA Lew was genuinely impressed with that article of yours on Northern Ireland. He said, "Here's a *brother.*"

BOYD *(Moved)* He didn't say that—did he?

DEBRA You see, I told him nothing—demeaning. *(Pause)* Just that we'd had some hard times—we fell out of love—we got divorced. And that was that.

BOYD *(Wincing)* That was . . . that. *(Pause)* As long as you're happy, Debra.

DEBRA *(Slowly)* I am very happy. Don't try to change that.

BOYD But I— *(Pause, looking at her with yearning, perhaps some disbelief, outrage)* I would never—

DEBRA Yes. Yes you would.

BOYD *(After a pause)* The scar isn't visible—is it?

DEBRA *(Touching her upper lip, involuntarily, then lowering her hand)* That depends upon how close you are.

BOYD, restless, gets to his feet; moves toward kitchen, glancing in that direction, as if worried that CLAYBROOK can overhear.

BOYD I'd heard—upsetting things—about him, and you. That's why I— that's one of the reasons why I—I'm here.

DEBRA   Well, you were mistaken. *(Sharply)* Who's been talking about me?

BOYD   Somebody said he was an unemployed jazz musician, living off you, and mixed up in drugs; somebody else said he was an ex-cop, mixed up in drugs; and maybe a pimp. *(Not noticing DEBRA's anger, laughing)* Burt Hartmann—I ran into him in Frankfurt, catching a plane—said he'd heard you were living with a breeder of pit bulldogs. *(Laughs)* The one consensus was—the guy was *black.*

DEBRA gets to her feet, quickly advances upon BOYD, and slaps him full on the face.

BOYD stares at her, his hand to his stung face; then, unexpectedly, he drops to his knees, takes hold of her ankles, embraces her legs, presses his face against her legs.

BOYD   *(Anguished, rapturous)*   These are so lovely—your shoes—your lovely shoes—Debra—I'm so sorry—

At this moment CLAYBROOK enters, with tray and drinks; an apron carelessly knotted around his waist. He stares at BOYD and DEBRA.

Lights out.

SCENE 4

Lights up. Later. There is evidence of drinking: a half-dozen beer bottles on the coffee table; a nearly depleted bottle of wine. CLAYBROOK, seated as before, has removed the apron and laid it on the table beside him. DEBRA, seated as before, is flush-faced and uneasy; sipping wine; frequently glancing at CLAYBROOK. BOYD, who is squatting by his duffel bag, taking out a portfolio, has removed his sport coat and looks disheveled but eager, happy.

BOYD   —Yes but each place is the worst, *the* very worst, in Africa. In Ethiopia—here— *(He passes photographs, at which CLAYBROOK stares grimly, adjusting his glasses, and DEBRA, wincing, can barely bring herself to look)* —I was "covering" the war—the drought—the famine—the starvation—the AIDS epidemic—me, and the other reporters and photographers, most of us white, some from the U.S. and some from West Europe—we all know one another, by now—covering the world's "trouble spots"— *(Laughs, wiping face with forearm, speaking rapidly)* —it caught up with me, made me sick in my *guts.* *(Pause, watching CLAYBROOK's and DEBRA's faces closely; then in an altered voice, with a bit of bravado)* But I filed the story anyway. "One of Boyd's best."

CLAYBROOK *(Moved)*   Lord Jesus have mercy!—this is powerful stuff. Makes the heartbreak I deal with what you'd call *negotiable. (Shows a photograph to* DEBRA, *who pushes faintly at his hand, not wanting to see)* Look at those eyes!—poor child.

DEBRA *(Quietly)*   If you can't do anything to help, it seems wrong to look.

BOYD *(Squatting on his heels, keeping his balance with difficulty)*   Right! Don't I know it! But—

CLAYBROOK   Where's the story coming out, Boyd?

BOYD *(Vaguely)*   It's—pending. *(Leafing through photos)* I spent Christmas photographing dying people—children especially. Close-ups like this. Faces, eyes. On film. To sell. Why else?—to sell. And there's the byline. *(Pause)* Back in New York, editors shuffle through the contact sheets, discard most of them. The rap is my shots are "too graphic"— or "not graphic enough." The closest to extinction the spark of life is in these kids, the more valuable the photo; but, if the spark of life is actually *out,* and all you have is a kiddy-corpse—no thanks!

DEBRA *(Impatiently)*   Oh, Boyd, let yourself *be.* It's all about you, isn't it?

BOYD *(Hurt)*   About *me?*

DEBRA   You know.

They exchange a significant look. DEBRA *shakes her head, just slightly.*

CLAYBROOK *continues to look through the photos; then, sensitive to* DEBRA's *feelings, collects them and hands them back to* BOYD.

CLAYBROOK *(With regret)*   Now's not the proper time, maybe. For these.

BOYD *(Almost defiantly, taking the photos back)*   When is the proper time, then?

CLAYBROOK *(Seriously)*   Well—some sacred time.

BOYD   Some what?

CLAYBROOK *(Holding his ground)*   Sacred time.

BOYD *puts the photos back in the portfolio, a bit carelessly; shoves the portfolio back in his duffel bag as if disgusted with it, or disappointed with its reception.*

BOYD *(Sitting on sofa, as before, taking up space)*   Some of us don't believe in "sacred time."

CLAYBROOK   There's true courage there, Boyd. In that work. And artistry too. Uh-huh, I'd say beauty—cruel beauty. *(Trying to be congenial)* Like Hell might be beautiful. If you've got the eye.

BOYD   If you're not in it.

CLAYBROOK *(To DEBRA)*   It's true what you say, Debra, seems wrong to *look* if you can't *act,*—like, *knowing* and *acting* shouldn't be separated. But, say you just bear witness—"they also serve who only stand and wait"—that can be a true course of action too.

BOYD *(Drinking)*   Debra doesn't buy that, Clay. She knows we're in it for the dough. "Media" men.

DEBRA   Don't put words in my mouth, Boyd, come *on.*

BOYD *(Slightly boastfully)*   My next big project is private—a book of my photos. "The Eye of the Storm" is the title.

CLAYBROOK   Fine title!

DEBRA *(Wanly enthusiastic)*   Is this Beacon Press?—the one you signed the contract with—?

BOYD   No, this is something new. *(Pause)* A better deal.

DEBRA   Well. I'm happy for you.

CLAYBROOK   And I am too, Boyd. *(Glancing at watch)* Uh!—it's *eleven?* How'd that happen?

DEBRA *(Making a motion to rise but sinks back as if dizzy, giggling)* Wow. If we don't get dinner on the table it isn't going to be *got* on the table.

CLAYBROOK and DEBRA confer, almost inaudibly; BOYD regards them as if from a distance.

CLAYBROOK *(Murmuring intimately to DEBRA)*   Sweetheart, you let me deal with the pasta, O.K.?—no need us both fussing.

DEBRA   I'll make it, hey c'mon, I'm not drunk—

CLAYBROOK   You toss the salad.

DEBRA   It's *tossed.*

CLAYBROOK   Get the water boiling then and call me—that angel hair, can't be overcooked.

DEBRA *(To BOYD, by way of teasing CLAYBROOK)*   He doesn't trust me, fears I'm gonna make a mush of his pasta. *(She gets unsteadily to feet; leans on CLAYBROOK; her shapely body inadvertently displayed)* His pasta—made it himself, on his machine.

DEBRA takes up some of the empties, moves stage left.

BOYD *(Voice raised, aggrieved, dramatic—his self-conscious "summing up")*   I thought that—reporting injustice, atrocities, suffering—I could make a real difference in the world. But one day I had to see— I was just *reporting.* Just a cog in the consumer machine.

This moment is lost, however: CLAYBROOK is watching DEBRA, who has picked up the empty bottles, fumbles and nearly drops them.

CLAYBROOK *(Warmly)*   Say Honey—you need some help there?

DEBRA (*Waving him back*) Honey *no.*

DEBRA *exits.* BOYD *is hurt, offended; from this point onward it is all he can do to control his deep rage; there is a moment of quiet; they listen to jazz.*

BOYD Man, that's beautiful. The greatest.

CLAYBROOK (*Nodding, tapping foot, keeping time with the music*) Mmmmm.

BOYD Uh—Ellington?

CLAYBROOK Peterson.

BOYD Who?

CLAYBROOK Oscar Peterson.

BOYD Oh yes! (*Listens*) You probably have a much larger collection, eh?—than just those CD's?

CLAYBROOK (*As if bemused at himself*) I have records—must be hundreds; I have tapes; I'm into CD's. Over at the other place.

BOYD The other place.

CLAYBROOK Down the "pike," in Trenton. Where I'm, y'know, located. (*Pause*) Till things get worked out.

BOYD Till things get worked out. (*Pause*)

CLAYBROOK (*Politely*) You're living in Washington—?

BOYD I'm living in— (*Shrugs*) —my car.

CLAYBROOK (*Not having heard*) Where's *that?*

BOYD (*Drinking, voice slurred, careless*) —living in my *bag.* (*A kicking gesture toward duffel bag on floor*)

CLARYBROOK *laughs, uncertainly.*

BOYD (*Almost hesitantly*) So, uh, Clay—O.K. to call you Clay?—my wife was your student, huh?

CLAYBROOK (*Carefully*) Debra O'Donnell—that's how I know her: "Debra O'Donnell"—was my student, yes.

BOYD (*Smiling*) Looks like, now, she's graduated.

CLAYBROOK She's getting her degree in May. But she's been working with County Services since last fall.

BOYD That's where you work too?

CLAYBROOK Debra's here in Passaic, I'm in Trenton—the state capital— like I said. I direct Family Services for the State.

BOYD (*Impressed*) The State! (*Pause*) "Debra O'Donnell"—not "Debra Boyd." That's how she identified herself, is it?

CLAYBROOK That's her name, friend.

BOYD She's—changed. A lot.

CLAYBROOK She's a fine, strong, good-hearted woman. Just needs faith in her own spiritual *self.*

BOYD   I'm happy for her . . .

CLAYBROOK *(Following his own line of thought)*   A human being, beneath his or her skin, has got to realize the spiritual *self*. "The Kingdom of God is within." That's what that means.

A beat.

BOYD *(Casually)*   That tiny scar on Debra's upper lip—sickle-shaped—you ever noticed?

CLAYBROOK *(Taken by surprise)*   A bicycle accident, Debra said—when she was a little girl.

BOYD *(Hiding relief)*   Well. O.K. 'Cause that's the truth, it *was* an accident. *(Pause; smiling ruefully)* My wife—ex-wife—is a, a somewhat destructive person—y'know? *(As CLAYBROOK listens noncommittally)* You saw us—a little while ago—sort of—fooling around?—me on my knees? *(Gestures toward the spot where he and DEBRA had been standing when DEBRA slapped him)*

CLAYBROOK *lifts his hands, or shrugs, in a gesture signaling that, yes, he saw, but isn't upset or proprietary.*

BOYD   I was—complimenting her on her shoes. Her beautiful new shoes. *(Pause)* That wizened little black nail on her smallest right toe—you ever noticed?

CLAYBROOK *hesitates, then shakes his head "no."*

BOYD *(Smiling)*   No? Never?

CLAYBROOK *shakes his head "no." But, despite himself, he's interested.*

BOYD   Next time, you'll notice. *(Pause)* *That* was no accident, the toenail. How it happened was— *(Leaning forward, confidentially; draws CLAYBROOK into leaning forward to hear)*—we'd just moved here, and things were a little rough, y'know how marital life can be?— *(Tries to cajole CLAYBROOK into nodding, but CLAYBROOK does not)* —my father told me, at my mother's funeral, he was drunk and sick but he knew what he was saying, "Son," he said, "days can be damned long but life goes fast and you never learn a thing"— *(BOYD breaks off to laugh, then succumbs to a fit of coughing)* —so anyway, we'd just moved here, into this house, Debra claims that I was involved in a "secret infidelity" at the time with a woman in New York but I was *not*—I swear, Clay, I was *not*—(A moment of anger, anguish) —it was just, just—the weight of daily, domestic life—how love's like a bright flame flaring up, y'know?—and this other, this weight, it's like a concrete *sky* crushing your chest—so you *love* people but can't, sometimes, bear them?—to be in the same room with them?—to hear them brush their teeth?—flush the toilet?—blow their noses?—walk across the floor?—*breathe?*

DEBRA reappears, stage left. She has come to fetch CLAYBROOK but pauses, listening.

BOYD *(Drunken, maudlin, anger beneath)*   I'd blow out my brains before I'd hurt that woman, I loved that woman, I never stopped loving her but it sort of—wore thin—not *out,* but *thin*—she thinks I stopped loving her but, I swear, I never did—*never.* Around that time, five years ago, my work wasn't steady 'cause of temperamental differences—never mind about *that*—*that's* a whole other story—and Debra had a job at a mall on Route 1, hated her job and hated her life and hated me I guess and every day, God knows why, she'd wear this pair of fake-crocodile shoes—high-heeled shoes with a strap—*(An almost lewd expressiveness)* —good-looking shoes, sort of sluttish—showing her legs, her calves—the way high heels are designed to do—and it turned out she was in pain wearing them—I mean *pain*—they were cheap, and they fit badly—almost, like, Debra was wearing them on purpose?—these glamorous-slutty shoes?—and the nail on one of her little toes turned black—blood accumulated under it—till finally she couldn't walk, she was in such pain, so she told me, and I examined it— *(Laughs, exasperated, perplexed)*—and I was so—stunned, kind of—couldn't imagine why she'd done it, how she could be so stubborn—and hurtful to herself. I hugged her, I guess—and I could feel the terrible rage in her. *(Pause)* At first, it looked as if the toenail would have to be surgically removed, then— *(Pause)* The podiatrist said he'd never seen anything quite like it.

Through BOYD's monologue, CLAYBROOK has been listening sympathetically, looking down at his hands.

DEBRA has discreetly withdrawn, and now reappears, smiling, flush-faced and perhaps angry, to fetch CLAYBROOK. She is carrying a glass of wine.

CLAYBROOK *(Quickly, looking up)*   Uh—you ready for me out there, Honey?
DEBRA   All ready. *(As DEBRA comes forward, she stumbles against BOYD's duffel bag)* Oh—!

BOYD is immediately on his feet, hurrying to her; takes her elbow.

BOYD   Christ, Debra, I'm sorry—damn thing's in the way.
DEBRA   Oh, it's nothing.

DEBRA has stubbed her toe but not seriously; she is rather more embarrassed than in pain.

BOYD *(Stooping to move the bag)*   Let me get this out of the—
DEBRA *(Stooping to assist him)*   I'll help—it's heavy—
BOYD *(Not wanting her to touch the bag, wrenching it from her grasp)*
   No, no I've got it—it's O.K. *(He hauls the bag up, places it on top of one of the boxes containing his possessions, gives the box a dismissive kick; he is panting, breathless, would seem to be acting a bit oddly)*
CLAYBROOK *(Knotting apron around his waist, approaching DEBRA)*
   Didn't hurt your foot, Honey, did you?
DEBRA *(Quickly, impatiently)*   No—of course not.

Lights out.

SCENE 5

Lights up, but subdued, in dining room area. It is later; BOYD, DEBRA, *and* CLAYBROOK *are seated at the table; candles are lit, and have burnt partway down. Two or three wine bottles on the table.* CLAYBROOK, *glass in hand, has been talking earnestly.*

CLAYBROOK   —no, it surely hasn't been easy, our urban tax base eroding, people who can afford to moving *out* of the cities, nobody moving *in*—and not what you'd call a mood of generosity these days. *(Pause)* It's the old story—a politician wants to stir up votes, he waves a flag, says he's going to cut down on the "welfare chiselers"—"welfare mothers"—hell, everybody knows what *that* means.
DEBRA *(Incensed)*   And denying indigent women abortions—even in cases of rape and incest. The states denying the federal government. Imagine!
CLAYBROOK   There's elected politicians—of both parties—pushing legislation to drop welfare mothers off the rolls, if they have more than one baby. *(Pause, angry smile)* Man, what're we supposed to do with these folks, let them *starve*? Out on the *street*?
BOYD *(A bit drunkenly, hoping to share in the emotion)*   Like they're starving in Africa!
DEBRA   Lew's got a plan, a special work-study program for welfare mothers, he's taking it to the state legislature next week; he's got some friends there, even among the Republicans, so maybe they'll listen.
CLAYBROOK *(Carefully)*   I'm optimistic—basically. My position has always been: I start with myself, a black man, O.K., and I am responsible for myself. Meaning I don't pity myself and I don't—ever—make excuses for myself. If I'm going to help my brothers and sisters—or

anybody—first I must help myself, and no excuses. *(Pause)* I got radical friends, though, black *and* white, believe that the only way to reform the welfare system—and the government bureaucracies choking us—is blow it all sky high. *(A sweeping gesture)*

BOYD *(Voice slurred)*   BLOW IT ALL FUCKING SKY-HIGH! Like back in the Sixties. With real bombs, maybe.

CLAYBROOK   Well, not with real *bombs.* Just re-think the whole structure, top to bottom.

DEBRA   Oh, Lew—easier said than done.

BOYD   The Sixties: people, then, had the courage of their despair.

CLAYBROOK   Despair?—naw. Despair never helped anybody. *I'm* optimistic, in the long run.

BOYD   Me, too. Things can always get worse. The fucking *sun* could come unhinged. *(Laughs)* Serve us right.

CLAYBROOK *(To BOYD, a bit sharply)*   Serve who right?

DEBRA *(Part teasing, part critical)*   Boyd is always looking to the Apocalypse, to set things right.

BOYD *(Pleasantly, but as if rebuked)*   That's how you'd sum me up, is it?

DEBRA   Of course not. I'm not in the habit of "summing people up."

CLAYBROOK   Yeah—"looking to the Apocalypse to set things right"— that's a temptation. Man, where I come from, is it ever.

BOYD   Where do you come from?

CLAYBROOK   North Philly.

BOYD   With a faint trace of—is it North Carolina?—*(Cupping ear, smiling)* Bet your folks came up from North Carolina, say, 1940?

CLAYBROOK *laughs, reluctantly acknowledges it's so.*

BOYD *(Pursuing it, smiling)*   I bet you got the highest grades in high school—hell, I bet you were valedictorian. *(As CLAYBROOK acknowledges, smiling)* I bet the hot-shot Ivy League schools were all over you—the way the Big Ten are all over the black athletes, begging you to accept their scholarship money—eh? *(As CLAYBROOK, embarrassed, concurs)* The admissions officers flew you to their campuses, put you up in the nicest dorms, sent the nicest most brilliant most "adjusted" minority students to recruit you—eh? And you had a hard time choosing between Harvard, Princeton, Yale, but you chose—

CLAYBROOK *(Wanting to cut it off)*   Yale.

BOYD *(Snapping fingers)*   Right! *(Pause)* I didn't get in.

DEBRA *(Eager to change subject)*   I guess—no one wants more food? *(Poking in salad bowl)* There's some salad—arugala—left. *(To BOYD)* Lew insists on real olive oil—from Italy. The kind we used to use, he poured it in the sink.

BOYD *(Pleasantly, a bit drunk, ignoring DEBRA's "we")* It's O.K., Lew—
I went to Cornell. My folks could afford it. And I worked.

CLAYBROOK That's—good.

BOYD I never resented it—"affirmative action." I saw the justice of it,
y'know?—the history behind it.

DEBRA *(Sharply)* It isn't "affirmative action," is it, when a student's
grades are good?—highest of the high?

CLAYBROOK *(To avoid controversy, genially)* Your talent for photography, Boyd—you never learned *that* in school. Real talent, you either
have it or you don't.

BOYD *(Slowly)* You either have it . . . or you don't. *(Pause)*

CLAYBROOK Trouble is, we all know how photographs can *lie*.

BOYD *(Defensively)* The photograph never lies.

CLAYBROOK Eh?

BOYD The photograph never lies. As a photograph.

CLAYBROOK C'mon, man. Some photographs are just trickery.

BOYD Compared to—what? *(A gesture around him)* "Reality?"

CLAYBROOK Working with the outsides—surfaces—of living things, people's faces, skin—what's deep, inside, isn't showing. Most of what we
see is accidents of light, fleeting impressions, moments—but, on film,
it becomes permanent. And that's a lie. *(Passionate)*

DEBRA *(Trying to lighten the tone)* Oh God!—I've seen some excrucia-
ting pictures of myself. Can't believe it's *me*!

BOYD That's just vanity, Debra.

DEBRA Yes? It is?

BOYD A photograph isn't *you*; it's a separate entity. *(Suddenly cool, ra-
tional: his intellect is a kind of weapon he has been concealing)* A com-
position—a formal work of art—has nothing to do with its subject's
perception of herself, or himself. If that was so, Matisse, Picasso,
Goya—any great idiosyncratic artist—would be judged by the most
trivial standards. *(Almost contemptuously)* People can't bear it, their
images get taken from them—used in ways they can't control. But
that's "art."

DEBRA *(Reacting)* Boyd's the quintessential photographer, Lew—refuses
to allow his own picture to be taken. You should see him, he actually
gets scared.

CLAYBROOK Why's that?

BOYD She's exaggerating.

DEBRA Oh—yes? *(Rises and goes into living room; picks up BOYD's camera, girlishly; BOYD follows anxiously after, trying to make a joke of
it)* Let's see! How's this work? *(Holding up camera which BOYD, not
wanting to be rude, wants to take from her)*

BOYD   Debra, please. Don't.

CLAYBROOK *(As if doubting this is a good idea)*   More pictures—?

CLAYBROOK *remains at the dining room table, amused, observing; while* DEBRA *tries to cajole* BOYD *into having his picture taken. She is charmingly, even flirtatiously, "high;" one senses that she is a woman who, in unguarded moments, can't resist provocation. A powerful sense too of how* DEBRA *and* BOYD *are still attracted to each other.*

DEBRA *(Giggling)*   How's this damn thing work? *(Fussing with camera)*

BOYD *(Reluctantly)*   Like this. *(Taking camera, demonstrating)* You push down here, you wait for the little red light—

DEBRA   What is it—Japanese?

BOYD *(Exasperated)*   That's what you always ask! *(Turning to CLAYBROOK, as if he is fearful of DEBRA)* Anything the least bit complicated, she asks—"Is it Japanese?"

DEBRA   C'mon, c'mon! Smile for the camera, Boyd!

BOYD *steps back, trying to smile.*

DEBRA *(Laughing)*   Boyd, you look ghastly! C'mon, *smile.*

BOYD *manages a grimace.* DEBRA *takes the picture, and* BOYD *takes back the camera, puts it aside.*

BOYD *(Getting revenge)*   Debra's father was an Army officer. It comes out, sometimes—she was an Army brat.

DEBRA *(Startled)*   Boyd, that's—silly. *(Pause)* I haven't seen my father in years.

CLAYBROOK   Well, I have yet to have the pleasure of meeting him.

DEBRA   Boyd had the pleasure—once.

BOYD   Does he know about—us?

DEBRA *(Quickly)*   Somebody in the family probably told him, *I* didn't.

BOYD   Lieutenant Colonel "Buck" O'Donnell. *(He makes a mock salute, shuddering)* Color-blind, they said of ol' Buck—treated whites and blacks equally: like shit.

DEBRA *(To CLAYBROOK)*   I've seen my father three times since I left home as a teenager. It's all ancient history.

CLAYBROOK   He's retired?

DEBRA *(Laughs ruefully)*   Retired from the human race, just about. He never did that well in the Army, as he'd wanted.

BOYD   Slight drinking problem, as I recall.

DEBRA   Boyd, it's ancient history.

BOYD   Debra doesn't like the military, sometimes it spills over into not liking men. *(Mysteriously)* Or, the obverse,—you know how opposites "attract"—liking them too much.

DEBRA   When have I ever not liked men!—that's ridiculous.

BOYD   I could think of a few times.

DEBRA *moves off from them;* BOYD *and* CLAYBROOK *watch her. She is the apex of a triangle that joins them.*

DEBRA *(In an altered tone, on the verge of bitter, yet bemused)*   All through my childhood we moved from one Army base to another. Texas, Florida, California, Minnesota, South Carolina . . . I'd make friends, we'd move. I never gave up, but my mother did. The Army bases were the same base. They were products of the same mind. There was the tall flagpole, there was the flag. The flag went up, the flag came down. At certain hours of the day, always the same hours, the enlisted men marched out to the artillery range. The gunfire from the range was like thunder. Rolling and dark-sounding, so you'd think the sky was black with clouds. So it was a shock to look up and see the sky empty, sometimes, and blue. *(Pause)* The thunder always came at the same time. It was an angry sound, but . . . it gave comfort, too. *(Pause)* I've been gone from that world since I was fifteen. I didn't run away, I walked. I had my mother's blessing even if she couldn't let me know. *(Pause) She* stayed.
BOYD *(Wistful mockery)*   There's a faithful woman! *(Pause)* Debra used to confuse me with the Lieutenant Colonel. I mean metaphorically.
DEBRA *(Neutrally)*   Boyd, I've never confused you with anyone but yourself.
BOYD *(Raising glass)*   I'll drink to that! *(Pause, as if this is a new idea)* I bought a second bottle of wine—let's open it.
DEBRA   Oh, no—
CLAYBROOK   A second bottle of *this*? *(Indicating* BOYD's *original bottle)*
BOYD *(Boastful)*   Pretty good stuff, eh? 1962 Bordeaux.
CLAYBROOK   Too good, almost, man. I mean—why don't you save it for another time?
BOYD *(As if casually)*   Maybe there's not going to be another time.
DEBRA   Of course there is.
CLAYBROOK   Sure, Boyd.
BOYD *(Almost too vulnerable)*   You mean that?
DEBRA, CLAYBROOK   Yes!

BOYD *looks searchingly at them.*

BOYD   I—I'm grateful. I won't hold you to it, but—I'm grateful. *(Pause)* When I called Debra last week, I expected her to— *(Pause)* —I don't know: hang up on me. Tell me to go to hell. Instead, she invites me— here. "Come have dinner with us, I want you to meet my friend Lew" . . . I have to admit, I wasn't expecting that.
DEBRA *(To* CLAYBROOK)   Boyd is always expecting people to behave the way, in their positions, *he* would. So he's always being surprised.

CLAYBROOK   Well, we all do a bit of that, don't we.

DEBRA *(Pushing it, pursuing her own thoughts)*   "You don't *really* mean that," he'd say. "You think you do, but you don't." *(Laughs)* "You don't like those people." "You *do* like these people"—meaning *his* friends. Always imagining he understood me, from above.

BOYD stands stricken.

CLAYBROOK   Well—that was then, this is now. What we need, folks, is a little nightcap.

DEBRA has been staring at BOYD.

DEBRA *(To CLAYBROOK, as if only peripherally hearing)*   Just a little, Lew. God!—I'm drunk.

BOYD   I'm not drunk, I'm . . . stone cold sober. A terrifying prospect at this time of night. *(Sits heavily)* Actually, I'm Boyd. Rhymes with "void."

CLAYBROOK   What kind of talk's that, man?

BOYD   You're a void if you don't have a soul. There's lots of us in that category. *(Laughs)* Makes things easier, actually.

CLAYBROOK   God is inside you, man, whether you know it or not. So enough this kinda talk, I'm gonna make us a little nightcap. *(Heads for kitchen)*

DEBRA rises to accompany him, carrying glasses, plates.

DEBRA *(An edge of impatience)*   Just *sit*, Boyd. Be *still*.

DEBRA and CLAYBROOK exit.

BOYD *(Calling after them, but unheard)*   That used to be *my* kitchen! *(Pause, then points stage left)* My bathroom where I laid the tile from Sears! My bedroom I'm banished from! *(Points in another direction)* My garage! *(Points down)* My basement that leaks! *(Louder)* My voice echoes here!—I'm the *ghost* here!

BOYD rises from the table, returns to the living room; appears to be headed in a collision-course with the stained-glass lamp, but, at the last moment, swerves; adroit on his feet as a basketball player.

BOYD *("Black" intonation)*   In you face!

BOYD goes to his duffel bag. Glancing over his shoulder, to see that he's unobserved, he removes an object from the bag that is wrapped in a towel. It is a revolver. He checks the chamber, squints along the barrel, spends a risky several seconds examining the gun; then shoves it into his trouser pocket. Glancing down, he sees that the object is too bulky; removes it and shoves it in his belt; but this too is conspicuous, so, finally, he pulls out his shirt, shoves the gun into his belt again, and hides it with the shirt.

BOYD *(Dampening his hands with his tongue, and smoothing down his hair; in a voice of gravity and menace)*   The Kingdom of God is within. The Kingdom of God is within. *(Pause)* THE KINGDOM OF GOD IS WITH-*IN*.

Lights out.

ACT 2

SCENE 6

Lights up. The living room area, some minutes later. (The candles have been extinguished on the table, and the dining area is in semi-darkness.) DEBRA, BOYD, and CLAYBROOK are back in the living room, though seated differently: DEBRA and CLAYBROOK are on the sofa, affectionately close; BOYD is in a chair to their right. His shirt tails out, BOYD looks disheveled but not dangerous; DEBRA has kicked off her shoes (And, as if unconsciously, moves and stretches her legs, even smooths the stockings with slow fingers—if she behaves in a sensuous, provocative way it should be very subtle); CLAYBROOK has removed his sport coat and appears to be quite warm, perspiration glinting on his face. (He may remove his glasses to polish them.) Jazz with a more hectic beat plays in the background. The long-stemmed rose in its vase is still on the coffee table.

CLAYBROOK has brought in a tray of ingredients for the nightcap—bottles, glasses, a tall shaker, a container of ice cubes, etc. He is genial, relaxed, expansive, hospitable; one of those people whom alcohol makes warm and childlike, yet volatile emotionally. His "black"/North Carolina accent is distinctly perceptible.

CLAYBROOK   Friends, this is a Flintlock I'm gonna conjure up, from my days tendin' bar on Seventh Avenue, workin' my way through *N.Y.U. (Stressing each syllable of N.Y.U.)* for the *Ph.D. (Stressing each syllable of Ph.D.—making the sounds comic)*

DEBRA   Bartender? You never said.

CLAYBROOK   *(Hand on her knee)* Lots of things I ain't said, Honey. *(Preparing the drinks, CLAYBROOK moves his hands in magician-style, basking in the attention)* First—three and three-quarters ounces bourbon: like so. *(Into shaker)* Next—two and one-quarter ounce apple-jack brandy: like *so.* Then—li'l bit of white Creme de Cacao. Li'l bit lemon juice. Li'l bit grenadine. O.K., now *shake. (Shakes liquid, eyes shut; both DEBRA and BOYD watch attentively)* O.K., friends, now you pour over ice cubes, and here y'are—straight from yo' man's hands.

BOYD, DEBRA, CLAYBROOK touch glasses ceremonially, and drink.

DEBRA   *(Between a sigh and a cry)*   Oh. God.

BOYD   *(Trying to sound sober)*   Man, this is *good.* What's it called?

CLAYBROOK   Flintlock.

BOYD *(Enunciating word)* "Flint-lock."

DEBRA   Some kind of old-fashioned gun?—musket? *(Laughs)*

BOYD   So, Clay, you were a bartender, too.

CLAYBROOK   Among my many dazzlin' gifts.

BOYD *(Almost boyishly)*   Are there—other things about you, too?—I mean—

CLAYBROOK *(A dismissive gesture of his hand)*   Nah, what you see is what you get.

BOYD   Well—that was the finest meal I've had in, in— *(Wipes at eyes)* — my *life.*

CLAYBROOK, DEBRA *laugh. They speak simultaneously.*

DEBRA   Oh, Boyd, *c'mon.*

CLAYBROOK   Listen to the man jivin' us!

BOYD   No, seriously, it was *good.* The meat, the sauce, the spices, the pasta—

DEBRA *(Proudly, but a bit teasingly)*   Lew insists on everything *fresh,* and I mean *fresh*—no canned tomatoes, no oregano or marjoram or basil out of jars. He's the real thing!

CLAYBROOK   The veal got overcooked, some. But the pasta turned out pretty good.

BOYD   You made the pasta yourself—didn't just *buy* it. *(As if marveling)*

CLAYBROOK   Only way you control quality, it's to do as much as you can, yourself.

BOYD   In food as in life! *(Pause, not mockingly but a bit ingenuously)* You take it all seriously, don't you? Making a meal, setting the table, coordinating the wine—all that.

CLAYBROOK *(Laughing)*   Man, I take *everything* seriously. "We don't pass this way but once."

BOYD *(Seeming non sequitur)*   A condemned man, he'll eat the proverbial hearty meal. A friend of mine did an article—interviewed Death Row prisoners and officials, in Texas. Number One favorite's T-bone steak and French fries. Some ask for lobster—first time in their lives. *(Laughs)*

DEBRA *(Shuddering)*   *I* couldn't eat, knowing I was to die!

A pause.

BOYD   Right. It's better not to know. *(A pause)* Veal marsala with angel hair pasta—a good Bordeaux—that's for me.

CLAYBROOK   You buy that wine by the case?

BOYD *(Laughs)*   Are you kidding? *That?*

CLAYBROOK   Some folks do. Like, an investment.

BOYD *(Slightly mocking)*   Folks you know in Trenton, New Jersey?

CLAYBROOK *(With disarming ingenuousness)*   Nah, hell. Guys I used to keep in contact with—from Yale.

BOYD   How come you're out of contact, now?

CLAYBROOK *(Shrugs)*   Ask them, man.

BOYD *(To DEBRA)*   So, "Debra O'Donnell"—you're getting a degree after all? I couldn't talk you into it—going back to college.

DEBRA   I wasn't ready. Then.

BOYD   What kind of a job d'you have—"County Services?"

DEBRA *(Enthusiastically)*   I'm assisting a case worker, and I work with a supervisor. Some of the clients, they report to *me*. I help them with, oh all sorts of things, simple things—like planning budgets—talking to landlords—asserting their rights. And within a family, say one member is dominating, or exploiting the others— *(Pause, to CLAYBROOK)* The other day, Lew, that woman I told you about?—the one whose husband broke her collarbone, said he was going to kill her? I got her into the shelter, her and her kids. *(Laughs sadly)* Imagine! Twenty-two years old, with four kids under the age of six!

BOYD *(Lightly ironic)*   That wasn't *your* problem, at least.

DEBRA *(Annoyed)*   I love my work. I'm just learning . . . It's exhausting, but it's worth it.

BOYD *(As if humoring her)*   You "feel you're doing some good in the world."

DEBRA   Yes. I do.

CLAYBROOK   You got a better agenda, Boyd?

DEBRA and CLAYBROOK have drawn just perceptibly closer together, as BOYD has been mocking DEBRA. Some small gesture of intimacy—DEBRA may pick a bit of lint off CLAYBROOK's sleeve.

BOYD *(Abrupt drunken ebullience)*   Soooooo, Clay my man! Dogs!

CLAYBROOK   Eh?

BOYD   Dogs! You breed pit bulls, eh?

CLAYBROOK *(Staring at him, unsmiling)*   Say what, Boyd?

BOYD *(Smiling, but confused—as if genuinely)*   Uh—I mean—you *don't* breed pit bulls. *(To himself)* He *doesn't* breed pit bulls.

DEBRA pokes BOYD in the leg with a foot, annoyed.

An awkward moment.

CLAYBROOK   What's this—*pit* bulls? *(Emphatically)* Hell, no, man, where'd you pick that up? Those are killer dogs, triflin' and dangerous. I'd vote to make the breed extinct.

DEBRA *(Alert, like a student)*   Extinct? A breed of animal? Can that be done?

CLAYBROOK *(Shrugging)* Why not, Honey? Pass a law. The U.S. Congress—let 'em pass a law. Civilized folks can do *anything,* passing the right laws. *(Winking)* Look what ol' Abe Lincoln did, folks shamed him enough.

DEBRA *(With exaggerated care, to avoid slurring words)* But, Lew, how can a breed of animal be outlawed? Isn't that, like, *geno*cide? In fact, there are laws protecting endangered species.

BOYD *(Eager to join in)* I don't think a pit bull is a species, it's a breed.

DEBRA So, all right, what's the difference? The poor dog doesn't choose his nature.

CLAYBROOK *(Gently, but forcibly, hand on her knee)* Look, Honey-girl, pit bulldogs ain't your specialty, so how 'bout droppin' the subject?

DEBRA They're some kind of bulldog, obviously. Something to do with— *(Vague)* —pits.

BOYD They're part terrier and part bulldog—

CLAYBROOK *English* bulldog. *(Mugging)* That's the nastiest kind.

BOYD *(As if to impress with his knowledge)* A pit bull is trained to attack all strangers and kill them, provoked or not. Whether the stranger is an elderly woman, or a baby, or—whatever. And they don't *bark*— that's the eerie thing about them. They give no warning, just leap at your throat.

DEBRA That's how they're *trained,* but I can't believe that's their *nature.*

CLAYBROOK *(Impatiently, hoping to drop subject)* The training *is* the nature, and the pit bulldog isn't natural, it's a hybrid.

DEBRA But, the individual dog—the *creature*! How can it be his fault?— her fault? All animals are innocent.

CLAYBROOK *(Voice rising)* I go for setters,—grew up with 'em. Yeah and collies. Dogs that, they look at you with their beautiful eyes, you feel life's worth livin'—right? Tell me it's a bourgeois sentiment O.K. it's bourgeois, tell me it's WASP, don't care. Lenin loved his dog above the Revolution—or was it Trotsky?—hell, could be Hitler!—the fact is, there's anybody or anything you can trust your life with, the dog is *it;* the only mammal that's *it.*

DEBRA *(Excited)* That's what I'm saying, that's what I'm saying—you don't *listen.*

CLAYBROOK Who brought this up?—let's drop it. *(A gesture of impatience; drinks)*

DEBRA *(To BOYD)* He's got a grudge against those poor dogs, that's how he *is*—strong opinions.

BOYD *(To DEBRA)* Why'd you tell me he liked them, then?—didn't you tell me?

DEBRA What?

CLAYBROOK What kinda shit's this?

DEBRA   I never said a word, Boyd.

BOYD   Must have been somebody else. Sorry.

The subject should be dropped; but DEBRA *unaccountably picks it up and persists. Half-consciously, she is enjoying the emotional attention, the frisson, of arousing* CLAYBROOK.

DEBRA   I just feel—

CLAYBROOK   Enough! *(Pause, then, speaking as we have not heard him speak before, angrily and ironically)*   Look, the pit bulldog is a macho breed, *black* macho breed, got it? That what we're talkin' about? Huh? Baaaad macho breed of killer-dog so black men get a charge walkin' the streets with 'em on leashes, sexy feelin', get it?—they give the word, the fucker's gonna tear somebody apart. Real baaad.

DEBRA   *(Hurt, angry)*   I don't care, I still—

CLAYBROOK   *(Coldly furious)*   You want the sociology, O.K. I'll provide the sociology, fucking-A right, the pit bull helps com-pen-sate for the male nigger in America being a dog himself but not a killer-dog, no way man, just a runty ole mongrel-dog not worth shit. You got it, Honey? Like havin' a big cock's s'post to com-pen-sate for not havin' nothin'— including, in fact, the cock. *(Contemptuous)*   Now you got it, Honey?

DEBRA *is stricken into silence, edging away from* CLAYBROOK. BOYD *is excited, trying to maintain control.*

BOYD   You don't have to be rude to Debra, Clay—you don't have to be rude.

CLAYBROOK   *(On his feet, upset, walking off, speaking loudly)*   Wasn't being *rude* to her, man, was just *explaining*.

BOYD   *(On his feet too)*   It—sounded rude to me.

CLAYBROOK   Well fuck you, man—whose problem's that?

BOYD   Just a—

CLAYBROOK   Don't you fuck with me, you—

BOYD   —a minute—

CLAYBROOK   *(Upset, exiting)*   Don't none of you fuck with *me*.

DEBRA *sits stunned on the sofa,* BOYD *is standing, fingers flexing. Oddly, his facial expression suggests extreme regret; almost as if he is about to cry.*

DEBRA   *(Hoarsely)*   I think you'd better leave, Boyd. Please.

BOYD   *(Calling)*   Clay?—uh, hey—Lew? Hey c'mon.

DEBRA   Haven't you done enough! *(Wiping at eyes)*

BOYD   Me? What'd *I* do? *You* set him off.

DEBRA   *(On her feet)*   That's the most—excitable—I've ever seen Lew, and you're to blame, Boyd, damn you! Bringing up pit bulls—who the hell told you about pit bulls?—which of our "friends?"

BOYD They're only concerned about you, Debra. Like me.

DEBRA *(Furious)* You! *(Approaching stage left, calling apologetically)* Lew?—honey?—oh Lew, please—

No answer. DEBRA *stands before the closed kitchen door, as* BOYD *joins her, takes her arm.*

BOYD If that's what the man is like, Debra—

DEBRA *(Fiercely)* That isn't what the man is like! He's—well—excitable. He has a temper. In class, a few times, he lost his temper—almost. But, tonight— *(Pushing* BOYD *away)* Get away! Haven't you done enough? *(Calling, as before)* Lew?—please? *(Before the kitchen door)* Lew, we're so sorry, both of us, we spoke out of ignorance— *(A pause; we hear* CLAYBROOK's *muffled voice, words unintelligible)* You know I wouldn't ever do anything to hurt or offend you, Honey—you know that— *(Pause, another muffled response, which* BOYD, *behind* DEBRA, *strains to hear)* Oh God yes, I do. Of course. What? *(Pause)* Please accept our apologies.

BOYD *(Cupping hands to mouth, guiltily, yet revelling in it)* I'm sorry, Lew—Clay—sorry as hell. Believe me!

Another pause. DEBRA *leads* BOYD *back into the living room. She wipes her face on a napkin. Distracted, begins gathering up glasses and bottles.*

DEBRA I've never seen him like that . . . he looked at me as if he didn't know me.

BOYD Well, maybe he doesn't. I mean . . . you know what I mean.

DEBRA It happened so fast . . .

BOYD He *has* got a temper. Man! *(Admiringly)* Nobody gets in his face.

DEBRA But that wasn't him—really. He'd been drinking.

BOYD North Philly, eh? That's dangerous turf.

DEBRA I've got to learn not to push him. You can't push a man like that.

BOYD You know what'd happen, I got in the car and drove to North Philly, tonight? When into a bar, tried to mix with the brothers? What'd happen to me?

DEBRA If it just didn't happen so *fast*. His changes . . .

DEBRA *drinks impulsively from one of the glasses; so does* BOYD.

BOYD *(Shivering)* Dead meat! Me. *(Pause)* His kind, they're not hypocrites.

DEBRA He's a man of pride, and we offended his pride. *(Holds out hand)* Look—how I'm trembling.

BOYD *(Taking her hand)* Debra, I'm so sorry. I wouldn't hurt you for the world.

DEBRA *(Easing away from him)* Is that—? *(Listens)* The back door? *(Listens)* He wouldn't just leave, would he? *(Stricken)*

BOYD If he did, where would he go?—where does he live?

DEBRA does not hear the question. BOYD begins to circle her as if stalking her. Touches the butt of the gun through his shirt.

BOYD He's been married, right?—has a family, right?—how do they feel about you?—"Debra O'Donnell."

DEBRA Boyd, take your things, please, and *go.*

BOYD I didn't come back for my *things,* Debra, I came back for *you.*

DEBRA What?

BOYD Tonight, I'm here, I came back for—you. *(Pause)* You, and me. *(Looks at her with longing)*

DEBRA *(Distracted, looking toward kitchen)* I might have been a stranger to him—the way he looked at me. I touched him, and he threw my hand off.

BOYD Didn't you hear? I said, I've come back for you, and me. Look at *me. (Grips her wrist; DEBRA can't twist away)*

DEBRA What are you saying, Boyd?—you promised it was over.

BOYD I was—wasn't—myself, then. Those months. You know what I was like. I said things I didn't mean, and you did, too.

DEBRA *(Half-sobbing, frustrated)* The people we were then, we're not, now. I'm never going back to that, again.

BOYD That one therapist, y'know, the woman?—on the Brunswick Pike? She said you had yet to get into contact with your anger, Debra, it wasn't just me you were angry with, but—

DEBRA Her? You were so contemptuous of her.

BOYD No, she was O.K.—*you* were threatened by her. "Get in touch with your anger"—

DEBRA *(Sharply)* That Sixties jargon! Those clichés! They're out of date, now. I hate "anger"—it isn't purging, it only makes things worse.

BOYD Telling the truth? That only makes things worse?

DEBRA There was anger in my family, and it was like—a kind of muteness. The more my father said, the more it destroyed things—and the less it meant. Just now, what Lew said, that wasn't *him;* that was—what we made him say. *(Voice rising)* Two whites, speaking in ignorance.

BOYD You can't rise above the color of your skin, in his eyes—no matter what he says.

DEBRA Never mind Lew and me, Boyd. Just never mind. It has nothing to do with you. *That's* over.

BOYD *(Quick response, veiled threat)* Nothing is over, Debra, until—it's over. *(Harsh laugh)*

DEBRA   Look, you can see: I have a new life now. I'm changed. I'm no longer "Boyd's wife."

BOYD   You're still my wife, my Debra. Oh yes.

DEBRA   No.

BOYD   The connection between us, it's like,—roots of trees, underground. You remember . . . *(Sexual pleading, on the verge of coercion)*

DEBRA   *(As if frightened)*   No! *(Pause)* I, I have a certain regard for you, Boyd—you know that. I respect and honor you, I *like* you, of course, yes and I feel sorry for you—but—

BOYD   I don't want your Goddamned pity, for Christ's sake. I want—you know—the way it *was*.

DEBRA   *(Ironically)*   The way it was, when?—the last few years?—that last week you were living here?

BOYD   No, the way it *was*. You know. *(Almost tenderly)* You know.

DEBRA   *(Quickly)*   No. That's over, that's gone.

BOYD   It is *not*.

DEBRA   I can't believe this—after you promised.

BOYD   Debra, I'm the one who loves you—not him.

DEBRA   Never mind him!—you don't know anything about him.

BOYD   I'm the one who loves you, I'm your *husband*.

DEBRA   *(Bravely, defiantly)*   Your face!—it isn't a face of love.

BOYD   *(An expression of barely controlled rage)*   If this is my face, it *is* the face of love, Goddamn you!

They struggle. DEBRA *tries to slap* BOYD, *but he grips that hand too.*

BOYD   *(Half-pleading)*   The other women never meant anything—I swear.

DEBRA   Yes, that was part of it.

BOYD   What? What was part of it?

DEBRA   You used them, and you used me. Nothing meant anything.

BOYD   I made mistakes. I acknowledge that.

DEBRA   We both made mistakes, and now it's over.

BOYD   Nothing is over, I said—until it's *over*. *(Pause)* No survivors.

DEBRA   Are you threatening me?

BOYD   I'm just telling you.

DEBRA   We were getting along so well, I thought—this evening—all of us. And now—

BOYD   *He* doesn't love you, that's for God-damn sure.

DEBRA   I refuse to talk about him with you. You don't *know*. BOYD   I know what I saw.

DEBRA   *(Half screaming)*   You don't know.

BOYD   Debra, please. Hey—c'mon.

DEBRA *(More calmly)*   I'll always be your friend, Boyd. But—
BOYD *(Unconscious of the import of his words)*   You're not my friend, you're my *wife*!

At this, DEBRA laughs, despairingly; BOYD, staring at her, finally smiles— a ghastly grin.

A pause.

BOYD   You don't believe me—but I do love you.
DEBRA *(Quietly)*   No, Boyd. I don't believe you.
BOYD *(With dread)*   You don't—love me? At all?
DEBRA   Not in the way you want.
BOYD   That's the only way there *is*.

DEBRA shakes her head "no." BOYD stares at her; grips her chin in his hand; seems about to kiss her; but, when she goes dead, unresponsive, he doesn't force himself upon her.

BOYD   Then it really is over, Debra? It's over—?

DEBRA does not reply, as she and BOYD freeze in their posture.

Lights intensify.

Lights out.

SCENE 7

Lights up. No music. Only a few seconds have elapsed: DEBRA and BOYD are in the same position, but now BOYD has released DEBRA, and DEBRA is rubbing her wrist, smoothing her disheveled hair, adjusting her clothing.

As she searches out her shoes, and puts them on, CLAYBROOK appears, stage left, entering from the kitchen. Both DEBRA and BOYD look at him.

CLAYBROOK enters the living room in a manner that might be described as rueful, yet not repentant. He is wiping his face with a white handkerchief or tissue.

CLAYBROOK *(After a beat or two, in stiff, "white" diction)*   I started some coffee—figured it's about time.
DEBRA *(Almost shyly)*   That's a good idea, Lew. *(He doesn't look at her, as if embarrassed. To BOYD)* Isn't that a good idea!
BOYD *(Ironic, with bravado)*   To sober me up, for the road?
CLAYBROOK *(Grimly)*   To sober us all up.

BOYD   You're kicking me out?—O.K., I don't blame you. *(Laughs awkwardly)* Clay, I mean Lew—I'm *sorry. (BOYD puts out his hand aggressively, but, looking elsewhere, CLAYBROOK discreetly ignores it)*

DEBRA *(Approaching CLAYBROOK, speaking hopefully, yet with composure)* I'm to blame, I guess—I feel like such a fool.

CLAYBROOK *(Squeezing DEBRA's arm at the elbow, a quick gesture of affection, an appeal for forgiveness, murmuring)* I'm the fool. Let's forget it.

CLAYBROOK and DEBRA exchange a significant look; as BOYD stands to the side, excluded.

BOYD   I guess—it's late.

DEBRA *(Politely)* I hope you don't have a long drive?

BOYD *(Quickly, as if with a double meaning)* Oh no. Not a long drive.

CLAYBROOK has been tidying up the coffee table, putting bottles, glasses, etc., on the tray; picking up crumpled napkins from the floor.

CLAYBROOK *(Trying to speak normally, though still in his "white" diction)* When you leave, I'll help you with those boxes. They're heavy.

BOYD *(As if boyishly)* Thanks!

DEBRA *(Trying not to show too overtly how vastly relieved she is)* I smell the coffee—is it mocha java?

CLAYBROOK   Yes, but a fresh package, not the old one.

DEBRA   Good. *(She takes the tray from CLAYBROOK, and the two appear, in that instant, domestic, companionable)* Thanks, Honey. I'll take care of everything.

DEBRA exits, to kitchen.

BOYD *(Seemingly nervous laugh)* Man, *you're* sure not to be messed with.

CLAYBROOK shrugs or grunts a reply. His back to BOYD, he is straightening cushions on the sofa; adjusts the stained-glass lamp by a fraction of an inch.

BOYD   It was those dynamite Flintlocks—that's what it was.

CLAYBROOK *(Bemused)* Maybe.

CLAYBROOK indicates that BOYD should sit. The men face each other, sitting in the chairs.

BOYD *(Leaning forward)* Well—it certainly was—is—generous of you, and Debra. Charitable. Having me here, tonight. The ex-husband, the ghost.

CLAYBROOK   O.K., man, that's O.K.

BOYD She's a good woman, and she deserves the best. I'm happy for her. *(Pause, smiles)* I'm not *happy*, but I'm *happy* for her.

CLAYBROOK O.K., man.

BOYD After the divorce, for a while—things were a little rocky for her. *(As if considering)* For both of us. *(Pause)* It was hard, she'd try to call me, I was out of the country, on assignment, out of contact. *(Pause, when CLAYBROOK doesn't respond)* Y'know, Clay, what you said before—"The Kingdom of God is within"—that made a strong impression on me. Thanks.

CLAYBROOK *(Cool smile)* Don't jive me, man, it's what everybody knows. Or, *don't* know—'cause maybe it ain't so. *(In a mock-"Negro" intonation)*

BOYD *(Frowning)* What do you mean?—don't you—believe? *(As CLAYBROOK shrugs noncommittally)* Your father's a minister, Debra said? "African Episcopal Baptist Church?" *(In BOYD's too-solemn intonation, this name sounds ludicrous)*

CLAYBROOK "African Methodist Episcopal Church."

BOYD *(As if to make a casual joke)* There's a difference?

CLAYBROOK *(A snorting sort of laugh)* Don't push it, man.

BOYD *(Leaning forward, eagerly, elbows on knees, as if speaking confidentially)* I wasn't—"jiving"—you, Clay. About "The Kingdom of God." It doesn't require a supernatural base, does it, or anything theological?—just, y'know, *psych*-ological? "Psyche" meaning "soul?" I was thinking— *(Runs hand through hair, a bit manic suddenly)* —you and I, maybe, you with your position—in the welfare department—

CLAYBROOK *(Interrupting)* Family Services.

BOYD —the kinds of things you see—and deal with—the two of us could collaborate—a book of photographs with a text—*(Seeing CLAYBROOK's negative expression)* —No?

CLAYBROOK In my profession, as long as you're *in* it, you don't exploit the people.

BOYD *(Hurt)* This wouldn't be "exploiting."

CLAYBROOK You don't use the people as material, that's all.

BOYD *(Deflated)* I see. *(Pause)*

DEBRA appears, bringing coffee things on tray. She seems to have freshened herself up: her hair is no longer disheveled, her look less harassed. She is wearing, not her glamorous high-heeled shoes, but flat-heeled sandals.

CLAYBROOK *(Smiling)* That smells *good*.

DEBRA *(Seating herself between the men, speaking brightly, to BOYD)* There's a new food store, Boyd, on Third Street—y'know, where the Italian bakery was? It specializes in all sorts of coffee, it's really wonderful.

BOYD   Is it! *(Smiles)*

DEBRA pours coffee, etc., for the three of them. BOYD, confronted with his cup, merely sits, smiles.

BOYD *(As if mischievously, like a small boy)*   Maybe I'll stick to—the other. I've got that bottle of Bordeaux in my bag.

DEBRA   Boyd, *no.* You have to drive.

BOYD   We could just start it, and I'd leave the rest of it for you. *(Half-hearted gesture as if to rise)*

DEBRA   Try the mocha java, Boyd, it's delicious.

BOYD *(Smiling)*   You know that sign you see, sometimes—aimed at commuters—"if you lived here, you'd be home now." *(Laughs)*

A moment's embarrassed silence. DEBRA and CLAYBROOK exchange a covert glance, which BOYD notes.

DEBRA, BOYD speak simultaneously; but BOYD prevails.

DEBRA *(Forced enthusiasm)*   So, Boyd, you're doing a book of—

BOYD *(To CLAYBROOK)*   I appreciated your response, Clay, to my photographs. That meant a lot to me.

CLAYBROOK   Well, it's good work.

BOYD *(Smiling)*   So why don't you want to collaborate with me?

CLAYBROOK   Eh? I said I couldn't.

BOYD *(To DEBRA, as if teasing)*   Clay snubbed me, just now. I suggested we collaborate on a major project—I'd do the art, he'd provide the text. "An unflinching look at America's underclass."

CLAYBROOK *(Trying to be pleasant)*   I didn't *snub* you, friend. I said I *couldn't,* for professional reasons.

DEBRA   Boyd, Lew doesn't have time.

BOYD *(Smiling)*   Oh I know! I can imagine. *(Pause) I* don't have time, either. Really.

CLAYBROOK   I'm not working just with the "underclass"—whatever *that* is. Family Services deals with all kinds of folks—*(Smiling)* —white folks too.

BOYD   That's what the book would do—combat stereotypes.

DEBRA   Maybe you could talk about it with Lew some other time.

BOYD *(Eagerly)*   I'd like that. *(Pause)* You know, *you* can perpetuate stereotypes too. *(Indicating CLAYBROOK)* It isn't just us.

CLAYBROOK *(Smile)*   Who's *me?*

BOYD   Talk of "whites"—"blacks"—*that's* irresponsible.

DEBRA   Now, Boyd—

BOYD *(Pointing at CLAYBROOK, smiling)*   For instance—*you* aren't black. I mean—not *black.* Even a really dark-skinned man isn't *black,* so why call yourself "black," then?

CLAYBROOK *stares at* BOYD *for a long moment, his expression impassive; he grips his coffee cup rigidly, however; sits very still.*

DEBRA   Boyd—!

BOYD   *(Speaking quickly, leaning forward)*   I mean—why not speak frankly? For once? A man like you, Clay, with your skin tone, it's absurd to call you *black*—you just aren't! I know, I know—there are historical factors—sure—but it's so extreme. Like primary colors—primary ways of thinking—no subtleties. Am I "white?" Is this— *(Extending hands)*—"white?" Hell, no. Somebody from another planet, arriving on Earth, would think we were all color *blind*.

CLAYBROOK   *(Shaking head, trying to remain calm)*   Man, you sure are one, aren't you?

BOYD   One what?

CLAYBROOK   One asshole-honky—sup-*reme*.

BOYD   *(Aggrieved)*   You're not addressing the issue! It's a, a, an epistemological issue!—how we *know* what we think we know, when it turns out we don't know know it 'cause it's wrong.

CLAYBROOK   *(As if to rise)*   Say what, man?—I'm tunin' out.

BOYD   Don't go! Sit still! Please! Don't— *(Pleading, yet with a threat beneath)* —condescend to me!

DEBRA   Lew, Honey, Boyd doesn't mean any insult, he just means— *(Embarrassed, concerned)* —what he *says*. He—

CLAYBROOK   I don't give a shit what he *says* long as I don't have to hear it.

BOYD   You're afraid! You're afraid! Man, you surprise me—you're *afraid*! To talk man-to-man, friend-to-friend, to speak the truth for once—like, "to bear witness."

CLAYBROOK   Friend-to-friend? *(Echoing* BOYD's *earlier remark, attributed to Roberto Durán)* —Get away, man, you're not my friend!

BOYD   'Cause you shut me out. That's why.

CLAYBROOK   Oh shit! Poor whitey! Ma asshole bleeds for poor whitey! *(Genuine laughter, loud)*

BOYD   What's so funny? What the fuck's so funny?

CLAYBROOK   People of color have got to JUMP UP AN' DOWN WITH JOY they get invited at last to the white-folks' house—my, my! Ain't we lucky! They shakin' our hands like our hands was *white*. Sayin, Skin color don't mean nothing to me, I'm color blind, ain't *I* hot shit! *(Laughs)* Sure, I was the scholarship boy—the "good" boy. 'Cause they was nice to me, they didn't need to be nice to my sister, my cousin—all the rest of 'em. *(Sudden savagery, pointing toward* BOYD's *portfolio)* Like that Third World–victim shit you're peddling!

BOYD   Huh? What?

CLAYBROOK   Share your income with your "tragic" victims—pay *them* for your pictures.

BOYD *(Excited)* I'm a, a—witness! You said that yourself! A—

CLAYBROOK Don't hand me that shit, whitey!

BOYD *(Excited)* What? *Whitey?* Why'm I *white,* c'mon tell me why'm I *white,* you think I'm *white,* what the fuck kind of insult is that, you think you're *black,* big-deal *"black"*—sit still!

BOYD takes out the revolver and points it at CLAYBROOK, who, about to get up, freezes. A beat or two of silence, astonishment. DEBRA gives a muffled cry, hand to mouth.

BOYD I'm not going to use this—I'm not a man of violence, don't make me use this, okay, man, don't make me use this, okay?— *(As if pleading)* —I just want to tell you, I want you to listen, I want respect—

CLAYBROOK *(Frightened, trying to be reasonable)* Hey, man, put that down—no need for that—hey?

Voices overlap.

BOYD You said I'm not your friend—well I *am*! I am your friend! I want to be! Goddamn it how can you shut me out?

CLAYBROOK Is that—loaded?

DEBRA Oh Boyd, my God—

BOYD *(Swinging barrel toward DEBRA)* It *isn't* me, it's you, and him, it's you two shutting me out—I'm backed in a corner like a rat—

CLAYBROOK Boyd, don't point that at Debra. O.K., man? Don't point that at her—please.

BOYD *(Excited, frightened)* I'm not, I'm not pointing it at anyone, I don't want to hurt anyone, don't push me! *(Swinging barrel in CLAYBROOK's direction)*

CLAYBROOK Man, nobody's pushing you—we're just sitting here talking, we're O.K., we're cool, nobody's pushing you, O.K.?

BOYD Just don't push me, O.K.?

CLAYBROOK Nobody's pushing you, Boyd, you're cool.

BOYD *(Veneer of calm)* I'm not a man of violence, I'm a, a pacifist, Debra will tell you— Stay still! *(CLAYBROOK has moved just slightly)*

CLAYBROOK *(Freezing, lifting hands)* Hey man—I'm cool.

BOYD *(To DEBRA)* See?—his hands?—the insides of his hands?—no blacker than I am. It's just crazy. It's tearing us all apart and it's just crazy, the craziest shit!

CLAYBROOK You're right, Boyd. You are right.

BOYD I *am* right, but none of you will acknowledge it. In Africa, I tried. I *did* try. And with guys I know, black guys—"black" they call themselves—back in college, too—"black"—"white"—you call yourself "black" so what's that leave us—"white?" And tonight I come as a, a brother—drove one hundred sixty miles and treated like dirt—condescended to—in my own house—shutting me out with your looks at each other, your—touches—of each other—think I'm blind?—shutting me, Boyd, out of this place used to be my own home for Christ's sake.

DEBRA   No one is shutting you out, Boyd. Please believe me.

BOYD   No, I can't. No more. You're with *him*—not *me*.

CLAYBROOK   Boyd, we could discuss this so much easier if—

BOYD *(Interrupting)*   I've seen human beings die. *(Snaps his fingers)* Like that!—gone. "Natural" causes—and not so "natural"—like, for instance, bullets. But *I* never aimed a gun at anyone before tonight. This is the—exigency!—you've brought me to! You, calling me "whitey" like I got no feelings!

CLAYBROOK   Jesus, Boyd, I'm sorry. I admit my ignorance.

BOYD *(Rapidly)*   You—a stranger—in my house—with her—sleeping with her—that's a, an outrage. Another man, he'd lose it completely—shoot you both dead—plead "insanity." "Self-defense"—I'm fighting for my life!

DEBRA   Boyd—

BOYD *(Waving gun)*   Tell him! C'mon tell him! How it really was, you and me—all those times! Hundreds! Thousands! You *know* you're not really going to love anybody but me—like it was—right here—*right here in this house. (A pause)* Tell him.

DEBRA *(Shrinking)*   Boyd, no—

BOYD   Get up! Do it! Tell the truth! For once! For once tonight! Tell him how it *was,* and how it never will be again—with any other man.

CLAYBROOK   Don't point that gun at her—

DEBRA   Lew, it's all right! *(Rises, to comply with* BOYD's *command, comes forward, frightened, and in a dilemma, her back to the men who stare at her)*

BOYD *(Almost pleading)*   Tell him!

DEBRA *must convey to the audience that she is willing to risk death for* CLAYBROOK's *sake—though, perhaps, what she says is not true.*

DEBRA   I . . . I can love another man. *(Pause)* I *do* love another man. As much . . . more . . . than I did you.

BOYD *(Stricken)*   That's a lie!

CLAYBROOK *makes a motion as if to protect* DEBRA, *and* BOYD *wheels upon him, the gun in his raised hand shaking. All freeze.*

BOYD   You're lying, Debra—you remember how it was for us, the two of us—in that room back there— *(Gesturing toward bedroom)*—those nights— Tell him the truth.

DEBRA *(Slowly, emphatically)*   I *can.* I *do.* I love another man . . . I love Lew.

BOYD   Liar!

DEBRA hides her face in her hands.

BOYD *(To CLAYBROOK)*   She's lying—for you! She'd die for you. *(Emotion draining from him, still holding the gun on CLAYBROOK, then weakens, gives up)* O.K. I'm fucked. I'm *over.* *(Laying revolver on coffee table)* You win, Clay my man—blow me away.

Silence.

CLAYBROOK   What're you saying, man?

BOYD   Take it, it's yours. *(Shoves gun toward him)* Here's "whitey"— blow me away.

CLAYBROOK snatches up the gun, as DEBRA makes a sound of protest and fear.

BOYD *(Terrified but reckless, goading)*   C'mon! Your turn!

CLAYBROOK *(Trying to speak calmly)*   Just get your things, and get out of this house, man!

BOYD   C'mon—pull the trigger. You scared?

DEBRA *(Weeping)*   Boyd, oh God. I can't believe this—

BOYD advances upon CLAYBROOK, who retreats.

DEBRA tries to interpose herself; BOYD pushes her aside; CLAYBROOK shouts as BOYD takes hold of her.

CLAYBROOK   No! Don't touch her!

BOYD   O.K. pull the trigger, it's loaded, black boy, big-shot nigger, c'mon *you* ain't scared, from North Philly *you* ain't scared, now's your chance to blow "whitey" away—

BOYD swings wildly at CLAYBROOK, who ducks the blow.

BOYD   GOD DAMN YOU PULL THE TRIGGER!

BOYD again rushes CLAYBROOK, who knocks him aside; BOYD falls to his knees on the floor, momentarily stunned. Hides his face in his hands. CLAYBROOK removes the bullets from the gun, drops them into his pocket, and tosses the gun away from himself and BOYD as if the touch is repellent.

CLAYBROOK *(Panting)*   Now get your ass out of here like it never *was* here!

A beat.

BOYD is panting; crouching; but all urgency has left him. He flicks his hair

*out of his eyes; shrugs; tries to laugh. He fumbles for his pack of ciga-
rettes, extracts a cigarette—then realizes he can't smoke here. Stuffs
cigarettes back into pocket.*

BOYD *(Faint smile)*   Mind if I use your bathroom, first?

Lights out.

SCENE 8

Lights up, subdued. Tone has changed. A few minutes later.

BOYD *is at the door saying goodbye; duffel bag over his shoulder, a box in
his arms.* BOYD *is both defeated and released; he looks for a final time at
the house he's leaving, and at* DEBRA, *who stands unmoving and expres-
sionless, before turning away.* CLAYBROOK *is helping him carry other
boxes out to his car. Both men exit,* BOYD *and then* CLAYBROOK. *Door remains open.* DEBRA *comes forward, fingertips to eyes. Then she drops her
hands, stands motionless.*

DEBRA *(Slowly, emphatically)*   I'm happy. I'm happy. I'm not going to
    cry—I'm happy.

A pause.

CLAYBROOK *returns. Lights on him and on* DEBRA. *They regard each other
in silence.*

Lights slowly out.

THE END

THE
PERFECTIONIST 🌿
A Comedy in Two Acts

Cast

TOBIAS HARTE—forty-eight
PAULA HARTE—forty-five
KIM HARTE—seventeen
WILLY REBB—early fifties
JASON HARTE—twenty
NEDRA MINSK—thirty-one

Setting

The affluent suburb of Mount Orion, New Jersey. The time is the early 1990s, over a period of approximately two weeks.

SCENE 1

Lights up. An empty corridor at the rear of a prep school auditorium. Red exit sign prominent. We hear the end of a student play.

GIRL'S VOICE *(Off-stage)*   Oh, don't have a cow, Al! You're old enough to be my grandfather anyway.

MAN'S VOICE *(Off-stage)*   It wasn't supposed to end like this!

GIRL'S VOICE *(Off-stage)*   It sure wasn't, Al—but, like, it *does*. Wow!

Rock music up, loud.

Thunderous applause (off-stage).

TOBIAS HARTE *appears, walking hurriedly. He has escaped the auditorium as soon as the play has ended. Angry, upset, not wanting to show it even to himself,* TOBIAS *removes a container of pills (blood pressure pills) from his coat pocket, and takes one. He is the "perfectionist:" a youthful, vigorous man of forty-eight; extremely handsome in a stiff, patrician way; impeccably dressed in a gray pinstripe suit with a vest, silk necktie and matching handkerchief in his lapel pocket. His hair is conservatively cut and touched with gray at the temples. His shoes shine.* TOBIAS *is an embodiment of a certain kind of American masculine-executive success—and also, as he himself can never forget, a man of the highest integrity.*

PAULA *enters, following* TOBIAS.

PAULA   Toby, what on earth—! Isn't this a fire exit?

TOBIAS *(Muttering to himself)*   My daughter! How could she! On a stage! In *public*!

PAULA *hurries to* TOBIAS. *She is a woman who takes appearances very seriously.*

PAULA   Toby, dear! What if you'd set off a fire alarm? What on earth is wrong with you?

TOBIAS With me? You sat through the same travesty I sat through: what's wrong with *you*, that you seemed to have enjoyed it?

PAULA Of course I enjoyed it—Kim was so—bold and inventive—and beautiful. It was meant to be enjoyed—it's a *comedy.*

TOBIAS *(With utter sincerity, shocked)* Nathaniel Hawthorne's "The Birthmark" is *not* a comedy, Paula, damn it! It is a profound, tragic work. *That* was what Kim led me to believe we'd be seeing tonight— a respectful adaptation. Not a shameful burlesque! If I'd known, I would have forbidden it.

PAULA *(Wryly)* Forbidden it?—Kim?

TOBIAS I remember, as an undergraduate, reading "The Birthmark" and being deeply moved. What a parable of man's fallen nature! Paula, Hawthorne is not meant to be "enjoyed": Hawthorne is a *classic.*

PAULA Toby, Kim did an adaptation. It wasn't meant to be the original.

TOBIAS Did you know what this was going to be, Paula?

PAULA *(Patiently)* Darling, Kim is seventeen years old; she is an honors student at one of the most demanding prep schools in the country; she not only adapted her little play, and directed it, she acted in it. I was a little startled at first, I will admit—and the dancing was a bit— much!—but didn't she look beautiful?—isn't she wonderful? Everyone loved her, didn't you hear the applause? And the laughter?

TOBIAS Well, I didn't laugh. I saw nothing funny in that travesty, and *I* didn't laugh.

PAULA Yes, and you were the only person in the audience who didn't. I'm afraid people noticed. Toby, why can't you be proud of one of our children for once, instead of hiding back here?

TOBIAS I am not hiding; I am composing myself. I *am* proud of my children, when they deserve it. *(Pause)* What a nightmare! Half of Mount Orion was in the audience—laughing like idiots. The kids I don't blame, but the adults—! Doesn't Hawthorne mean anything to them? The Armbrusters—the Orkins—several members of the board—they must have grandchildren at the school. And they all know Kim is my daughter.

PAULA Oh, Toby—you sound like an old prig. And you aren't, at all: you're young.

TOBIAS *(Dryly)* A young prig? *(A new thought has struck him)* Paula, do you think Kim may have sent that play as part of her college applications?

PAULA Well, don't ask her tonight.

TOBIAS Do you think she has jeopardized her academic future?

PAULA *I* think you've been working too hard, again. You feel the pressure: Dr. Flamm's resignation, your imminent appointment as Director. *(As TOBIAS winces, out of modesty and annoyance, gesturing for PAULA to be discreet, and both glance over their shoulders)* Oh, don't be silly, no one can hear. And what if they did? It's an open secret that Tobias Harte will be named the next Director of—

TOBIAS   The Board of Trustees has to approve first. You know that.

PAULA   For God's sake, Toby, the Board worships you. If only you'd learn to relax.

TOBIAS   Sometimes I wish I could climb up out of my body, and have done with all this nonsense. *(Gesturing at his body)* Maybe, then, I could get something *done*.

PAULA   *(Touching his forehead)*   You're feverish, and all over a harmless little entertainment. As if Kim did all that work just to sabotage you! Please come with me backstage, and then we're all going to Laurent's for a light supper. You do remember, we'd planned?—A little celebration, for Kim?

TOBIAS   Now? *(Checking his watch)*   At ten P.M.? I'd planned on going over to the office for a while.

PAULA   *(Almost angry)*   Tonight? Damn it, Toby, you're impossible.

KIM appears, bouquets of flowers in her arms. She is flushed with excitement, still in her costume. With both dread and childlike anticipation, she approaches her parents.

KIM   Mommy?—Daddy? What are you doing back *here*?

PAULA   Oh, honey, you were wonderful. You were just—wonderful!

Much overlapping as KIM hurries to PAULA, to be embraced, etc. TOBIAS looks on, smiling stiffly; flexing his fingers.

KIM   Mommy, Daddy—thank you for the flowers! And I got more— look, from the kids in the Drama Club, and from—

PAULA   What a surprise! What a—delight! Darling, we're so proud of you! We had no *idea*.

KIM   Was I O.K.? Could people hear me?

PAULA   The audience loved you. Honey, congratulations!

KIM   *(Voice dropping)*   Daddy didn't like it.

TOBIAS   Kim, of course I—was impressed. I—*(Pause)*—did like it. *(Pained smile: but he is trying)*

KIM   *(Tragically)*   No, you didn't like it. Oh!

TOBIAS   Honey, I did. I found it very—bold, and imaginative, and— experimental. Ask your mother—

KIM   You hated it! You hated my play!

TOBIAS   Kim, I said—

PAULA   *(Overlapping)*   He did like it, Kim, really he did. He was—laughing as much as I was.

TOBIAS   Well, maybe not quite so much as you were, Paula. But—

KIM   Daddy hated my play! That I worked so hard on! Oh! *(Crushes flowers against her, hides her face in them)*

PAULA   Kim, honey, no. Your father loved it, and I loved it—

KIM   Everybody hated it. I wish I was dead!

PAULA   Sweetie, no! This is a *happy* time—

TOBIAS *(Trying)*   I found much to admire in it, Kim, really. Maybe if I saw it again—

KIM *(Tearful)*   Oh, don't tell Kitzie and Brooke. *Their* parents thought it was great.

TOBIAS *(Losing patience with her)*   Kim, please. This isn't the time to be emoting, you're not on stage now. Your little play was what it was; you can't seriously think it was "great." And you and Kitzie and Brooke are amateur actors, aren't you? You can't expect to be—

KIM *(A pretense of calm)*   All right, Daddy, what did you hate about it? Where did it fail?

TOBIAS   I didn't hate anything about it. I don't think it failed—I think it probably succeeded, in what it set out to do.

KIM   You hated that, then?—what it "set out to do?"

TOBIAS   Well, you did subvert a great American classic; you made a feminist burlesque of a tragic tale of Hawthorne's.

KIM   It *is* a feminist burlesque of Hawthorne, so what?—Hawthorne sucks. Hawthorne may be a buddy of yours, Daddy, but—

TOBIAS, PAULA   Kim!

KIM   HAWTHORNE SUCKS AND ALL THE KIDS THINK SO!

TOBIAS   Watch your language, young lady.

PAULA   This is supposed to be a happy time, I've made reservations at Laurent's—

KIM *(Wildly)*   I can't believe this I want to die. Oh! *(Throws down flowers)* I'm so ashamed!

TOBIAS   Kim, don't be childish. Pick those flowers up.

KIM   You hate me!

TOBIAS *(Pained)*   We've been over this—you can't emotionally blackmail your mother and me by claiming we "hate" you whenever we disagree with you.

PAULA *(Quickly)*   Kim, honey, you must be starving. We're all overexcited. I made reservations at Laurent's for fifteen—enough for your friends, too.

KIM   Oh! I couldn't eat, now!

JASON HARTE, KIM's twenty-year-old brother, enters. He is a lanky, good-looking young man with long, calculatedly disheveled hair; in bleached and tattered jeans, a coat or a jacket over a designer T-shirt; expensive running shoes. Though cautious of TOBIAS, JASON seems temperamentally unable to resist provoking him, if only by his presence.

JASON   Hey Kim!—that was cool. Wow! *(Pause)* What are you all doing back *here*, through the fire door? This is weird.

KIM   Daddy hated my play.

TOBIAS   I did not. I—

PAULA   Wasn't it wonderful, Jason? Wasn't Kim just simply terrific?

JASON   Everybody's looking for you, Kim—what's going on? *(Sees flowers on floor)*

KIM   I'm so—ashamed.

PAULA   *(Hugging KIM, scolding)*   Honey, stop. Don't be childish. *(PAULA picks up flowers, gives to KIM who accepts them reluctantly)* Let's go to Laurent's—please.

JASON   Shit, Kim, everybody loved the play. You heard the applause, didn't you? Congratulations. *(Kisses her cheek)* I wish I could think of ingenious stuff like that! But it had a point, too, y'know?

KIM   *(Drying eyes)*   You liked it, Jason? *You* thought it was O.K.? We sort of flubbed our lines a few times, but—

JASON   Nah, nobody could tell.

KIM   You *did* think it was O.K.? *(Dropping her voice)* Daddy hated it.

TOBIAS   *(Losing patience)*   Daddy loved it!

PAULA   You *are* coming with us to Laurent's, Jason, aren't you? As we'd planned?

JASON   Aw Mom, I'd love to, but—

PAULA   Don't say you have other plans—

JASON   *(Overlapping)*   —I've got other plans—

WILLY REBB enters. He is a large, exuberant, generous man; losing his hair, but sporting a youthful mustache; aggressive, warm, noisy; a back slapper and brisk handshaker. Clothes are important to him: they are those of an aging preppie, with bowtie and matching handkerchief. A lawyer— shrewd and watchful beneath his busy social manner.

REBB   *(Swooping upon KIM like an uncle)*   There she is! The girl of the hour! Congratulations! I loved it! All of Mount Orion loved it! *(Kisses KIM's cheek, hugs her)* Funny as hell—an all-girl Hawthorne revue!

KIM   *(Delighted)*   Oh Willy—you liked it?

REBB   Liked it? I stayed awake for it—first play or concert I haven't fallen asleep in, in years. Say, I didn't know you could *act,* Kim. And dance—wow! *(Wriggles hips)* That was something, I tell you. *(To the others)* Congratulations, Harte family! Minnie was so sorry to miss this—sends her regrets.

REBB energetically kisses PAULA's cheek; shakes TOBIAS's hand with a slightly teasing mock-formality. TOBIAS tries to be sociable.

REBB   Paula—lovely!—as usual. A new dress?

PAULA   Yes, I thought—it isn't every day my own daughter makes her stage debut.

REBB   Quite right! Yes! What a night! *(A sly smile)* You're looking glowering, Toby—something wrong?

TOBIAS shakes his head no. PAULA intercedes.

PAULA *(Quickly)*   Oh, you know Toby, Willy—there always *is* something, isn't there. *(Brightly)* We're fine.

REBB *(To TOBIAS, conspiratorial)*   Didja see the Piranha brothers in the foyer?—I had lunch with them yesterday. I'll keep you posted, podna.

TOBIAS   The—who?

PAULA *(Quickly)*   Never mind business, now. Are you coming to Laurent's with us, Willy? Please do!

TOBIAS *(To REBB)*   Did you say the —Piranha brothers?

REBB *(To PAULA, big smile)*   I guess I could be inveigled into it, Paula.

KIM   I'll go change. Thanks, Willy! *(A parting hug)*

JASON *(Has been edging away)*   Yeah, well, O.K., cool—I'm outa here.

PAULA *(Calling sharply after him)*   Jason, what is more important to you, your friends or your—

JASON *(Exiting)*   See ya!

PAULA   —family . . .

REBB   God, Jason's grown. Good-looking, too. *(Chuckling, with a lewd undertone)* This generation of kids—their sex lives are a lot different from ours, eh?

PAULA *(Ignoring this)*   Jason so rarely does anything with his family any longer, I can't understand why.

REBB   He's at home, though, is he? Taking a semester off from Dartmouth?

TOBIAS *(Dryly)*   That's a way of putting it.

REBB *(Seeing that PAULA has been hurt)*   Hell, kids his age— they're just finding themselves. Each generation it takes longer, you ever notice? My great-grandfather came over from Liverpool, alone, aged sixteen—by twenty-five, he was married, had children, was on to making his first million. *My* son—he's twenty-five—has just left home—but— *(Comical shiver)*—I think he's only circling the block. You wait, though, Jason will turn out fine. *(Pause)* Why are you all out *here*? Something wrong? *(Innocently)*

PAULA   Oh, whatever could be wrong!

REBB *(Chuckling, slapping TOBIAS's shoulder)*   Yessir—that's the Tobias Harte glower! Now—a smile. *(As TOBIAS forces a smile)* Well, your daughter's got quite an imagination, old boy.

TOBIAS   Yes. So I've been told.

REBB *(Pushing it, as if innocently)*   Hmm! These kids sure do surprise us, don't they? I love it.

PAULA   Kim is so bright, and so eager. She wants to go into the foreign service, or "environmental law."

REBB   So does my youngest. Every other kid you meet these days, it's "environmental law." Goddam gridlock out there in the environment. *(Pause)* Well, I thought Kim was great, and the other kids, too. I love them, that age. I acted in high school, too, had a helluva happy time in plays. Then—*(He sighs loudly, shaking his jowls)*—the curtains closed and it was *real life.*

Silence.

REBB   *(To* TOBIAS, *undertone)*   Hmmm! Has Dr. Flamm heard anything further from D.C.?—I keep watching the *Times.*

TOBIAS   *(Annoyed)*   It's supposed to be confidential, Willy. Dr. Flamm will be mortified if the appointment falls through.

REBB   *(Slyly)*   He wouldn't be the only one, eh?

PAULA   *(Quickly, to change subject)*   Willy, it's good to see you. Just let me— *(She adjusts his bowtie, which is slightly crooked)* There, that's better. How *is* Minnie?

REBB   D'you mean since the hysterectomy, or since the sciatica?

PAULA   Oh dear—I thought it was colitis.

REBB   *(Genially)*   They're all well, all of 'em. Doing fine.

PAULA   How did you even know Kim's little play was on tonight?

REBB   *(Laying his forefinger along his nose)*   Willy Rebb always knows about things—and people—that matter to him.

PAULA smiles, pleased. TOBIAS is annoyed.

TOBIAS   *(Abruptly)*   Paula, Willy—I'll walk over to the restaurant; I could use some fresh air.

PAULA   But it must be two miles! And it's chilly.

TOBIAS   It will do me good. *(Starts to walk off)*

PAULA   *(Taking a step after him)*   Toby—

TOBIAS   *(Pauses, turns)*   Yes, Paula?

PAULA   *(Kissing him on the cheek)*   I'll see you at Laurent's as soon as— you arrive.

TOBIAS exits with a wave of his hand, his step springy, energized.

PAULA   *(To* REBB, *incensed)*   Oh I know he's going to "drop by" the office—I know.

REBB   *(A look of distaste)*   Tonight? Now? Office? *Work?*

PAULA   Didn't you see him smiling when he left? The more successful Toby has become, the more obsessive.

REBB   *(Mock-sage)*   "Success is like riding a bicycle—if you stop pedaling, you fall over."

PAULA   Oh Willy, if only he could learn from you. Success should bring with it a little healthy complacency. *(Laughs sadly)* Remember when

Toby had that terrible kidney stone attack, and refused to go into the hospital until he collapsed in agony—and, even then, he took his laptop computer with him in the ambulance?

REBB   Maybe Tobias Harte is a secret masochist?

PAULA   Masochists derive pleasure from pain. Toby tries not to derive pleasure from pleasure.

REBB *(Wistfully)*   Still, he loves you. You love him.

PAULA *(As if amazed)*   We've been married twenty-two years—!

PAULA and REBB move slowly to the exit, deep in conversation. We sense their long intimacy. REBB is in love with PAULA and PAULA, while not quite reciprocating, is comforted and flattered.

PAULA   What happens in the next week or so will determine the rest of our lives, and it scares me. Toby has this "vision" of what he will do as Director!—I'm afraid it will kill him. The other morning he was smiling in his sleep, but agitated, kicking about and I woke him, and he said he'd been dreaming that the new library wing had been built— "Paula," he said, "it was *beautiful.*"

REBB *(A look of distaste)*   God, that's sick. *(Neutrally)* Still, you love him.

PAULA *(Sighing, as if helpless)*   Oh, yes. He's perfect.

As they exit, lights out.

SCENE 2

Lights up. Two evenings later, in TOBIAS HARTE's study in his home. His desk is stacked with papers, but he has cleared a space for his Digitronic home blood pressure measuring kit. TOBIAS is taking his blood pressure, but with difficulty. He is in his shirt-sleeves, trying to fasten the cuff of the instrument on his upper arm; it slips loose. He repositions his elbow atop the desk; mutters to himself; tries not to become agitated. He reads instructions from a booklet propped up before him.

TOBIAS   "Microphone mark over pulse point . . . wrap cuff . . . one finger inserted . . . same height as heart . . . rubber bulb, pump . . . " *(He begins pumping the rubber bulb, vigorously)* Ow! Damn! *(Cuff slips loose again, apparatus falls to floor)*

A knock at the door and PAULA pokes her head inside; enters.

PAULA *(Seeing the apparatus)*   Oh, that! Don't you want some help, darling?

TOBIAS *(Ironic)*   I was doing fine until you interrupted.

PAULA   Why is it on the floor?

TOBIAS   Paula, it fell. It squirmed from my arm, and fell.

PAULA *(Picking up apparatus, deftly wrapping cuff around TOBIAS's arm)*
Why didn't you call me for help? You've had this contraption for three
months, and you've yet to do it correctly. Have you rested five minutes?—you're agitated, I think.

TOBIAS   This is my restful state. Any more, and I'd be comatose. *(As
PAULA pumps the bulb, TOBIAS winces)* Ow! That hurts.

PAULA *(Scolding)*   How can I get a reading if I don't exert pressure? *(She
tries again, peering at the gauge)* Oh dear—this is odd.

TOBIAS   What? I'm dead?

PAULA   All I get is zeros . . . no, thirteen over zero. Something's wrong.

TOBIAS   The microphone mark is off the pulse point.

PAULA *(Absorbed)*   I'll try again. Hold still. *(Pumping, etc., TOBIAS grits
his teeth, but sits stoically)* Now it says—oh, God!—this can't be.

TOBIAS *(In dread)*   What?

PAULA *(Hurriedly)*   I'll try again. *(Procedure as before)*

TOBIAS   Can't we stop? Maybe you could do a spinal tap instead.

PAULA *(Absorbed)*   Toby, relax. You know, I *like* this. I should have been
a nurse, instead of a—whatever it is I am. Toby, remember?—you
came into the Red Cross Bloodmobile, on Harvard Square? I was a
volunteer aide and you were—so handsome—so strong and confident—twenty-three years old, a Ph.D. student in something I'd never
heard of—you were perfectly brave until you happened to see the bag
filling with blood, and you fainted. Just like that! I'd been warned it
was always the men who fainted, not the women, but you were my
first. *(Smiling in reminiscence)* It took ten minutes to revive you.

As TOBIAS starts to faint, PAULA grabs him. Forcibly lowers his head.

PAULA   Oh, dear! "Lower head to knees"—like this.

After a few seconds, TOBIAS revives; gets to his feet; tears the cuff off.

TOBIAS   Enough!

PAULA   We'll do it in the morning—that's the proper time anyway.
(Pause) Toby, I'm concerned about Jason. He's been acting
so . . . oddly lately.

TOBIAS   How could you tell? Has he left off wearing his earring?

PAULA   Since the night of Kim's little play, when he didn't come home until almost dawn, haven't you noticed—he's so withdrawn. I mean
withdrawn when he's visible; most of the time he's out of the house. I
try to speak with him but he avoids me. He won't look me in the face.

TOBIAS   Jason hasn't looked me in the face for years. I'd assumed it was
some sort of aesthetic statement.

PAULA   You joke about Jason because you're so bitter about him—don't interrupt, please, it isn't helpful. *(Wringing hands)* Something has hurt our son; he looks wounded. Even his appetite is depressed . . .

TOBIAS *(Making an effort)*   Paula, I am not bitter about Jason, I am concerned about him. A young man who hopes to be an "ecological programmer" and whose room looks like a nuclear waste dump—a young man who gets a C minus in a course called "Deconstructing *Batman*"—a young man who drops out of college his junior year to live at home and work as a busboy at the Mount Orion Inn—of course I'm concerned. When I was Jason's age—

PAULA *(Quickly)*   Oh, I know! But you had the advantage of not having *you* as a father.

TOBIAS *(Incensed, puzzled)*   What do you mean? *(Pause)* I had my own father.

PAULA *(Reciting, not unkindly)*   When you were Jason's age, you had three jobs, and you were in college; you took five courses, including Classical Greek, Advanced Calculus, Voltaire Not in Translation—oh, I know! But Jason is, as Willy said, of another generation. *(Pause)* You didn't even notice, Jason's hair is cut. But so strangely. And he looks—well, ravaged, somehow. A—spiritual wound—I'm just so worried about him.

TOBIAS   Wait—what about his job at the Inn?

PAULA *(Evasively)*   Oh—Jason, um, resigned, a while back. I'm sure we told you.

TOBIAS   Resigned? *Quit?* His busboy job? He's unemployed *again?*

PAULA   I'm sure we told you.

TOBIAS   Let me guess why: busboying at the Mount Orion Inn wasn't "intellectually engaging" enough for our son?

PAULA   No, that was *not* why Jason . . . resigned. The job *was* intellectually engaging, in fact, because all the other busboys had B.A.'s and one had a Ph.D. in—Sociotopology, I think. And he could practice his Spanish with the waiters. No, the reason Jason quit was because he knew it was embarrassing *you.*

TOBIAS   *Me?*

PAULA   Jason knows you judge him harshly; he knows you're disappointed in him. No, don't interrupt. When Dr. Flamm brought you and your colleagues to lunch at the Inn one day, Jason was so ashamed, he thought the sight of him embarrassed you. "I can't put Dad through that again," he said. He's so *sensitive.*

TOBIAS   He quit his job to spare my feelings? *(Incredulous)* But—I didn't even *see* him, Paula. If I did, I looked right through him—I was preoccupied.

PAULA   Yes, Jason was hurt. You invariably look through our son—unless you look *at* him. And then you find fault.

TOBIAS *(Dryly)*   Obviously, I should wear dark glasses.

PAULA *(Conceding)*   Jason *does* make communication difficult.

TOBIAS   Yes. He lies.

PAULA *(Incensed)*   But not intentionally, I'm sure. I think sometimes he forgets what truth *is*. And Kim, too. It isn't somehow so transparent as it was in the past.

TOBIAS *(Eloquently)*   "Truth is of all time, it is for all men, it has only to show itself to be recognized, and one cannot argue against it."

PAULA   Really! Who said that?

TOBIAS   Voltaire.

PAULA *(Half-sob, frustrated)*   Oh why are we always talking about him! Will you speak with Jason, Toby? Shall I bring him in?

TOBIAS *(Alarmed)*   In *here*?

PAULA   I'll catch him before he slips out— *(Moving to exit)*

TOBIAS   Paula, wait, I— *(PAULA exits)* —I'm afraid to be alone with our . . . son.

TOBIAS paces about as if, indeed, he is afraid. He adjusts his necktie, smooths his shirt, hair.

TOBIAS *(Ironically, to himself)*   Voltaire also said: "A long dispute means that both parties are wrong."

PAULA is glimpsed pushing JASON into his father's study; she does not come inside herself, though TOBIAS wishes she would. JASON enters reluctantly, gaze downcast. His eyes are ringed with fatigue; he is unshaven; sloppily dressed and lacking the insouciant ease of the previous scene. His hair is jaggedly cut. A single gold earring glints in his right earlobe.

TOBIAS, JASON *(Mumble)*   H'lo.

TOBIAS   How are you?

JASON *(Overlapping)*   How's it goin'.

TOBIAS   Why—er—don't you have a seat? *(Pointing to a chair)*

JASON   Nah, I'm O.K. But—uh—you? *(Pointing to chair behind desk)*

TOBIAS   No, I'm fine.

JASON *(Mumble, overlapping)*   I'm fine.

Silence.

TOBIAS, JASON *(Abruptly, simultaneously)*   Guess I missed you at dinner?

TOBIAS   I had to work late—sorry.

JASON   Yeah, well—I didn't make it either. *(Pause)*

JASON sights the blood pressure kit on the desk, and reacts fearfully.

JASON   Geez Dad—what's *that*?

TOBIAS *(Quickly putting the kit aside, or in a drawer; embarrassed)*   Oh, nothing!

Silence.

JASON *(Shy, dreading sidelong glance)*   There isn't anything wrong with you, Dad? Like—uh—your heart—

TOBIAS *(Overlapping briskly on "heart")*   Certainly not, Jason. I'm fine. And—you?

JASON *(Quick mumble, hand through hair)*   Oh yeah—fine. Real good.

Silence.

As if their conversation is over, TOBIAS *and* JASON *speak simultaneously, with relief;* JASON *edging toward door.*

TOBIAS, JASON   Well!—uh—

JASON   —guess I'll be going, Dad—gonna meet some friends—

TOBIAS *(Overlapping)*   —good to see you, son—

JASON *would exit except, at the door,* PAULA *is waiting; we see rather than hear them confer;* JASON *is then pushed forcibly back into the room.*

JASON *(Ill-at-ease, nervous mannerisms)*   Uh, Dad—I, uh—

TOBIAS *(Back at desk, startled)*   Oh—you're back?

JASON   Dad, I got something to, uh—tell you, like.

TOBIAS *(Forced smile)*   Well, sit down!—like. Please.

JASON *slinks into the chair, slouching;* TOBIAS *straightens his shoulders pointedly, to suggest to* JASON *that he sit up, too; which he does with a spasmodic effort; then, by degrees, he slouches; and again* TOBIAS *straightens his own shoulders. Throughout their conversation, father and son "negotiate" this matter of posture.*

JASON *is clearly disturbed about something, and shamed, yet at the same time he exudes an air of sullen defiance. His relationship to his father is complex and his moods mercurial: even as he approaches* TOBIAS *in appeal, he shrinks away; or is repelled by the older man's unconscious rigidity.*

An awkward pause.

TOBIAS *(Forced geniality)*   Well, Jason! It's been a while. You say you have something to tell me?

JASON *(Gazes downcast, picking at a tear in his jeans through which a patch of skin shows)*   I . . . I'm so ashamed. I . . . *(Pause)* I can't.

TOBIAS *(Uneasy, yet more genial)*   Well, that's a, a start. That's a strong start. *(Pause)* What are you ashamed of, Jason?

Silence.

TOBIAS   Shame is a powerful emotion. A driving force for civilization. Without it, we wouldn't be human, would we? *(Pause)* Was it something you did, Jason, or something done to you?

JASON *(Wiping at nose, mumbling)*   Kinda, like, both.

TOBIAS *(Hand to ear)*   What?—don't mumble.

JASON *(Louder, with anguish)*   Both.

Silence.

TOBIAS   And when did this occur? Recently? *(As JASON nods, gaze still downcast)* How recently?

JASON   The other night, uh, after Kim's play, I—it was then.

TOBIAS   Was this, er, did this episode, I mean had it, was it—something sexual? *(This is very difficult for TOBIAS to utter, so he says it with an air of abandon; a ghastly smile)*

Silence.

TOBIAS *(Encouraging)*   "The only shame is to have none"—Pascal. *(Pause)* In translation.

Silence.

TOBIAS *(Encouraging)*   I was afflicted by shame too, as a boy, as young as six or seven, if I didn't get perfect scores on tests . . . and then at puberty, I was miserable with shame for obsessive thoughts, habits . . . *(Pause)* Just the other day, I was ashamed of myself for being impatient with a colleague at the Institute. And so—I understand, Jason. I'm with you.

Silence.

TOBIAS   Your mother happened to mention you'd quit your job? I'm hoping this means you'll be returning to school next semester? *(Pause)* BUT I'M NOT PUTTING ANY PRESSURE ON YOU. *(Pause)* We can discuss the subject, where you might transfer, any time, I assume you've sent for brochures, application forms, a damned shame we have to go through the process again so soon but since Dartmouth didn't work out, well . . . Dartmouth didn't work out. *(Pause; JASON's silence is beginning to make him angry)* I've failed too, Jason, lots of times: I know what abject failure is, yes I do: I'm with you. *(Pause)* Once, when I was nine years old, it started to sleet while I was delivering newspapers, this was in Morgantown, West Virginia, I rode my bicycle for miles in the dark, in the sleet the wind-chill factor dropped the temperature to minus six degrees and I had only one more block to go when I . . . collapsed. *(Shakes head, shuddering)* I was so ashamed, I started to cry in the emergency room. My fingers and toes were near frozen but WHAT I FELT, SON, WAS GOOD OLD-FASHIONED SHAME. *(Pause)* As you know, my relations with my father were a bit, er, formal, yes, but I respected him, and was determined to repay his debts after he died and after our deceitful Uncle Morgan absconded with the insurance money *and* what remained of the stock in my father's bankrupt shoe store, I've never confided in you perhaps the depth of my determination, it was an obsession fueled by shame and the fear of shame, and so when I received offers of scholarships from Harvard, Princeton, Yale, Berkeley, Chicago and one or two others, I had to make the decision: would I go to college, or would I work forty hours a week? *(Pause)* I decided to do both.

JASON, who has fallen into a open-eyed trance or stupor, has begun to snore.

TOBIAS   Jason! Are you listening?

JASON snores again.

TOBIAS *(Incredulous)*   Are you asleep? With your eyes open?

He waves a hand in front of JASON's face, and JASON continues to stare glassy-eyed.

JASON wakes himself with a loud snort.

JASON *(Quick mumble)*   Right, Dad. I hear you. Cool.
TOBIAS   You were asleep with your eyes open.
JASON   I was *not*. I was here all the time.
TOBIAS   You snored, Goddamn it. Do you snore while you're awake?
JASON   Who snored?
TOBIAS   What was I saying, then?
JASON *(Flat, rapid, mechanical voice, gestures mimicking TOBIAS's)*
   When I was your age, I never took less than six courses at Harvard; I was never off the Dean's list, and I was never in the infirmary. Waking at four thirty A.M. I would hike three miles to my job at a meat packing plant where I handled raw sides of beef weighing nine hundred pounds while I recited my Latin lesson to myself then I would return to my dorm before my roommates were even awake where I would quickly shower to get the blood and gristle off and then hurrying to my eight o'clock class in Advanced Metaphysical Poets I would devour a stale bun from the Day-Old Bakery on Harvard Square (I could not afford room *and* board at Harvard *and* send enough money back home to my widowed mother) and feel, crossing the Yard, an inexpressible sweetness and joy knowing myself, Tobias Harte, to be blessed. Later I would toil in the gloomy depths of the Widener Li-

brary and still later, well into the night, in the hellish depths of Weld Hall, I would shovel coal into a roaring furnace; yet I had time to be editor of the Crimson, president of the Debate, Latin, and History clubs, captain of the track team, and a faithful volunteer in the University Christian Fellowship Mission to the Maimed and Hopeless of the Greater Boston Area. My credo was Aristotle's—"All things in moderation."

TOBIAS *(Shaking JASON)* That was the continuation!—I hadn't gotten to that point yet. You *weren't* listening.

Silence. TOBIAS is hurt and indignant; JASON sullenly apologetic.

TOBIAS *(Trying a new tack)* Well, er—your mother says you got your hair cut?

JASON *(Derisive laugh)* This—? On purpose—? *(He grabs his hair, which has been jaggedly cut, one side shorter than the other)* Nah, somebody did it to me. With a rusty shears. Got me here, too. *(Indicating a scratch, bruises on his neck)*

TOBIAS What on earth—? Who did that to you?

JASON I was assaulted, like.

TOBIAS Who did it, Jason?

JASON *(Reluctant, ashamed)* This, uh—woman. A woman.

TOBIAS A woman—?

JASON *(In a rapid mutter, eyes downcast)* Her name is Nedra I don't know her last name she's renting the carriage house on the Eaton estate *she* came on to *me* where we ran into each other in the park she invited me back to her place and we got high and, uh, she seemed like she liked me O.K. so next night I went back and there was some kind of disagreement and she got excited and went at me with the shears and she's saying she might bring r-rape charges— *(Ends out of breath, panting)*.

TOBIAS *(Stunned)* R-rape charges?

JASON *(Childlike appeal, frightened)* I didn't do it, Daddy!—I didn't! I didn't do anything—almost.

TOBIAS *(Faintly)* Jason, my God. What . . . didn't you almost do?

JASON *(Rapid recitation, as before)* The first time, she asked me there, and, uh, we got high, she supplied the, uh, substance, and, uh, we kinda, uh, made love and that was O.K. I thought then the next night I went back and she hardly let me in the door she's like different pretending not to know me and I was, uh, I guess I got a, a little forceful I guess, I'd had a few beers and I don't know what happened then she's screaming for me to get out, I got excited and I don't know—knocked her down maybe. And she went crazy and hit me. And she got these nasty old shears and—assaulted me.

TOBIAS   You broke into a woman's house and attacked her? Is that what you're saying?

JASON *(Protesting)*   I knew it! I knew you'd take her side!

TOBIAS   I'm not taking anyone's side—

JASON   You hate me! I knew it!

TOBIAS   Jason, please be calm. Tell me what happened.

JASON *(Incoherently)*   I don't know what happened! It's, like, it was all in a dream! One night she liked me real well, the next night I should've figured she was crazy and gotten the hell out but I made a bad mistake I guess I got excited but I didn't r-rape her—oh Dad don't let them arrest me! I don't want to go to jail!

TOBIAS   You say she hasn't notified the police yet?

JASON *(Miserably)*   I don't think so—I'd be arrested, wouldn't I?

TOBIAS   Were there any witnesses?—anyone who saw you go in her place, come out?

JASON   Well, uh, the first night, actually, uh, there were some others guys she invited back, too, but, uh, they left, and, uh—I stayed. 'Cause she asked me to. Then the next night, I came back alone.

TOBIAS   That night—last Saturday night—you came back uninvited to this woman's house—she didn't want you to stay but you did—and then what did you do?

JASON   What happened was some kind of a misunderstanding, like?—and she got all emotional and went after me with the shears.

TOBIAS *(Sharply)*   I didn't ask you "what happened"—I asked, "What did you do?"

JASON *(Protesting)*   She assaulted *me*, Dad! Almost poked my eye out! She hates men! She said she was gonna— *(Pause)* —castrate me if I ever came back.

TOBIAS *(Trying to remain calm)*   Jason, let me get this straight: last Saturday night you went to a woman's house, the carriage house on the Eaton estate, —I hope to God the Eatons don't know about this, they're in the top five percentile of the Institute's donors—and got into a struggle of some kind? *(Enunciating carefully, distastefully)* Knocked a woman *down*? And did you then force yourself upon her?

JASON   S-say what?

TOBIAS   You know perfectly well what I mean: forcible penile penetration: rape.

JASON   No!

TOBIAS   Yet she accuses you of it?

JASON   Dad, she's crazy, she's—far out. *(Pause)* Shouldn't we get a lawyer?

TOBIAS   A lawyer. I see.

JASON   Isn't that what—guys do? At times like this?

TOBIAS   "What guys do"—"times like this."

JASON *(A small, cringing-dreading voice)* Maybe she wants money?

TOBIAS Whose money?

JASON *(Emotional, childish)* I'd pay you back, with interest, Dad!—compound interest! I promise! You can break my fucking kneecaps if I don't!

TOBIAS *(Sharply)* Watch your language, son. Jason, who is this woman?

JASON I don't even *know.* I mean, she's real secretive. She's new here in Mount Orion, only staying for a few months she says. Came up to us in the park where we're hanging out, some of the guys and me, y'know, and she's got a camera and asks can she take our pictures— we're just what she wants for her project. *(Striking a pose, unconsciously)* "Disaffected Suburban-Caucasian Youth of the American Fin-de-Siècle." *(Pronounced "fin de seeckle")*

TOBIAS *(Passing hand over eyes)* My God.

JASON "Fin-de-siècle"—that means, like, end of the century? —kinda, like, decadent?

TOBIAS *(Losing his temper)* I KNOW WHAT FIN-DE-SIÈCLE MEANS.

Silence.

JASON *(Whining)* Like I said, I tried to talk to her, Dad—she tells me to fuck off. Calls me a rapist. Can't we get a lawyer, Dad? Please? Willy Rebb, maybe? *He'd* understand. *(Pause)* Dad, I'm sorry. I DIDN'T DO ANYTHING, BUT I'M SORRY. You want me to get on my knees? *(On his knees, shuffling to TOBIAS)* Want me to fucking *beg? Grovel?*

TOBIAS Jason, stop. For God's sake—

JASON *(Sobbing)* You don't love me you hate me you wish I'd never been born Kim's your favorite Kim's always been your favorite you don't give a shit about me you don't believe me do you!

TOBIAS Watch your language! *(Pause, tries to speak calmly; with comic solicitude)* Jason, of course I love you. You're my son. Of course I believe you. *(Pause)* Though this is by far the worst thing you've ever done even if you haven't, as you insist, done it. This is by far the worst thing I could ever have imagined you doing. *(As JASON melodramatically collapses on floor, at his feet)* This is why I never wanted a personal life. A private life. A domestic life. A life of feeling, and not of intellect. *(Pause)* But of course I love you, son. I'm your father.

Lights out.

SCENE 3

Lights up. The Harte family room, same time. KIM *in shirt and jeans is lying on her stomach on the rug, with various brochures, application forms, papers spread out before her.* PAULA *stands over her. Tense atmosphere.*

KIM *(Petulantly, tossing down pamphlet)*   WHY should I submit myself —my *soul*—to the fascist SAT exam?—fill out all these groveling applications? *(Pushing papers, etc., from her)* Wesleyan, Brown, Yale, Princeton, HARVARD—Big deal!

PAULA *(Wringing hands)*   But, Kim, all your friends and classmates are—

KIM   That's what I mean, Mom! Everybody who *exists* is applying to the same places! It's, like Mount Orion Day School is going to reconstitute itself—hundreds, thousands of kids just like us—The Class of nineteen ninety-eight. Shit!

PAULA   Young lady, watch your language!

KIM   Oh, don't have a cow, Mom. *I* think it's craven and immoral to have all these special aids— *(Waving booklet)* —"The SAT Study Manual"—"How to Improve Your I.Q. in 10 Quick Steps"—just to get into college. What about poor kids from ghetto schools, how're they gonna compete?

PAULA   It does seem unfair, but . . . as John F. Kennedy himself once said, "Life *is* unfair."

KIM *(Incensed)*   That was back in the old, ignorant days, when people weren't politically enlightened, like we are now. Besides, John F. Kennedy was a *womanizer*. It all came out in *People Magazine.*

PAULA *(Angry)*   John F. Kennedy was much more than a "womanizer," Kim. He was a brave, idealistic man—the last of the macho liberals. I forbid you to be flippant about him.

KIM   Oh, Mom, don't have a—

PAULA   If I hear that obscene expression one more time—

KIM *(Rolling away from her on the floor, taking up a glossy advertisement and unfolding it; now dreamy)*   Wow—"Venice Beach Rep"— "workshops in Radical Theatre, Theatre of the Absurd, and mime"— *no* SAT exam, *no* transcripts, just an audition. Our drama coach Sol Schwartz took a workshop there last summer, and said it was fantastic. And the tuition's one tenth of what you and Daddy would pay for college.

PAULA   We've gone over this, Kim. It's out of the question. "Venice Beach Rep"—!

KIM *(Dreamily taking up another ad)*   O.K., closer to home—"East Village Experiment"—"a limited number of internships in acting, playwriting, directing, stagecraft, and building maintenance"—"Theatre of Cruelty and Alienation"—"Children's Guerilla Puppets"—wow, you and Daddy could come in to New York and see a production any-time. Sol Schwartz knows the Artistic Director here, he can get me an audition any time by just picking up the phone. And I'd be an intern—*no* tuition and fees.

PAULA   And no salary, either—you'd be working for nothing. You'd be exploited.

KIM   I'd be an *intern*, Mom.

PAULA   That's just a trendy word for *exploited*.

KIM   And I wouldn't be exploited, going to college—twenty-five thousand dollars a year tuition?

PAULA   Honey, that's different. That's—education.

KIM   What about *you*?

PAULA   *(Immediately defensive)*   What about me?

KIM   You went to college, and—well?

PAULA   *(Stiffly)*   I had other goals. I was engaged before I was twenty-one.

KIM   Yuck, Mom!

PAULA   In those days it was—different. We didn't have much choice to be pro about.

KIM   Maybe you were exploited, too. You just had a different word for it.

PAULA   *(Quickly)*   This discussion is not about me, Kim—it's about *you*. Oh! What are you doing?

KIM   *(Begins to tear up application forms, histrionically)*   I WANT TO GO INTO THE THEATRE. I WILL DIE IF I CAN'T GO INTO THE THEATRE.

PAULA   *(Shocked, taking up pieces of the applications and trying to fit them together)*   What have you done! You've torn up Barnard!

KIM   *(Tearing others)*   Here's Stanford! Princeton!

PAULA   Stop!

KIM   *(Flinging pieces into the air like confetti)*   Harvard!

PAULA   Oh! That's your *father*! *(Picking up pieces, distressed)* Oh, darling, this is madness. This is your *future*.

KIM   *(Near tears)*   Sol Schwartz says I'm the most talented student he's ever *had*. And you and Daddy just don't *care*.

PAULA   Honey, of course we care—we love you. We don't want you to make some rash, hideous decision at seventeen and ruin your life.

KIM   Ruin my *life*? At my age?

PAULA   Your father and I enrolled you in the Mount Orion Pre-School Academy when you were eighteen months old, as soon as you could take the I.Q. tests—the competition was cutthroat! But from pre-school to this very moment— *(A sweeping gesture of her hand)* —your way has been assured. In America, there's no sympathy for those who fall off the track and let the competition rush past.

KIM *(Bold naïveté)* I want to go into the theatre for *love,* not *competition.* I *scorn* competition. Anyway, if I'm an intern in, like, the East Village Experiment, it won't cost you and Daddy a penny.

PAULA *(Dubiously)* But—where would you live?

KIM *(Airily vague)* Oh, somewhere in New York.

PAULA The Village is frightening enough, but the East Village—! I worry about *diseases.*

KIM *(Exasperated)* Mom, give me a break! Sol Schwartz is urging me to go into the theatre, I'm supposed to tell him, "My mother is worried about diseases?"

PAULA Well, honey, I can't help it, I *am.*

KIM There are diseases all over, Mom. The United States is, like, a sick place.

PAULA *(Snobbishly)* I mean New York-type diseases. *(An aria)* Here in Mount Orion, we have a different class of disease: we have migraine and melancholia; we have anorexia, bulimia, and Epstein-Barr Syndrome; we have mania, and myopia, and passive-aggressive husbands; tennis elbow and jogger's knee; high blood pressure and alcoholism and ulcers; omnipotence and impotence—and nothing in between. We have depression, and suppression and nymphomania—*non*-practicing. And if we have drug dependency, it's *legal* drugs. We have *physicians.*

KIM That's what I mean—sick. You take Xanax—and there's nothing even wrong with you.

PAULA *(Incensed)* I do not take Xanax! I've been cutting back.

KIM Hey c'mon, Mom—everybody's mother takes Xanax in Mount Orion.

PAULA They do?

KIM What's to be, like, embarrassed about? Jodi Carstairs came home the other day after school and almost freaked out: the burglar alarm was going full blast, one of those weird whooping ones— *(KIM imitates)* —and the sprinklers too, all over the house—and there was their toy poodle Tiffany dead on the living room rug! Poor Tiffany had set off the burglar alarm and was electrocuted in the process, and the singeing fur set off the sprinklers in the ceilings! And there's Mrs. Carstairs so mellowed out on Xanax, she's sitting in the solarium reading Danielle Steele when the police arrive. Wild!

PAULA Mimi Carstairs!—I don't want to hear it. *(Pause)* What did the police do? *(Phone begins to ring)*

JASON enters.

PAULA Hello? *(Immediate change of tone)* Oh—Willy! What a coincidence, I was just thinking of you. Did you hear about Mimi Carstairs? *(To Kim)* I'll take this upstairs.

PAULA *exits.*

JASON *(Distracted at first)*   Uh, hi Kim—how's it going?

KIM *(Pouting)*   Oh, Mom's just having her usual cow. *You* know.

JASON *(Flinching as he sees college applications on rug)*   God, that shit! *(Shivers)* Applying to college is the pits. I think it did, like, real lasting psychic damage to me. *(Touches head)*

KIM *(Bravely)*   I've decided I won't go through with it. Nobody can make me. I WANT A CAREER IN THE THEATRE NOBODY CAN STOP ME IF I WANT IT BAD ENOUGH.

JASON   Wow, that's cool! Is that a saying from somewhere, or did you just make it up?

KIM *(Theatrically)*   My heart just . . . yearns so . . . when I think of the theatre. "Moscow! To Moscow! There's nothing in the world like Moscow!"

JASON *(Puzzled)*   Moscow? How come?

KIM   I want to write my own theatre pieces and perform them. I know I can do it! *(Pause, bites thumbnail)* Do you think I'm . . . deluded?

JASON *(Forcefully, like a big brother)*   Nah, you can't let yourself think like that. *Just go for it.*

KIM   "Go for it!" *(Hugging herself)* Oh, I know it's the right decision, I just *know. (Pause)* I'm scared of what Daddy will say.

JASON   Don't tell him what you're gonna do; tell him what you've done. A *fate accom-plee. (Confidentially)* That's my plan.

KIM   Your plan?

JASON glances over his shoulder to make certain no parents are within earshot. Squats down beside KIM, speaks excitedly.

JASON *(A deep breath)*   I have some news, too, Kim. I'm like, just emerged from the—Dark Night of the Soul. You heard of that? *(Shivers)* These past forty-eight hours.

KIM *(Biting thumbnail)*   Dark Night of the Soul!—oh, wow. You're scaring me, Jason.

JASON *(Reproachfully)*   Not that anybody around here would notice. I was gonna tell Dad, but—forget it! This is not a household where spiritual anguish is noticed.

KIM   Hey, c'mon—we noticed you missed dinner. We just thought, y'know, you ate at McDonald's, with your friends.

JASON *(Incensed)*   A Dark Night of the Soul is more than missing a meal, for God's sake! It's . . . interior. Unfathomable. Like . . . *(Searching for the perfect metaphor)* . . . going through a car wash, all those big bristly brushes, NAKED. *(Now on his feet, pacing about, scarcely able to restrain his sense of self-importance)* It's, like, I died, Kim. I DIED AND WAS REBORN.

KIM   Up in your room—?

JASON *(Snappishly)*   What's it matter where, for God's sake! I told you, it's *interior.* *(Pause)* I had this dream vision, like, where there was so much weight pressing on me I kind of . . . impacted . . . and suddenly I saw my own body from the outside! Like my soul slipped out of my body! I thought, "Am I dead? Is this death?" And, this *is* weird, I mean, whew! *weird!*—there comes floating this beautiful woman or maybe a guy—creamy light-skinned black but not, y'know, *black*—I look and can't believe what I'm seeing—"Michael Jackson? Coming for *me?*" except he, or she, was kind of blurry, took my hand and smiled at me and whispered, "Don't be afraid, Jason," so I wasn't afraid, and he, or she, led me through a tunnel all glittering like jewels, and we came out into a space that was filled with light, and I realized that my escort, this beautiful person, was an angel leading me into the presence of God. *(Breathless)* An angel that looked just like Michael Jackson!

KIM *(Rapt, wide-eyed)*   Oh, Jason!

JASON *(Pacing about)*   Then God swept over me. "Jason, you must change your life"—God told me. Not in actual words, but—inside my head. "You have sinned, Jason, and now you must change your life." But He wasn't angry, Kim, He was, like, loving. *(JASON wipes at his eyes)*

KIM   What's God look like?

JASON *(Importantly)*   God is a spirit, Kim, a—force, energy. Like the sun. Like the sun spilling liquid fire through our veins. He's outside us, and inside us—He *is* us.

KIM   Wait, Jason. You refer to God as "He." Is that right? I mean, if God is a spirit . . .

JASON *(Snappishly)*   That's not the crucial thing, it's the vision He gave me, to change my life.

KIM   How can a spirit be "He?"—I'm just asking.

JASON   The voice sounded male, for God's sake. You want to hear the rest of my vision, or not?

KIM   You said the voice was inside your head, so how was it *male?*—I'm just asking.

JASON *(Temper flaring)*   You want me to call God "It?" I should call God, this force, like, that transfigured my soul—*"It?"*

KIM *(Doggedly)*   In school, we have to say he/she—"he-slash-she." Of course, that's just referring to human beings.

JASON   YOU WANT TO HEAR THE REST OF MY FUCKING VISION, OR NOT?

KIM *(Chastened murmur)*   Yes, Jason.

JASON   So—God sort of flew me to this place—far from here, in the country—and I saw myself, again—purged of sin. I was healthy, and tall, and proud—walking in the sunshine in the coarse-woven robe of a monk! With a rope belt around my waist! In sandals! I understood that I was a Trappist monk, that I'd taken a vow of poverty, chastity, obedience, and silence for the rest of my life. It was me Jason Harte, but—transformed.

KIM *(Suddenly recalling)* Uh—isn't that from the documentary we saw last week on PBS?—the Trappist monastery at Gethsemane, Kentucky? Where Thomas Merton was a monk?

JASON *(Annoyed)* It went deeper than that! The documentary, like, awakened this other—*yearning*. In my soul.

KIM *(Stunned)* Jason, you want to be a Trappist monk? You?

JASON No way I'm *not*. God has spoken.

KIM Don't you have to be a Catholic, first?

JASON They can convert me when I get there.

KIM You're just . . . going? Shouldn't you, uh, apply first?

JASON I figure, God might've sent them a vision, too, the head monk there, to prepare them for me. It's, like, political asylum from the heartless materialist secular-suburban Caucasian world of my birth-right. *(Pause, excited)* A Christian brotherhood—male bonding with God! It'd be a big deal for the Trappists, too, y'know?—*People Magazine* might cover it, "Sixty Minutes" . . .

KIM Oh, God. Mom and Dad are both going to have a cow.

JASON I already tried to tell Mom—"God sent me a vision," I said—and she, like, blushed. She blushed! You can't talk about God in Mount Orion, your own mother's embarrassed. Like soiled sheets, or something. As for Dad . . . *(Shudders)* That's why I'm going to Gethsemane, Kentucky, for political asylum. See, there's some heavy shit on my, uh, soul, like . . . I'm in some trouble, I guess . . . I don't know how it's gonna turn out . . . I JUST KNOW I GOTTA GET OUT OF HERE. Tonight . . . when you guys are sleeping . . .

KIM Jason, you're scaring me! What did you *do*?

JASON O.K. I admit I did . . . something. I guess. I used another person wrongly, I committed a sin. I see that—yeah. But she won't let me apologize. And Dad right away takes her side. I go to that man in ut-ter despair and a sickness unto death, and what's he tell me?—"Shame is a powerful emotion, Jason." Quotes fucking Aristotle! For sure, he hates me! "This is the worst thing I have ever imagined you doing, Ja-son." THIS IS HOW MY FATHER CONSOLES ME IN MY HOUR OF NEED. *(Pause)* My suitemates at Dartmouth last year, *they* prac-tically raped a drunk freshman girl on the fucking green, for God's sake, *their* fathers show up the next day with their lawyers threaten-ing a counter-suit for libel—that's the kind of *faith* some fathers have in their sons! That is what is absent from my life.

KIM My God, Jason, did you rape a girl?

JASON *(Moving off, shamefacedly)* No! No! No! *(Pause)* She isn't a girl.
KIM *(On her feet, stricken)* My brother is a rapist? A sex fiend? Wait—
JASON *(Waving her away, exiting)* I'm out of here—"To Gethsemane!"

Lights out.

SCENE 4

That night, in the carriage house rented by NEDRA MINSK. *A single large studio-room that serves as a workroom/living room/bedroom. On the walls are blown-up posters of stark black and white images (Depression-era photos by Walker Evans, perhaps). A cluttered work bench with camera equipment, negatives, prints, etc. Rock music of an exotic, sultry type may be playing; we hear a heavy, pulsing downbeat.* NEDRA *leans over the workbench, examining photographs which she is mounting and arranging in a sequence. The room is sparsely furnished and clothes may be strewn about. A pair of large gardening shears is visible, though inconspicuous.*

NEDRA *is a passionate young woman of thirty-one, extremely striking, and with an air of tightly-coiled sexual energy; her features are dramatic, intense. Full-bodied springy hair. A volatile person whose emotions are close to the surface, masking more subterranean layers of personality. Her sexual aggression is meant to intimidate, yet has an element of play in it.*

NEDRA *wears black—skin-tight top, leotard—with a scarf knotted around her waist or neck; she is barefoot, and her toenails are painted to match her fingernails and lipstick—dark maroon.*

A knock at the door, stage right. NEDRA, *absorbed in her work, does not answer. Knock recurs.*

NEDRA *(Yelling over the music)* If that's you, you sorry prick, nobody's
    home.

Silence.

NEDRA *returns to her work, her movements reflecting anger. After a beat or two, the knock recurs, hesitantly.* NEDRA *drops what she is doing and strides to the door; opens it, suspiciously, on a chain.*

NEDRA Yes?
TOBIAS *(Much intimidated)* I—I'm sorry to— I'm the father of—Jason
    Harte—
NEDRA *(Incensed)* Father of who! *That* shit? Get out! *(About to shut the
    door)*

TOBIAS *(Urgently)* Please, may I—speak with—

NEDRA You can speak with the cops, that's who you can speak with. *I* don't have anything to say to you!

TOBIAS But I—

NEDRA rushes to pick up the shears; returns to the door and unlatches the chain; opens the door; and, as TOBIAS steps inside, brandishes the shears at him.

NEDRA I told your son, and I'll tell you: don't fuck with me, mister. I don't take shit from anybody, got it?

TOBIAS is utterly astounded by NEDRA. He backs away from her, colliding with a chair, and nearly falls down.

NEDRA *(Threatening him with the shears)* Want to be a "victim?" Want to know what it feels like? I'll make a WOMAN of you.

TOBIAS *(Horrified)* No, wait! No—

NEDRA *(Incensed)* See how you like it! *(Clicking the shears at TOBIAS's groin.)*

TOBIAS backs away, panicked; collides with a pole lamp.

TOBIAS Please, I assure you—that isn't necessary. I'm really—harmless.

NEDRA So was Baby Face. Where's he now, hiding out in the bushes?— in Daddy's car? I told him to get out of my face PERMANENTLY.

TOBIAS Jason is nowhere near. I've come alone.

NEDRA *(Angrily, self-righteously)* To try to talk me out of filing charges?—well, fuck that! Nobody puts pressure on *me*.

TOBIAS *(Quickly)* Oh, no! I can see that.

NEDRA Nobody ever tells me what to do. Even if it's the right thing to do.

TOBIAS I can see *that*.

NEDRA What did you say your name was?

TOBIAS Tobias Harte. Jason's father . . . *(He puts out his hand to be shaken, but NEDRA is holding the shears; he withdraws his hand)* And you're Nedra—?

NEDRA Nedra Minsk.

TOBIAS *(Feeble geniality)* Well, I'm . . . very happy to . . . meet you. Except, under these circumstances . . . *(Pause)* Do you really need that weapon?

NEDRA A woman always needs a weapon, because a man always has a weapon. *(She lets the shears fall on a table)* So, what do you want?

TOBIAS This is a terrible, tragic thing that has happened. I'm sure it must be a—

NEDRA No, it isn't.

TOBIAS No, it isn't—what?

NEDRA   A misunderstanding.

TOBIAS   My son Jason simply isn't the kind of—

NEDRA   How do you know? When's the last time you saw him with an erection?

TOBIAS   *(Slight wince)*   Not recently . . .

NEDRA   And to your next question—no.

TOBIAS   "No?" What did I ask?

NEDRA   Would I be willing to settle out of court. NO.

TOBIAS   *(A bit dazed)*   Yes, —no: of course not.

NEDRA   *Rape* is *rape, no* is *no*, a woman says "no" what does she mean?

TOBIAS   "No"—?

NEDRA   "NO." *(Pause)* So there's nothing to discuss.

TOBIAS   There's nothing to discuss . . . ?

NEDRA   If I didn't despise the white fascist cops in this town I'd have filed charges by now. I'm undecided . . . I'm *not* vindictive.

TOBIAS   You're not vindictive . . .

NEDRA   I'm thirty-one years old, I've outgrown merely personal rage. It's generic rage I'm into.

TOBIAS   "Generic rage"—?

NEDRA   Must you be an echo? Can't you think of your own words? Everything I say, you repeat.

TOBIAS   I'm sorry, I . . . seem to be overwhelmed. I'm not accustomed to . . . being overwhelmed.

NEDRA   "Tobias" is a dog's name, isn't it? How'd you get named it?

TOBIAS   *(Startled)*   A dog's name—?

NEDRA   Actually, I mean "Toby." "Toby" was the name of a dog once, when I was a kid, not ours but next door . . . It seems weird to me, parents naming a baby "Tobias."

TOBIAS   I suppose they didn't do it deliberately.

NEDRA   *(Peering at him)*   You're *sure* you're at the right place?— you don't look like you'd be that kid's father, somehow.

TOBIAS   *(Faintly)*   There wouldn't be more than one of us out tonight, would there?

NEDRA   More than one what?

TOBIAS   Distraught father of a son accused of . . .

NEDRA   *(Mockingly)*   Can't you say it, Tobias?—"rape."

TOBIAS   "R-rape."

NEDRA   Not "r-rape": "rape."

TOBIAS   *(Clears his throat)*   "Rape."

NEDRA   C'mon, like a man: "RAPE."

TOBIAS   "RAPE."

NEDRA   You're almost there: "RAPE."

The music on the tape has run out; there is an abrupt silence.

TOBIAS *(Loudly)* "RAPE."

NEDRA   Great, so . . . what's there to discuss? We're in agreement.

TOBIAS *(Agitated)*   But it couldn't have been . . . r-rape . . . could it . . . really? Jason is such a, so . . . incompetent. *(Pause)* Miss Minsk—*Ms.,* I mean—*Ms. Minsk*—would you agree to see Jason?—in my company of course?—he wants to explain—apologize—clear up this terrible— confusion. I've never seen the boy so upset, frightened—

NEDRA *(Flaring up)*   He's upset? He's frightened? What about *me?* I'm the fucking victim! *(On her feet, moving about aggressively)* I could be pregnant,—I could have AIDS.

TOBIAS *(Stunned)*   Oh, not AIDS, surely. I can attest to that.

NEDRA   *You* can attest to that? Who the hell are *you,* some kind of med- ical wizard? I'll get a court order to force your precious Jason to have a blood test, I don't have to take *your* word for it.

TOBIAS   Of course, of course. *(Passes a hand over his eyes, gropes for a chair as if suddenly faint)*

NEDRA *(Less vehemently, though still suspiciously)*   Jesus, you're *white.* You O.K.? *(She shoves a chair to* TOBIAS, *who sinks into it weakly)* I suppose it *is* a shock, for a Mount Orion citizen, to discover his own flesh and blood is a rapist.

NEDRA *moves to the rear while* TOBIAS, *trying to recover his composure, gazes out toward the audience.*

TOBIAS   I never wanted a personal life. *(Pause)* I knew it would be distracting.

NEDRA *takes a bottle of spring water from a small refrigerator; pours glasses of water for herself and* TOBIAS; *comes forward.*

TOBIAS *(As if trying a new tack)*   Miss Mink—Ms.—

NEDRA   It's Minsk.

TOBIAS   I mean—Minsk. Ms. Minsk—

NEDRA *(Coolly)*   "Minsk" was my father's name, "Nedra" is my name. So call me "Nedra," O.K.?

TOBIAS *(With difficulty)*   "Nedra"—Jason just told me about this to- night, I had no idea. HE says he has tried to see you . . . call you. You refuse to—. Of course, you have every—. *(Pause, in anguish)* My God, what a nightmare! If only it hadn't happened!

NEDRA *(Bemused)*   "—hadn't happened?" Yes, well, it *has. (Hands him a glass)*

TOBIAS *(Surprised)*   Oh! Thank you. *(Nearly drops glass)*

NEDRA *(As if to explain her own solicitude)*   Well, I figure, you're look- ing kind of . . . pathetic, *(Peering at him)* Wow, your hand sure shakes. Is that real? It's like, vibrating.

TOBIAS *(Apologetically)*   I guess I'm . . . overwhelmed. *(Drinks, dribbles water, wipes at himself, etc.)* Oh! Sorry! The taste is unexpectedly tart.

NEDRA   You older guys are something!

TOBIAS   Yes, well . . . what we lose in energy, we gain in technique.

NEDRA   What are you, a lawyer or something? *(TOBIAS shakes head)* Doctor? *(He shakes head)* Executive in some megabucks corporation? *(He shakes head)*

TOBIAS   Administrator. Of a research center.

NEDRA   Research? Like with chemicals? Germ warfare? Experimenting on animals? Destroying the ozone?

TOBIAS   Oh no, no! —we concentrate on *ideas.* We're harmless.

NEDRA   Your son said, you're disappointed in him 'cause he isn't turning into you. Says you're a BIG DEAL. HOT SHIT. Eh?

TOBIAS coughs, drops water glass, water spills on shoes, etc.

TOBIAS *(Wiping up, with handkerchief, clumsily)*   Sorry.

NEDRA   Yeah, you really look . . . ashy. Like a mannequin with the DT's.

TOBIAS   A what?

NEDRA   Mannequin. Store dummy. *(Pause)* You notice, I don't help people clean up their messes. You spill: you mop. I've got the instinct, for sure,—it's like sex, in a woman: right in the pit of the belly. *(Clutches self)* Somebody spills something, I want to help clean up. But I don't. I've overcome it.

TOBIAS   You've never been a mother, then.

NEDRA *(Sharply)*   No, I have not.

TOBIAS *(Ruefully)*   Instinct has always been my downfall.

NEDRA   To clean up other people's messes?

TOBIAS   What other kind are there? *(Pause)* The instinct to do the right thing, the . . . necessary thing. *(Grimly)* The perfect thing.

NEDRA   Wow, aren't we noble! *(Laughs)* Like junior says, HOT SHIT.

TOBIAS *(Flustered)*   Miss—Ms.—Nedra—do you mean to be insulting?

NEDRA   Yes.

A pause.

TOBIAS *(Swallowing pride)*   Well . . . you, er, succeed.

NEDRA   I tell the truth, I don't bullshit.

TOBIAS *(Quickly)*   Oh yes! I'm . . . sure. *(Pause, then with dread)* What did Jason do here, last Saturday night?

NEDRA   What did he say he did?

TOBIAS   He . . . says he did not force you. Into any kind of . . . inti-mate—

NEDRA   Fucking. *(Pause)* Go on.

TOBIAS He admits he . . . he'd been drinking. The two of you . . . struggled. *(Miserably)* He . . . knocked you down?

NEDRA Go on.

TOBIAS He . . . claimed the two of you had been intimate . . . the night before.

NEDRA *(Flaring up, defensively)* What's that got to do with it?

TOBIAS Well, I . . . suppose he thought . . . he'd be welcome, the next night.

NEDRA What do I care what *he* thought!

TOBIAS I'm just trying to explain a twenty-year-old's perspective, not to justify it. He admits he may have been overexcited.

NEDRA I get excited too, but I don't rape people. *(Pause)* So, then what? He knocks me down, then what?

TOBIAS *(Pained)* He said you "went crazy" and "attacked" him with a pair of shears. You cut his hair—which I'd say was a good thing. *(NEDRA does not respond to the "humor")* And you chased him out.

NEDRA And that's it? Well, he left out some crucial minutes there.

TOBIAS I was afraid of that.

NEDRA Like, I told him "stop" and he didn't. I told him "get out" and he didn't. Saying how he loved me, he was crazy about me, got me on the floor. Ripped my clothes. Stuck his knee between my legs. *Raped* me. *(Breathless)* Like, all that your precious Jason left out.

TOBIAS *(Hand over eyes)* Oh God.

NEDRA *(Just slightly qualifying)* Of course, there are degrees of rape.

TOBIAS Degrees—?

NEDRA Why's this such a revelation to you, Tobias—you're a man, aren't you? *(As TOBIAS winces)* Maybe he thought it wasn't rape, maybe he wasn't thinking at all. That's not my problem. I came to Mount Orion as an experiment, to do a photography project. Not on assignment—for myself. A lily-white American suburb, houses selling for as high as two million dollars—

TOBIAS Not very many, surely. *My* house—

NEDRA *(Not hearing, dramatically)* —a pocket of decadence in a culture of shame. Racial prejudice, misogyny, fascist-Republican politics—

TOBIAS But Mount Orion has been integrated for thirty years.

NEDRA *(Mild incredulity)* Only superficially—skin deep! Your blacks, Asians, all *white*. *(Shivers)* I look at myself and it freaks me out—"Am I next?"

TOBIAS *(Having gotten to his feet to dab at water on the floor, now moves about, with a hesitant but growing curiosity)* So you're in Mount Orion photographing "Disaffected Suburban-Caucasian Youth of the American *Fin-de-Siècle*."

NEDRA Hey, how'd you know?

TOBIAS I even know what *"fin-de-siècle"* means. *(Peering at prints on worktable, genuinely surprised and impressed)* Why these are—remarkable.

TOBIAS's interest in her work makes NEDRA *uneasy, yet is obviously flattering. She's ambivalent about giving this man any opening—isn't he the enemy?*

NEDRA *(Partly blocking his view, pushing some prints aside)* Yeah, well—they're O.K. Not what I came here for exactly, but—O.K.

TOBIAS *(Selecting a print)* My God, is this Jason? *My* Jason? He looks so . . . transformed somehow. *(Staring)* I almost wouldn't know him.

NEDRA *(Curtly)* Probably you haven't looked at him in a long time.

NEDRA, *wanting to take charge, sorts through prints and shows some to Tobias. Obviously proud of her work.*

NEDRA The weird thing, kids like your son are so eager to have their pictures taken. Like they'll be made real, or something. You know how primitive people fear the camera, think their souls will be stolen from them?—these kids, they're hoping the camera will *give* them souls. *(Handing* TOBIAS *prints)*

TOBIAS These friends of Jason's—the Trevor boy, Billy Wingate—they all look . . . significant, somehow. *(Pause)* What is Jason doing here?

NEDRA Pissing into a fountain. I caught that light streaming through the leaves so it's, like, dreamy, see? This arc here balances this one. *(Pauses, as she admires her work)* This one, it's Michelangelo's David, get it?—the way the kid's head and body are posed. A lucky shot.

TOBIAS *This* is my son?

NEDRA The human body is beautiful, you see it right. It's just personalities that get in the way.

TOBIAS I don't know him at all.

NEDRA *(An abstract air, studying the prints)* The human form as a transcendent aesthetic object . . . it's maybe, we just inhabit our bodies, we haven't earned them. *(Pause)* But that isn't the kind of photography I want, right now.

TOBIAS What do you mean?—these are excellent. You're very talented.

NEDRA *(Quickly)* Oh, shit. "Talented." If I can't make the camera do what I want it to do . . .

She takes the prints back and drops them on the table, as if dismissively; rubs temples, eyes.

NEDRA It's like it has a will of it's own, y'know? I came to Mount Orion to expose it, not to find beauty. *(Self-mocking)* "Nedra Minsk's corrosive social satire"—"pitiless vision"—*(Pause)* These spoiled-affluent-Caucasian bourgeois kids! You get to know them, you can't help liking them. *(Pause)* Some of them.

TOBIAS   Is that a weakness, liking people?

NEDRA   It is when it fucks you up. *(Pause)* You want a little more—? *(Lifting her water glass)*

TOBIAS *(Courteously)*   Thank you, no, I'm still—damp.

NEDRA   So you're not close to your son, eh?

TOBIAS   Not exactly.

NEDRA   That's O.K., I wasn't close to my father, either. It's probably a good thing. With some fathers, I mean.

NEDRA pours herself more water and drinks it thirstily.

NEDRA   He's got a mother, though?

TOBIAS   Who?

NEDRA   The rapist.

TOBIAS *(Pained)*   I wish you wouldn't . . .

NEDRA   Does he?

TOBIAS   Of course. Yes.

NEDRA   She knows you're here?

TOBIAS   Not exactly.

NEDRA   She knows about the situation, though?

TOBIAS   Not exactly.

NEDRA *(Ironically)*   So, what's it?—not worth her attention, yet? She's some real sensitive lady *her* feelings should be spared?

TOBIAS *(Stiffly)*   Paula knows something upsetting has happened, but not what.

NEDRA   So, who's gonna tell her?

TOBIAS   I will, if I must.

NEDRA   She's close to her son, she'd want to know. *I'd* want to know if it was a kid of mine. *(Pause)* You're thinking I'm vindictive, I'm the enemy, I'm *not*. *(Pause)* I maybe exploited them, winning their trust, you might say. I look younger than my age. *(Pause, begins to speak rapidly)* What happened was, I'd been hanging out with these kids, maybe three weeks off and on, then last Friday night I invited some of them back here, and Jason was one of them; the one I chose to . . . stay the night. Good-looking kid, and sexy as hell. *(Shaking her head)* Guys that age, God!—it's like squirting, y'know, that lighter fluid stuff on a fire.

TOBIAS *(Uncomfortably)*   Is it.

NEDRA   The reaction's always a little more than you can count on.

TOBIAS   So—Jason was the one you "chose?"

NEDRA   Just that once. We, er, got along . . . it was good. I was lonely.

Yeah I *was* weak. Then the next night, late, he shows up again, uninvited, and drunk. Saying I had to let him in, he didn't have anywhere else to go. I let him in for a while then saw what it was, I told him please go away, I tried to be nice.

TOBIAS   And . . . he wouldn't go away?

NEDRA   He *was* leaving, then he grabbed me, almost cracked my ribs, like a giant baby, and strong. My mistake was . . . *(Sudden change of tone, as NEDRA moves restlessly about)* Fuck it, no: it wasn't my mistake. I AM NOT THE GUILTY PARTY. *(Her voice has risen, now she makes an effort to speak more calmly)* O.K. to tell the truth what happened exactly, I don't know, I've got a temper and this kid, he's combustible, we both sort of . . . blacked out. *(Pause)* I remember I got the shears, and . . . I cut his hair? *(Laughs shrilly)* Lucky for him that's all I did.

TOBIAS   There *was* evidence of . . . sexual intercourse?

NEDRA   *(Defiantly)*   Sexual *assault.*

TOBIAS   Have you seen a doctor?

NEDRA   What doctor? Why? *(Arms crossed over her body protectively)*

TOBIAS   If you were injured—

NEDRA   "If?" "If?" What the fuck are you saying, mister—"if?"

TOBIAS   I only meant—

NEDRA   Here, you want to see? You want evidence? *(Yanking up top, tugging down pants to show that, indeed, she is bruised: her breasts, midriff, stomach. Behavior that is both desperate, and yet exhibitionistic. Taunting TOBIAS, who is stunned)* Want to stick, your fingers in my *side?*

TOBIAS   Nedra, Nedra, I— *(Approaching her)* Is there—? Anything I—?

TOBIAS has approached NEDRA, who now faces him aggressively; he begins to back up. Clumsy, comic: A repetition of his colliding with the lamp pole, the chair.

NEDRA   *(Menacing fists)*   Didn't get what you came for, eh? Playing on my sympathy, eh? *(Slaps or punches him)* How d'you like it, "To-bi-as?" Yeah, how d'you like it?

TOBIAS   "Wait, I—" "Please" "N-Nedra—"

The enraged woman pursues him. He backs up across nearly the width of the stage, stumbling and swaying; trying to fend off NEDRA without exactly touching her.

NEDRA   *(Ecstatic)*   Why'd you come here? What did you want? This, eh? This? Eh? *(She strikes him in the face, and his nose begins to bleed)* A little blood, how'd you like it!

TOBIAS   Damn you!

NEDRA *(Pursuing him)*   How d'you like it!

TOBIAS *(Catching her in an embrace, pinioning her arms)*   I like it.

Lights out.

ACT 2

SCENE 1

Lights up. TOBIAS's *office.* TOBIAS *is at his desk, impeccably dressed and deeply absorbed in his work, preparing notes for a meeting; looking through long strips of computer printouts that coil along the floor. We hear* NEDRA's *music.* TOBIAS *is distracted by a thought—rises to his feet—becomes entangled in the printouts—kicks his way free and goes to the window to look out dreamily. When he hears* WILLY REBB *coming, he hurries back to his desk and assumes his previous pose.*

WILLY REBB *is hearty and good-natured as usual, but guarded beneath; he suspects trouble. He wears a checked sports coat, a red vest, a yellow bowtie and matching lapel handkerchief. He holds aloft the first page of the Metro Section of* The New York Times, *where the lead story is headlined:* MT. ORION, N.J. INSTITUTE DIRECTOR CHOSEN TO HEAD D.C. RESEARCH CENTER. *Dr. Sylvan Flamm's photograph shows a white-haired "distinguished" gentleman.*

REBB *(Blustering into office)*   Whooeee! Here it is! At long last! Terrific news, eh? *(His big smile is met by a somewhat forced smile of* TOBIAS's*)* Of course, you knew, Toby—?

TOBIAS   Dr. Flamm called me yesterday morning.

REBB *(Whistling)*   That's a long time to keep a secret, in Mount Orion! And, um, for Paula, too—?

TOBIAS   I didn't tell Paula immediately.

REBB   Didn't tell your own wife? *(Shakes head)* Well, it's damned good news—we all move up a notch, eh? Sylvan is delighted: down in D.C. no one will notice the man's a little, um, shall we say, out to lunch. *(Forefinger to lips)*

TOBIAS *(Protesting)*   Dr. Flamm has been an excellent director—a man of the highest principles—

REBB *(Applauding)*   Quite right, Toby! *(Comes to shake* TOBIAS's *hand vigorously)* An "eloquent induction speech by the incoming Director!" And when are *you* taking over, podna?

TOBIAS   I've taken over. I've been going through Dr. Flamm's files. *(Indicates paper, etc., on desk)* I've found some things that have . . . disturbed me greatly.

REBB *(Overlapping, not hearing, pumping* TOBIAS's *hand)*   Dear friend, I congratulate you. I am so truly happy for you. The Board's unanimous choice. *(Finger to lips)* Yes, I know, I know!—"confidential." But, um, the Board consulted me, and, um, well—I spoke from the heart, of the—Harte. *(Laughs)* "From the *heart,* of the *Harte.*" *(As TOBIAS smiles minimally)* Hell, I just told the truth. "Toby Harte is the only man for the job—yessir." *(Pause)* You're looking ecstatic, as usual, eh?

TOBIAS *(Sincerely)* I *am* pleased, of course. I've worked for this . . . for many years.

REBB Mustn't overdo it, eh. "All things in moderation"—as Fatty Arbuckle said. *(Laughs heartily)* Well, hell, *I'm* happy. A man of your ideals, heading the Institute! Your integrity! Just when our fund-raising campaign is bearing fruit! *(Sly humor)* Why, who would have predicted, in a freezing sleet storm in Morgantown, West Virginia, many years ago, when a nine-year-old boy entrusted with the delivery of the morning paper failed to complete his route . . . failed to deliver his papers . . . collapsed while frantically pedalling his bicycle . . .

TOBIAS *(Startled, stung)* Who told you that?

REBB . . . failed so ignominiously, poor little bugger, who'd've predicted he'd end up Director of the Mount Orion Institute for Independent Research! My, yes.

TOBIAS I didn't realize I'd told you that. *(Solemnly)* Well, the future did look grim.

REBB I spoke with Paula on the phone just now, to congratulate *her.* She says she can't wait to remodel Hill House.

TOBIAS I've told Paula, there will be no remodeling of Hill House for some time. I've spent the weekend drafting a new austerity budget. Beginning today.

REBB After lunch, I hope. *(Checks watch)* Sorry I'm late, old friend. I've been on the phone all morning with Melva Upchurch—Whew! *(Waggles little finger in ear, to indicate that the woman is loquacious)* I'm starved.

TOBIAS *(Startled, severe)* Melva *Upchurch?*

REBB Byron Upchurch's mother, you know.

TOBIAS You're still pursuing *that*—? I thought I'd convinced Dr. Flamm—

REBB *(Smoothly)* Toby, my friend, let's have lunch; we can discuss it then. You made reservations, I assume? Laurent's?

TOBIAS No, actually not.

REBB The Mount Orion Inn, then—?

TOBIAS I'm afraid not.

REBB *(A bit crestfallen)* Well—the Institute dining room *is* quite elegant, overlooking the, the lake, or whatever it is out there. It's just the wine list that's, um, a bit below par.

TOBIAS *(Who has been taking deli containers, a plastic bottle of spring water, plastic cups, plastic forks, white paper napkins, out of a desk drawer)* We're eating in my office, Willy. Have a seat.

REBB *(Appalled)* Eating—here? We're having lunch—here?

TOBIAS *(Without irony)* Actually, I always eat my lunch here. I like to work right through. It's quite pleasant, really . . . sometimes I look out at the scenery.

REBB *(As if in shock, stock still)* We're having lunch—here? Eating—here? On today of all days? Why, this was to be a celebratory lunch, Toby, I'd thought.

TOBIAS It *is* celebratory—there's extra cole slaw, and an extra pickle for you. There's a choice of white meat turkey, tuna salad, and my usual egg salad—the turkey's on rye, the others are on whole wheat, dry. The spring water has tincture of lemon. *(Pours water into plastic cups, etc.)*

REBB *(Slowly)* Toby, I'd heard rumors that . . . sometimes . . . you ate lunch at your desk . . . but I'd naturally assumed it was some sort of smear spread by your enemies.

TOBIAS That's bracing to hear.

REBB What is?

TOBIAS That I have enemies. When a man is unopposed, when things get too easy for him, it isn't salutary; he can become complacent. "Pay attention to your enemies—for they are the first to discover your mistakes." Antisthenes. In translation.

REBB Who?

TOBIAS A fourth century B.C. Greek philosopher. *(Indicating chair)* Willy, I've slotted you in for fifty minutes, and we have a good deal to discuss . . . some very crucial things to discuss. *(Tense smile)* You're already twenty minutes late.

REBB *(A bit sullenly)* If Sylvan wanted to see me on the hour, he always meant twenty past. *(Sits)* Well, this is, er, an historic occasion: *déjeuner sur le desk* with the incoming Director of the Institute. If I'd known, I might have brought a brown bag.

TOBIAS *(A genial host, handing REBB a napkin, spreading out items on a desk)* Well! Dig right in. I'm famished too, I've been up since five thirty. This is the turkey, this is the tuna fish, this is the egg salad. They've learned to go light on the mayonnaise.

REBB I get my choice?

TOBIAS Actually, you can have two sandwiches if you like. I splurged a little.

REBB But you want the egg salad.

TOBIAS *(Hesitantly)* Why, no . . . not at all. *You* have the egg salad if you want it.

REBB The egg salad, and one other? I can have?

TOBIAS   Of course, Willy. Go ahead.

REBB   But the egg salad is your favorite, Toby. I sense it.

TOBIAS   Oh no, it's just a habit, I suppose. *(Pause)*

REBB   I'll take the turkey, then.

TOBIAS   No, really, if you want the egg salad—

REBB   Absolutely not. I wouldn't hear of it.

TOBIAS   It's just that . . . egg salad reminds me of . . . grammar school. My lunch bucket, thermos . . .

REBB   Lunch "bucket"—?

TOBIAS   That's what they were called in Morgantown, West Virginia.

REBB   What was in the thermos?

TOBIAS   Tepid milk.

REBB   *(Shuddering)*   Sounds delicious.

TOBIAS   It wasn't meant to be tepid, the thermos didn't exactly work. *(Unwrapping sandwich with boyish enthusiasm)* There was a certain . . . odor . . . to the inside of a lunch bucket, impossible to describe. My mother scrubbed it out periodically, but the odor came right back.

REBB   An odor of . . . egg salad sandwich?

TOBIAS   And slightly rotten banana. And waxed paper used so many times it was crinkly and opaque.

REBB   This plastic wrap isn't quite *it*, eh? You can see through it. *(Pause, biting into sandwich)* The turkey's fine . . . maybe a little dry.

TOBIAS   We can share the wastebasket, Willy. Move right in. *(Shifting his swivel chair about)*

REBB   *(Fastidious disdain)*   The wastebasket?

TOBIAS   I usually eat over it. That way, my desk isn't defiled by crumbs and such. *(Leaning over wastebasket as he eats)* Did you want mustard? *(Hands REBB a packet)* Go easy, though, it's high in sodium.

REBB   *(Maneuvering himself awkwardly to the wastebasket)*   You really should have a wastebasket with recesses for knees. *(Eating)*

TOBIAS   Oh, this one is good enough for me.

REBB   . . . Salt?

TOBIAS   Salt substitute. *(Handing it to him)*

REBB   Um. Delicious. You really couldn't get anything like this at Laurent's.

TOBIAS   The egg salad is fine. Maybe just slightly crumbly today.

REBB   That's one of the hazards, without mayonnaise. *(Lifting water cup)* Well, Toby, here's to you: congratulations! It couldn't be happening to a more deserving man. *(Drinks)* Mmm. The "tincture of lemon" is . . . subtle. I *like* it.

TOBIAS   *(Drinking)*   I always used to get plain, but the other day . . . someone turned me on to this.

REBB   Turned you on, eh? *(Sipping)* I like the carbonation, too. There's always something devil-may-care about *bubbles.*

TOBIAS   Here, help yourself to the cole slaw. It's a little too sweet for me.

REBB   *(Eating, with plastic fork)* Mmm!

TOBIAS   Please take the tuna fish sandwich, and the pickles. Both pickles are for you.

REBB   Both? That's generous. *(Devouring an immense pickle)* Nothing like kosher dill, eh!

TOBIAS   A little too salty for me.

REBB   Hmmm, yes. Paula mentioned . . . your blood pressure, eh? Or is it the ulcer? Colitis? —No: colitis is my Minnie, isn't it. *(Lifts pickle, brandishes it suggestively)* This I'll wrap for later. *(Patting lips, sighing)* Well, quite a feast. You'll have to come over to my wastebasket— I mean, my office—next time.

TOBIAS   *(Tidying up, wrapping things in napkins and placing neatly in wastebasket)*   I hope you weren't disappointed, Willy. We have so many serious, and confidential, things to discuss . . .

REBB   *(As if to deflect the subject, adroitly)*   May I—? *(Pours himself and TOBIAS more water)* Unless this will make us too giddy.

TOBIAS   No, fine. I'm . . . thirsty, too.

REBB   Good old Toby—I s'pose you ran five miles this morning, before coming to the office?

TOBIAS   Only three. *(Pause)* If we're finished with lunch, Willy, we—

REBB   *(Brightly deflecting subject)*   Hey, how's the family? Forgot to ask.

TOBIAS   Who?

REBB   You know: wife, children . . . when you leave the office, and go home, they're *there.*

TOBIAS   *(Vaguely)*   They're fine. Willy, this is painful for me—

REBB   *(Excitedly)*   Paula mentioned, just now when I called, that a reporter from the *New York Times* wants an interview with you. And the *Newark Star-Ledger* wants to do a feature on your entire family. You're a New Jersey celebrity!

TOBIAS   *(Distressed)*   But this is terrible. The appointment isn't official until the Board announces it. I hope Paula was discreet.

REBB   *(Ambiguously)*   Your wife, of all women, is the most discreet.

TOBIAS   *(To himself)*   I can't allow things to swerve out of *control.* *(Pause, vague and polite)* And how is . . . Minnie?

REBB   Wonderful!—that's to say, no worse. *(Confidentially)* Minnie may be hallucinating a wee bit lately. Since the hysterectomy, she's been on massive estrogen dosages. You have to wonder what that will do to a woman, eh? *(Shudders)* She told me she saw a man she swore was you, Toby, on the access road out beyond Ridge Road—y'know, behind the

Eaton's? Day before yesterday, she said. This person crossed into the woods and disappeared. Minnie had been playing bridge with her group at Fanny Eaton's and was driving home. I said to her, "Why on earth would Toby Harte be skulking around in the woods out there?" and Minnie got huffy and said, "How would I know?" Women are so damned illogical.

TOBIAS *(Not looking at REBB)*   That certainly wasn't me.

REBB *(Seems to believe him)*   Just what I told Minnie.

TOBIAS *(Agitated)*   I only jog between six and seven A.M. and I only jog on the Institute trail . . . the hourglass path through the woods . . . *(Gestures to indicate hourglass shape, repeated)* . . . eleven times around and it's three miles exactly. *(Pause)* Willy, we really should talk about the matter at hand. *(Grim, posture rigid)* The reason—reasons—I asked you to come by.

REBB *(Rubbing hands ebulliently, disingenuous smile)*   Shoot, podna.

TOBIAS *(Looking through documents on desk)*   You've been chief legal counsel for the Institute for fourteen years, and involved in fund-raising for the past six years. Dr. Flamm always expressed the highest confidence in you, and trusted you . . .

REBB *(Genially)*   Why, I sure hope so. What are you getting at, Toby?

TOBIAS *(Frowning at a sheet of paper)*   I've discovered some puzzling irregularities in various files. Faculty "expenses" for which there are no receipts; columns of figures added up incorrectly—but never to the disadvantage of the party involved; pilfering of toilet paper, Kleenex, and soap from the Institute restrooms—

REBB   But we have *liquid* soap in the restrooms—

TOBIAS   —and Dixie cups. Last night, consumed by curiosity, I called Dr. Steilvogel, the renowned Biblical scholar, to ask what on earth three thousand nine hundred and ninety-eight dollars for "F.D." was, for August, billed to the Institute, and he admitted that F.D. is his pet dachshund Fritzie Dog. She had to have emergency surgery . . . *six* mastectomies. Dr. Steilvogel claimed that, since Fritzie is crucial to his life, and he is crucial to the Institute, the expense was justified.

REBB   These Biblical scholars! Always think they have a *mandate*.

TOBIAS *(Shift in tone)*   As for you, Willy . . .

REBB *(Just slightly flustered)*   Eh? Me?

TOBIAS   . . . the irregularities are more elusive, but potentially far more serious.

REBB   Irregularities—?

TOBIAS *(Hesitantly)*   Certain of your expense account items, Willy. What's this, back in February of last year— *(Shows him a print-out of numbers)* two thousand three hundred and seventy-seven dollars for "s.s. for v.t.g."

REBB (*Studying the item*) Hmmm! "s.s. for v.t.g." Oh yes—"secretarial service for visiting Tokyo gentlemen." You remember, Toby, the two Sushibito men. I was in charge of hosting them.

TOBIAS (*Indicating a stapled receipt*) Secretarial service from the "Nonpareil Escort Agency" in Newark?

REBB Oh, no, that must be a mistake.

TOBIAS Here's the receipt. Your signature.

REBB Maybe it's a forgery?

TOBIAS (*Leafing through papers*) A case of 1962 Bordeaux . . . car rental in Coral Gables, Florida . . . receipts from the Four Seasons, Le Cirque, the Oak Room at the Plaza . . . But what upsets me most, Willy, is this. (*Showing* REBB *a copy of a letter*) What do you make of it?

REBB (*Putting on reading glasses, scanning letter*) Hmmm! A copy of a letter from you to Ezra Piranha . . . two September of this year . . . encouraging him and his brother in establishing the Piranha Center for Ethical Studies at the Institute. The promise of a twenty-one million dollar endowment. (*Big smile, removes glasses*) Marvelous, my friend!

TOBIAS (*Grimly*) Except that I didn't write this unctuous, fawning, salivating letter.

REBB But here's your signature.

TOBIAS That is not my signature, and you know it. This is a forgery.

REBB (*As if scandalized*) No! What? (*Peering at letter*) Toby, this is your handwriting.

TOBIAS It's forged, Goddamn it.

REBB But this is your signature. Look—(*Takes up another item on* TOBIAS's *desk, squints at it*)—see, here's your signature, too; they're almost identical.

TOBIAS Because this one was copied from my signature, to make it "almost identical."

REBB (*As if naive*) But, Toby, how can you tell? (*Looking from one to the other*) I'm damned if *I* can.

TOBIAS BECAUSE I DIDN'T WRITE THE GODDAMNED LETTER, AND I DIDN'T SIGN IT.

REBB Then who did?

TOBIAS Don't you know?

REBB (*Huffly*) I hope you're not accusing Dr. Flamm. After all he's done for you!

TOBIAS Willy, you're the one who's been associating with the Piranhas for years.

REBB Not for years—just since last year. Piranha Construction did the renovations on our house, added a rec room, solid oak beams and hardwood floors—you've seen it. All the materials discounted. And when we build here—

TOBIAS *(Takes back letter, slaps it down on his desk)* Willy, I believe *you* forged my signature.

REBB *(Astounded)* What! You're accusing me of—forgery? Of dishonesty?

TOBIAS You deny it?

REBB This is dangerously close to slander, Toby. *(On his feet, pacing about, belligerent)* How can you!

TOBIAS You deny it?

REBB I . . . qualify . . . it. It may have been perceived by both Dr. Flamm and I that a letter of some sort, from you, as Assistant Director, was expected by Mr. Piranha. A matter of protocol, courtesy . . .

TOBIAS And since I would never have written such a letter, you wrote it for me?

REBB *(Faltering a bit)* A, er, letter came to be . . . written.

TOBIAS *(Voice quavering, on his feet too)* You know how I feel about the Piranhas—they're crooks. We don't want their money.

REBB Other institutions in the area, including the Mount Orion Theological Seminary, don't take your high moral tone. The Piranhas' money is fine with them.

TOBIAS The Theological Seminary? I don't believe it.

REBB The Piranha Chair of Christian-Humanist Values. Eight million dollars.

TOBIAS I'm . . . shocked. Ezra and Elias Piranha will be indicted soon for stock market manipulation, fraud . . .

REBB *(A retort)* But they aren't indicted yet.

TOBIAS Men who cheated investors, including elderly pensioners, of eight million dollars—

REBB *(A new tack)* Toby, where's your compassion? Don't you believe in forgiveness?

TOBIAS But the Piranhas haven't confessed to their crimes—

REBB *(As if reasonable)* Can't you forgive them anyway?

TOBIAS I refuse to allow the Institute to be compromised. We are not a conduit for laundering criminals' money!

REBB Toby, Ezra and Elias Piranha are not *criminals;* they are contemporary American *businessmen.*

TOBIAS *(Agitated)* I can't believe that Dr. Flamm knew about this. I can't understand it . . .

REBB Oh, for Christ's sake, what's to understand? The Institute needs money; we all benefit; it's in the cause of civilization—advancing knowledge. Look at it that way. *(Pause)* Who the hell do you think paid for your fancy desk here?—your scenery out the window?

TOBIAS *(Caught by surprise)* Who?

REBB Money earmarked for "development" by Sushibito of Tokyo.

TOBIAS But, *that's* a legitimate business—isn't it?

REBB All businesses are legitimate if they get big enough.

TOBIAS *(Earnestly)* Didn't most of us come to the Institute out of idealism? *I* took a pay cut—

REBB *(Big smile, enthusiastic)* Toby, we're still idealists! We haven't lost our youthful vision. Except we need BIG BUCKS to implement it, eh? *(Slaps fist viciously into hand)* Gotta beat out the fucking competition.

TOBIAS *(Almost pleading)* But—to beg; to fawn upon; to flatter; to—

REBB *(Nodding)* —kiss ass, right!—

TOBIAS —it's demeaning, it's corrosive to the soul. It's—

REBB *(Booming)* —a challenge. To maintain the highest ideals, while kissing the donor's ass. *That's* the challenge!

TOBIAS *(Passing hand over eyes)* I can't believe what I am hearing.

REBB Huh! You never even showed up at your daughter's party after her play, the other night. Poor sweet kid kept looking for you—"Where's Daddy? Where's Daddy?" *That's* moral?

TOBIAS *(Taken off guard)* I, I—lost track of the time—I didn't mean not to go—

REBB *(Self-righteously)* Paula had to comfort the stricken little girl, and I had to comfort Paula. *That's* moral?

TOBIAS Just a minute, Willy—

REBB "Morality is what *other people* are deficient in," eh?

TOBIAS Who said that?

REBB *I* said that. And not in translation. *(Pause)* Toby, now that you're the Director, you should know—we've been running things in a certain, er, elastic manner, for years.

TOBIAS I don't believe it. I was here: Dr. Flamm trusted me.

REBB He trusted you with the "intellectual" side of things, not development. He . . . feared you.

TOBIAS Feared me! Why, I worshipped the man.

REBB That's why he feared you. *(Pause)* We all do.

TOBIAS *(Hurt)* I can't believe this . . .

REBB No doubt you're going to climb on your high horse, too, like old Diogenes, about the Upchurch A.D.E. Research Center—so we might as well discuss it now.

TOBIAS The Upchurch—what?

REBB *(Flamboyantly, pointing out the window)* Yessir!—right out there it will be, glittering in the sun—where, now, there's wall-to-wall Canada geese crapping up the lawn. We'll commission Bob Venturi—or Mike Graves—to design it: the forty million dollar UPCHURCH A.D.E. RESEARCH CENTER OF MOUNT ORION.

TOBIAS   A.D.E.—?

REBB   "After Death Experience." The cutting edge of today's science—medical, theological, ethical. Ideal for our Institute, ever pioneering into new challenges. Melva Upchurch is determined to fund research in the field in memory of her son Byron—who died so tragically last year in a "gun accident."

TOBIAS *(Voice rising)*   Willy, this is even more unconscionable than plotting to get an endowment from the Piranhas! Plotting to get an endowment from a distraught, elderly woman whose son committed suicide—

REBB *(Sharply, courtroom style)*   That has yet to be proved, sir!

TOBIAS   —while under indictment for fraud, income tax evasion, bribery—Have you no shame?

REBB *(Passionately)*   After Death Experience is a bold, beautiful, heartening area of research, no matter what cynics think. Melva Upchurch had an A.D.E. herself a few years ago: she was under general anesthetic for, er, facial surgery—a little tightening and polishing—and suddenly her heart stopped—she *died*—and slipped out of her body—and hurried on winged feet through a tunnel of glittering jewels—emerging in a place of pink, radiant light—the sumptuous Crystal Room of the Cotillion Club! There, her relatives and friends who had already passed over greeted her; one among them more radiant than the rest, in a gold brocaded dinner jacket, glittering with gems—none other than the late Liberace! He danced a single waltz with her, and turned her aside, saying, "Melva, your time is not yet at hand!"—and sent her back through the tunnel to her awaiting body—and life. *(Wiping at eyes)* And so, reluctantly, Melva Upchurch returned to life again, but never forgot her After Death Experience. *(Pause)* This is the sort of thing she wants to share with the world.

TOBIAS   Willy, I asked you: have you no shame?

REBB *(Wiping brow with handkerchief)*   That, sir, I take to be an insult.

TOBIAS   But you haven't answered my question.

REBB *(Dignified pout)*   I have plenty of shame.

TOBIAS *(Taken off guard)*   Well . . . er, integrity, then. Have you no integrity?

WILLY REBB, though exposed, brazens his way out of the scene with panache. He draws himself up to his full height for a grand exit.

REBB   Integrity, Tobias, in America today, is a mere vestigial organ—like an appendix. You might have it, but it's utterly useless; and one day it just might do you in.

A beat of startled silence.

TOBIAS   I can't believe what I'm . . . hearing. Willy, I'll have to dismiss
  you.
REBB *(Loftily sneering)*   Oh-no, no, podna, Willy Rebb is not "dismissed:" Willy Rebb *quits.* Effective instantaneously.

REBB exits.

Lights out.

SCENE 2

Lights up. TOBIAS's *office, as before; but it is late in the day (A suggestion of
waning light through the window) and* TOBIAS *is disheveled. His suit coat
off, he is struggling to measure his blood pressure, and having difficulties.*

TOBIAS *(As cuff slips from his arm, etc., muttering)*   Damn!

*He manages to get the cuff back on. Telephone rings. He answers it with
the cuff on his arm.*

TOBIAS *(Tries for his usual dignified diction)*   Yes? Oh—Martha. *(Pause)*
  No, I'm still going over the records. I'm going over my going-over of
  the records. *(Computer print-outs slip to floor)* Tell the auditor I'll see
  him at four thirty. *(Pause)* It's five forty-five now? *(Amazed, peering at
  watch, then at window)* Five forty-five P.M.? But which day? *(Pause)*
  Tell him I'll see him tomorrow morning at eight thirty promptly.
  Thank you! And Martha—no more calls today, please. *(Hangs up)*

TOBIAS *returns to the blood pressure kit. Pumps the bulb, peers at the
gauge, etc.*

TOBIAS Hmmm. Two hundred and three systolic, fifty-nine diastolic. Is
  that good, or not so good?

Telephone rings. TOBIAS *answers reluctantly.*

TOBIAS Martha, didn't I— *(Listens) Another* urgent call? *(Listens)* Who?
  (Listens) Oh. Yes. Send her right in.

TOBIAS *rips off the cuff and pushes the equipment into a desk drawer; un-
noticed, the rubber bulb on its tube hangs down. He hastily rolls down his
shirt sleeves but hasn't time to put on his suit coat as* NEDRA *enters.*

NEDRA *wears attractive but subdued clothing; black-tinted stockings;
"ethnic" jewelry. Her hair is somewhat tamed and she carries a large
leather bag into which she has shoved her camera.*

NEDRA and TOBIAS *stare at each other wordless for a long moment. They are clearly excited to meet—but stricken with shyness.*

NEDRA, TOBIAS   Well! Hello . . .
NEDRA   Tobias . . .
TOBIAS *(Quick overlapping)*   Ms. Mink . . .
NEDRA *(Nervously aggressive)*   Minsk. *MINSK.*
TOBIAS   —Minsk.
NEDRA *(Quick overlapping)*   Actually, it's—
TOBIAS   Nedra—I know. *(Pause)* A lovely name.

They shake hands, shyly, yet eagerly; each anxious, though NEDRA *is better at hiding her emotions.*

NEDRA   And "Tobias"—
TOBIAS *(Laughs awkwardly)*   Actually—Toby. A dog's name.
NEDRA *(Protesting)*   Oh, no: a classic name. Like—Tobias Mann?
TOBIAS   Thomas Mann. *(He gives "Thomas" the German pronunciation)*
NEDRA *(Edgy cheeriness)*   Him, too.

This initial repartee is breathless; now NEDRA *begins to be a little more at ease, moving into the office, as* TOBIAS *continues to stare at her.*

NEDRA   Some terrific space you've got here, Toby! Like Jason says, you *are* a big deal, eh?
TOBIAS   I think Jason meant that as irony. *(Seeing that* NEDRA *is peering at the things on his desk, and hoping to deflect her attention)* Can I get you anything, Nedra? Spring water with tincture of lemon . . . ? *(Pawing around on top of desk)* I have half an egg salad sandwich on whole wheat bread . . . a dill pickle . . .
NEDRA *(Indicating the blood pressure bulb, dangling from a drawer)* What's that thing?
TOBIAS *(Hastily shoving it into the drawer)*   A, uh, thing—a rubber thing.
NEDRA *(On the edge of distaste)*   A rubber—*thing?*
TOBIAS *(Awkwardly joking, which is not his style)*   A thing sort of thing, a, uh, *entity*—of rubber.
NEDRA   It was moving.
TOBIAS   No! It *was* . . . ? It's safe in here. *(Makes certain drawer is shut tight)* I mean, we're safe . . . out here. *(Awkward laugh)* Please have a seat, N-Nedra. May I offer you—? *(Indicating water bottle)*
NEDRA *(Suspicious)*   It isn't some sort of . . . obscene sex toy, is it? That thing?
TOBIAS *(Quickly)*   It never has been.
NEDRA *(Doubtfully, sitting in a chair beside the desk)*   Well, O.K.

Brisk and a little pushy in her actions, NEDRA *doesn't wait for her host to pour her water; she pours her own, and some for* TOBIAS.

TOBIAS *(He accepts a plastic cup from* NEDRA *and drinks thirstily)* Thank you.

Telephone rings. TOBIAS *answers it reluctantly.*

TOBIAS *(Trying to be courteous)* Martha, what *is* it—! *(Listens)* A— trapper? *(Listens)* Trappist? Trappist *monk?* *(Incredulous)* An "urgent call" from the head of a Trappist monastery—for me? *(Listens)* No, there must be some mistake. The poor man is fundraising in the wrong place. Tell him the Institute doesn't have a dime to spare. *(Hangs up; to* NEDRA*)* I'd have sworn Trappist monks take a vow of silence.

NEDRA But shouldn't you have talked to him? A monk?

TOBIAS *(Indicating his hands are shaking, he's nervous)* I'm not in any state to communicate with a man of God.

NEDRA *(Self-conscious laugh)* I, well, I . . . I'm . . . I guess I'm . . . what you'd call antsy.

TOBIAS "Antsy"—?

NEDRA Like, y'know—"ants in your pants?" *(She squirms a bit, as if to demonstrate)* My mother'd get nervous, us kids squirming around, like at dinner, y'know, it'd set off my old man and he'd get—some-times—so she'd, well, I mean basically she'd—she was a well-meaning woman, a good woman, just sort of overwhelmed by, by marital fate—well, she'd make a joke of it, she'd say, "Nedra, have you got ants in your pants?"—so we'd laugh. *(Laughs, a bit shrilly)* Rationally, I know I don't have ants in my, my . . . or anywhere . . . I know . . . but . . . sort of . . . *(Laughs)* I can feel them.

TOBIAS *(Suddenly)* Me, too.

NEDRA You? But you sit so still, your posture's so perfect . . . like a . . .

TOBIAS Mannequin.

NEDRA I was going to say . . . statue.

TOBIAS I've got ants, but I don't show it; I sit in the ants; I show them who's master. *(Pause)* Tiny red stinging ants.

NEDRA *(Half reproachfully)* You don't show it. *(Pause)* Well, I won't stay long, I know you're busy . . . *(As if to rise)*

TOBIAS *(Quickly)* Oh, no, I'm not busy: I'm not at all busy. *(A sweeping gesture of his hand has the unintended effect of knocking papers to the floor)* It's . . . slow here this afternoon. *(Scrambles to pick up papers;* NEDRA *helps)*

NEDRA What is all this . . . ?

TOBIAS Records, audits, transcripts . . . I'm trying to catch up on Insti-tute history.

NEDRA Well! I . . . saw your picture in the paper: congratulations.

TOBIAS *(Tonelessly)* Thank you. Yes. It's the goal I've been working for, for years. Since the age of nine . . .

NEDRA Well, the reason I'm here is: I want to set your mind at rest. I've decided not to press charges against your son.

TOBIAS *(Gazing at her)* My son?

NEDRA You know—Jason. The tall lanky kid with the hair.

TOBIAS Of course—*Jason. (With infinite relief)* You're not going to press charges? Thank you, Nedra!

TOBIAS takes NEDRA's hands in his, deeply moved.

TOBIAS Thank you—what wonderful unexpected news—

NEDRA *(Quick overlapping)* Hey, don't thank me—

TOBIAS —the happiest news I've had in—years—

NEDRA *(Overlapping)* —thank yourself, I'm doing it for you.

NEDRA withdraws her hands from TOBIAS's. He looks at her searchingly.

TOBIAS For me? *(Pause)* But no, you shouldn't, Nedra—I mean, for *me.* If Jason is guilty—

NEDRA Look, I made my decision and that's that.

TOBIAS —he should be punished. It's a matter of justice—

NEDRA *(Appalled)* Toby, for God's sake: do you want your son in jail?

TOBIAS No, no, certainly not. But—

NEDRA *(Sharply)* Guilt is just a legal term. Moral responsibility is the real issue. I think Jason knows that, now. *I* know it. *(Pause)* It's a matter, not of legal absolutes, but of moral degrees.

TOBIAS But—I didn't put pressure on you, Nedra, did I? *(Pause)* The other night—

NEDRA *(Quickly)* I make my own decisions.

TOBIAS The other night did . . . occur . . . didn't it? *(Pause)* Or did it?

NEDRA *(Beginning to be emotional)* I MAKE MY OWN DECISIONS.

TOBIAS *(Quickly)* Yes, I . . . surmised that. *(Pause)* And you were . . . are . . . right . . . not to have allowed me back. Under the circumstances.

NEDRA *(Incensed)* I want to lead a moral life, by my own terms. I *will* lead a moral life . . . by my own terms. Even if . . . *(Pause, looking at TOBIAS; then looking away)* . . . it's hard.

TOBIAS Nedra, I . . . the other night . . . since then . . . though I realize it can . . . should . . . have no consequences . . . the other night, what happened between us . . . has been . . . vivid . . . in my life. *(Pause)* It has rearranged my life. *(Pause, seems about to reach out to her, but hesitates)* But that shouldn't affect your judgment, Nedra.

NEDRA *(Sudden reversal, defiant)* Then what should?

TOBIAS stares at NEDRA. Telephone begins to ring.

TOBIAS *(Disoriented, answering after several rings)*   Hello?—no, sorry— no one's here right now. *(Hangs up clumsily, receiver slips off)*

NEDRA   Actually, Jason came to see me the other day. We straightened things out. He was on his way to—Kentucky?—

TOBIAS   *Kentucky?*

NEDRA   Well, maybe I heard wrong: he said he was going to stay with some brothers of his . . .

TOBIAS   Jason doesn't have any brothers. There is only one of him.

NEDRA   Stone cold sober, he's a sweet, kind of sad kid. He told me how sorry he was for how he'd behaved with me and asked for forgiveness. I figured what the hell, he *is* sorry, I'm *not* vindictive . . . He'd had some kind of vision, I guess—God spoke to him.

TOBIAS   *God?*—spoke to *Jason?*

NEDRA   He said the vision had "altered every molecule" of his being. He was going to change his life, and owed it all to me. He got down on his knees . . . I could see you in him, in his eyes; and I was, like, em- barrassed of myself, for having taken such a hard line. I asked him would he promise to respect women the rest of his life, and if, say, a woman's drunk, or high, or not exercising free volition, say she's depressed . . . would he promise not to take advantage of such weak- ness? He said yes, so I said, it's a deal.

TOBIAS   *(Moved)*   That's very generous of you, Nedra.

NEDRA   *(Quickly)*   Since my marriage broke up I've been susceptible to thinking "Men are the enemy," which is what a lot of women think today—with good reason. But I . . . guess I don't believe that, one hundred percent. You're not *all* bastards and motherfuckers.

TOBIAS   We're not?

NEDRA   I guess my principles as a feminist are, like, provisional.

TOBIAS   *(Elated)*   It was David Hume who said, "Nature is too strong for any principle."

NEDRA   Who—?

TOBIAS   The great eighteenth-century Scottish philosopher who refuted Kant and the laws of causality . . . *(Pause)* He was a gross fat man who played billiards.

NEDRA   Good.

NEDRA rises, and TOBIAS quickly rises too, as if to urge her not to leave.

NEDRA   Well—I just wanted to wind things up, Toby. My project is fin- ished and I'm leaving Mount Orion on Monday morning.

TOBIAS   Leaving Mount Orion? But you only just arrived.

NEDRA   I never stay in one place long, that *is* a principle. How about you?

TOBIAS   I've been here— *(As if counting rapidly on fingers)*—forty-eight years.

NEDRA   Forty-eight—? No!

TOBIAS   I mean, no, I've been here—eighteen years. My age is forty-eight.

NEDRA   *(Glancing about)*   I was reading in the paper, this is a hot-shot place, eh? No teaching, just—intellects? Doing research on what?

TOBIAS   *(Rapid recitation)*   The Mount Orion Institute for Independent Research in the Humanities and Sciences is a privately endowed non-profit research institution dedicated to "the finest, highest, and best to be discovered without consideration of monetary reward or public acclaim"—"with no compromise in ideals, and no challenges too venturesome." Nestled in the idyllic hills of Central New Jersey, on two hundred acres, the Institute is but an hour's train ride to New York City and within easy access of Newark International Airport. Its faculty, devoted to pure research, consists of seventy-five Senior Fellows appointed for life, and ninety Junior Fellows appointed for shorter terms. Expanded to its present size in 1949, the Institute has regularly published ground-breaking studies in the fields of—*(Speaking so rapidly now, his words are like those of an old-time auctioneer's, virtually run together in a single stream)* anthropology/archeology/art/astrophysics/classics/economics/hellenic studies/linguistics/philosophy/politics/psychology/religion/sociology/history—*(Now slowing down a bit)* —sociolinguistics/psychohistory/biopsycho Biblical studies/neurotopology/anthro-psycho-eco-historical-astro-physical-socio-cognitive-semantics. *(Pause)* The last are relatively new fields.

NEDRA   You're happy here, running all that?

A pause.

TOBIAS   *(A bit tonelessly)*   I have exciting plans for the future.

NEDRA   *(Peering out window)*   Terrific view. What's all that rippling gray stuff?

TOBIAS   The backs of several thousand Canada geese.

NEDRA   Wow. How'd you get so many?

TOBIAS   It started with just two. *(Smiles)*

NEDRA   *(A bit self-consciously)*   You do look . . . happy.

TOBIAS   That's because you're here.

Pause.

NEDRA   I thought I saw you a few days ago, out where I live . . . I ran out, but you were gone. Into the woods . . . ?

TOBIAS   *(Embarrassed)*   That wasn't me. *(Pause)* I mean, it was, but . . . it wasn't supposed to be.

NEDRA   How's that?

TOBIAS   It was supposed to be, not me, but someone who resembled me. Most joggers in Mount Orion, above the age of forty, look alike.

NEDRA *(Frankly)* I wouldn't mistake anyone else for you, Toby. You're one of a kind. *(Removes camera from bag)* D'you mind? Not for professional—just, like, a memento?

TOBIAS *flinches as* NEDRA *takes her first shot, using a flashbulb.*

TOBIAS *(Belatedly)* I'd rather you—
NEDRA *(Unhearing)* Relax. Like you were a minute ago. *(Takes another flash shot)*

TOBIAS *nervously checks his tie, smooths down his hair, etc. His expression is wooden, grim.*

TOBIAS I'd . . . rather you didn't, Nedra.
NEDRA Over by the window . . . yeah. Like that. *(Another shot)* You're a good-looking man, you don't look a day past fifty . . . C'mon, smile.
TOBIAS *(Stffly)* It's natural to fear the camera, since our photographic likenesses are always posthumous. They outlive us.
NEDRA *(Impressed, lowering the camera briefly)* That's exactly how I feel, too. I don't let anybody take *my* picture.
TOBIAS *(Hesitantly)* I've never told anyone this, Nedra, not even my wife, but . . . my father died suddenly at the age of forty-nine; and I'm convinced . . . *(Suddenly fearful)* . . . terrified . . . I will die at that age, too.
NEDRA *(Immediately sympathetic)* Hey, don't talk that way.
TOBIAS *(Grim smile)* I'm resigned to my fate; at the same time, scared as hell.
NEDRA But that's just superstition. You're too smart for that.
TOBIAS *(Wanting to believe)* I am, I *am.* Yes. *(Visibly shudders)*
NEDRA *(Repositioning* TOBIAS *to take another photo)* Relax! *(Takes photo)* Ummm—that *was* a bit grim. When's your forty-ninth birthday?
TOBIAS One week from this Saturday. *This* Saturday, I will be formally inducted as Director of the Institute.
NEDRA How'd your father die so young?
TOBIAS A stroke. High blood pressure. *(Pause)* He was an alcoholic, too.
NEDRA Yeah? *My* old man, too—a drunk.
TOBIAS When I was a child, I fervently believed that, if I was good, if I worked hard and got high grades and was, say, "Outstanding Boy" in seventh grade, it would make a difference: my father would stop drinking. My mother was always saying, "We must try harder—we must pray." *(Pause)* It didn't work. We prayed, and he drank. I always thought it might be . . . me . . . at fault. Long after I knew that I made no difference to my father, I continued as I'd done—determined to be perfect. I only dared to try things I knew I *could* do. I might have

wanted to be—well, something like you . . . a photographer, an artist . . . writer . . . But I couldn't risk failing. My mother was the same way . . . She died young, too.

NEDRA   *My* mother took a lot of shit for years, then finally kicked my father out. Smartest thing she ever did. It's like the sun was shining again! We all went to Reno for the divorce, and Mom got a great job as a blackjack dealer. Wild!

TOBIAS *(Amazed)*   You didn't feel guilty about it?—him?

NEDRA *(Matter-of-fact)*   Why the hell should I, or any of us?

TOBIAS *(Struck by this)*   Yes.

NEDRA   My husband—*ex*—tried to lay a guilt trip on me, too. Like *I* was responsible for him fucking up his career, cuffing me around—

TOBIAS *(Shocked)*   Your husband beat you?

NEDRA *(Quickly)*   Never mind. It's over. It was a mistake.

TOBIAS   We all make mistakes. We all get married.

NEDRA *(Briskly)*   I never stay in one place long, anyway. My philosophy is, human beings are all constructed along lines of fracture: hit us just right, we crack. So it's best to remain a moving target.

TOBIAS   Since the other night, I've been . . . thinking of you . . . somewhat obsessively. Nedra, I . . .

NEDRA *(As if mishearing)*   I've told you: I take advice from nobody. Even if it's the right advice.

NEDRA *strides to the door; then turns back, impulsively.* TOBIAS *has been gazing after her.*

NEDRA   Um . . . did you say you had some kind of sandwich? I missed lunch, I'm starving.

TOBIAS *(Eagerly)*   Yes! Here! Somewhere— *(Pawing through clutter on desk)* Egg salad sandwich on whole wheat—with extra alfalfa sprouts—Here. *(Hands it to her)*

NEDRA *(Suspicious)*   Light on the mayo?

TOBIAS   *No* mayo. That's where the alfalfa sprouts come in—they sort of imbricate the ingredients into a satisfying texture.

NEDRA *(Taking sandwich from him)*   There's a bite missing.

TOBIAS   That was just me.

NEDRA *(Taking a bite)*   Mmmm!—delicious. There's a real art to egg salad, y'know? After Mom's divorce we were so poor sometimes she'd make egg salad sandwiches for us mixing in the eggshells. They're high in calcium and Vitamin D.

TOBIAS   Yes! And that great, gritty texture . . . you know you're really *chewing* something.

NEDRA *(Shaking* TOBIAS'S *hand, attempting to be nonchalant)*   O.K., thanks! I'll send you some prints, Toby—as a memento.

TOBIAS *(Stricken)*   A mere—memento? Wait.

TOBIAS is going to kiss NEDRA goodbye, but the intercom buzzer rings loudly. He moves away from her guiltily.

NEDRA   Goodbye!

NEDRA exits.

TOBIAS   Goodbye . . . ! *(Looking after her)*

Lights fade as the intercom rings again and TOBIAS crosses distractedly to answer it.

TOBIAS *(Rattled)*   Hello, there's no one here—I mean, yes, *I'm* here—

Lights out.

SCENE 3

Lights up. Several days later, the afternoon of the Saturday of TOBIAS's induction as Director of the Institute. TOBIAS's study at home. He is working at a word processor, stacks of papers on the desk beside him. But he is restless, goes to a window to look out; paces about.

As PAULA enters, agitated; shutting door behind her, TOBIAS quickly crosses to desk to sit as before.

PAULA *(Shocked, furious)*   Toby, how could you! Lie to *me*! Deceive *me*!

TOBIAS *(Startled)*   Paula, why—what on earth—?

PAULA *(Magnificent in her outrage)*   Lying to *me*!—why, you don't even know *how* to lie! I had to teach you!

TOBIAS   Paula, w-what do you mean? Lying about—

PAULA   It's all over town! And the induction ceremony tonight! Oh how could you, Tobias Harte! Practicing deception! On me!

TOBIAS *(On his feet, trying to placate)*   But, Paula—I *was* going to tell you—I only just—After tonight—

JASON enters, stage right. He carries a duffel bag and is wearing rumpled clothes. Unshaven, sullen. Seeing him, PAULA cautions TOBIAS.

PAULA   Shh! Jason's back! *(Transformed, runs to embrace JASON)* Jason! Darling! You're home!

JASON *(Clearly hoping he'd be spared this, enduring her embrace without reciprocating)*   Aw, hey Mom . . .

PAULA   My darling boy, my baby love, oh! you're back!—you've lost weight. You're haggard!

TOBIAS *(Off to the side, looking puzzled)* Back—?

JASON Aw, Mom . . .

PAULA Why didn't you tell me where you were going! I'm so hurt that you would confide in your sister and not in me. *(Peering anxiously at him)* Are you all right? What did they *do* to you in the monastery?

TOBIAS Monastery—?

JASON *(Losing patience)* Aw, Mom, I gotta use the bathroom, I've been on the fucking bus for three days!

PAULA *(Automatically)* Watch your language, Jason. *(Now loving)* My sweet dear baby boy! What a scare! "Run away to God," Kim said. Jason, I'm your mother and I'm so hurt: you get your religious yearnings from *me*, I once seriously thought of entering a convent . . . How could you not share your secret with *me*?

JASON *(Trying to get past her)* Aw, Mom, shit . . .

PAULA *(Automatically)* Watch your language, Jason.

TOBIAS *(Overlapping)* Excuse me, I seem to be—in the dark, here. You "ran away to God" to a monastery, Jason?

JASON *(Incredulous)* Didn't you miss me?

TOBIAS Why, I—I— When did you run away exactly—

JASON *(Hurt, incensed, to PAULA)* His only son runs away to join a Trappist monastery and devote his life to God and he doesn't fucking *notice*?

PAULA *(Quickly)* *Watch* your language, Jason. *(Another tone)* Dear, your father has been so busy, I didn't want to worry him.

JASON He didn't *miss me*?

PAULA Why, yes he did, didn't you Tobias, yes—just last night, your father was home for dinner, I could tell he was wondering where you were—weren't you dear?—he *noticed* the empty chair—didn't you?— *(As TOBIAS nods emphatically)* —and then the phone rang.

JASON *(To TOBIAS)* Your only son is missing for four fucking desperate days and you don't notice! You only notice my—*sins*!

PAULA *(Framing JASON's face in her hands)* But what did they *do* to you, Jason?

JASON *(Aggrieved)* They only let me stay one night, 'cause I was all hungry, and wet, and cold. They told me . . . aw, never mind, I gotta use the bathroom.

TOBIAS *(Protesting)* Jason, I notice you all the time. I've been thinking about you almost constantly since—

PAULA *(Hanging on JASON as he tries to get away)* The head monk, or whoever, called here, Wednesday . . . *I* thought he was a bit snippy. For a monk who has taken a vow of silence. You expect a meeker class of person.

KIM enters through the door JASON is trying to exit from.

KIM *(Squawking with delight)*   Jason! You're back! Oh, wow!

KIM runs to embrace JASON, too. Both PAULA and KIM overlap in the following exchange.

PAULA   Poor baby's lost weight! So pale!—haggard! And we're not Catholic—no one in the family!

KIM   What happened? What'd they say? What's it like there? Are you going back?

JASON   Aw, shit . . . I gotta use the bathroom.

KIM   Are you going to be a monk, you think? Is God still talking to you?

PAULA   You're back in time for the Institute banquet—tonight, your father is inducted as Director.

JASON *(Sullen)*   I'm not going, I'm crashing. Three days on the fucking bus—Gethsemane, Kentucky to Mount Orion, New Jersey. And the toilet's broken. *(To KIM)* You still got some of those college applications?—I'll use them.

KIM *(Disappointed)*   What? You're returning to college?—to conformity?

PAULA *(Anxiously)*   The monks didn't . . . baptize you, did they? With holy water on your forehead?

JASON manages to extricate himself, exits. KIM rushes after.

KIM *(Exiting)*   Jason, this is crucial: is God still talking to you?

TOBIAS and PAULA remain, looking at each other. PAULA runs her hand dramatically through her hair.

PAULA   I just want you to know, Toby, that I—am—furious—with—you.

TOBIAS   My God, Paula, I'm so, so sorry—I'll make a clean breast of it right now—I didn't want to hurt you—

PAULA *(Overlapping on "you")*   Listen! You lied to me! You told me Willy resigned his job, but in fact *you fired him*. Didn't you!

TOBIAS, expecting another accusation, is thrown off balance.

TOBIAS   Why, I—Willy?!

PAULA   Practically our dearest, closest friend—you *fired*!

TOBIAS   Paula, please. Willy *did* resign from the Institute. Are people saying otherwise?

PAULA   Everyone in Mount Orion is talking of nothing else: how Tobias Harte betrayed the very man who'd advanced his career—his dearest, closest friend.

TOBIAS   "Dearest, closest friend"—? Willy Rebb and I have never much liked each other.

PAULA   All the more reason, then, to keep the friendship up. You know what Mount Orion is like. Oh, Toby, how could you!

TOBIAS   Paula, I didn't fire Willy . . . exactly. I'd brought up some
. . . infractions . . . of which Willy was guilty, and which he did not
deny; he became angry, and . . .

PAULA   Of course Willy became angry: he's a man with pride. You can't
treat him like one of your Institute fellows who cares only for his
work, or Truth, or something! *(Incensed)* What "infractions" is Willy
guilty of?

TOBIAS   Paula, these things are confidential. You know I can't tell you.

PAULA   Why can't you tell me?—I'm your wife.

TOBIAS   It's for Willy's protection, too. I would never betray con-
fidentiality.

PAULA   Oh, don't be ridiculous! Willy has told me plenty of Institute secrets over the years and I'm not even his wife.

TOBIAS   What secrets?

PAULA   *(Carelessly)* Oh, all sorts of silly . . . sad . . . hilarious . . .
astounding . . . classified secrets. Willy knew he could trust me, even if
you don't.

TOBIAS   *(Horrified)*   *Classified* secrets?

PAULA   Oh, salaries and such; and who informed on whom; and where
Dr. Flamm took his two-week fling years ago with that—what *was* the
name?—the anthropologist from—

TOBIAS   *(Overlapping)*   Dr. Flamm?—*fling*?

PAULA   *(Gesturing)*   That cute dimpled little Hawaiian—Dr. Guppy. With
all the hair.

TOBIAS   *(Profoundly shocked)*   Dr. Guppy is a *man*, Paula.

PAULA   Well, Dr. Flamm must have known, don't you think? Anyway, he
had the fling, and he came back. It's old history now.

TOBIAS   Dr. Guppy is a *man*, Paula.

PAULA   You see? You just get upset. It's better for you not to know. Willy
knows he can trust *me*.

TOBIAS   Paula, this is very upsetting—

PAULA   It *is* upsetting, your unconscionable behavior with Willy. And,
oh!— *(Checks watch)* —the banquet begins in four hours!

TOBIAS   But—what have you been hearing about Willy, Paula? He refuses to return my calls.

PAULA   *(Half-sobbing)*   He won't call me back, either. Oh, how could
you! When we've been so happy!

TOBIAS   *(Puzzled)*   Who has been happy? Paula, what are you talking
about?

PAULA   What are *you* talking about? You don't know the first thing
about the very man you fired!

TOBIAS   *(Trying to take PAULA's hand, but rebuffed)*   Paula, dear—I'd
hoped you might be supportive. I know Willy has many friends in

Mount Orion, but, believe me, he is *not* what he seems . . . If the Institute wanted to press charges . . .

PAULA Press charges! Toby, my God! *(Drawing away)* Willy would slap a countersuit on you for libel. Don't try it! *(With satisfaction)*

TOBIAS Paula, you've always been critical of Willy, yourself . . .

PAULA *(Maudlin)* His bowties and hankies! His cologne! *(Almost crying)* His moustache that's like a caterpillar! *(Pause)* But not *Willy.* Not deep inside, where he's *Willy.*

TOBIAS *(Appalled)* Where he's *Willy?* That hypocrite?

PAULA We are discussing a man's soul, Toby. This is not Ethics 101 at silly old Harvard.

TOBIAS Paula, I can't believe this—you're taking Willy's side against *me?*—against *Harvard?*

PAULA Oh, you! Everything has to be perfect with you! And *you* are perfect! *(Pause)* It's the reason I fell in love with you, and the reason I've fallen out.

TOBIAS Fallen out—? You don't love me?

PAULA I'm stuck with you, aren't I? The best-looking man in Mount Orion—the most successful, and admired—the best dressed. I'm stuck with you.

TOBIAS Paula!

PAULA *(A bit wildly)* Oh, I don't mean it—I haven't meant anything I've said since puberty. Of course I love you. *(Pause, can't resist continuing)* I'm your wife, of course I love you. I can't just give *up.* *(Pause)* Or can I?

TOBIAS Paula, what are you saying, Paula?

Phone begins to ring.

PAULA You know what I'm saying. *(Answering phone)* Hello?

TOBIAS I'm so sorry, Paula, I've upset you. I'm to blame.

PAULA *(Incredulous, then aghast)* What? What? *What?* *(Drops the receiver, backs off, hands pressed against her mouth)*

TOBIAS Paula, what is it?

TOBIAS tries to comfort PAULA, but she pushes him away.

PAULA *(Stunned, hoarse voice)* WILLY HANGED HIMSELF. WILLY IS DEAD. *(Rushes off)*

TOBIAS *(Stunned; hangs up phone)* Oh God, what a tragedy! Poor Willy . . . I'm to blame.

TOBIAS's knees buckle; he sits on the arm of a chair; stares into space. Pulls at his collar as if choking. Takes out his vial of pills, fumbles, and the pills scatter on the floor. He makes no move to retrieve them.

KIM, humming cheerfully, enters the room; she is carrying several books. She is oblivious of TOBIAS's agitated state.

KIM   Daddy, I need your expert advice. I can't decide between Ophelia, Hedda Gabler, and a monologue from *In the Boom-Boom Room.* For my audition? At East Village Theatre? *(When TOBIAS doesn't reply)* Daddy, the audition is *Monday. (Pouting)* My entire life might be determined by this audition and you don't care, do you?! You don't even hear me! *(Peering at him)* Golly gee, Daddy—you look like you lost your best friend.

TOBIAS   *(Wakes from his trance)*   Kim, honey—we've had an upset, but things are going to be all right. *(Stunned, waking, with increasing emotion)* I love you, honey, you know that, don't you?

KIM   Gosh, Dad, what's wrong?

TOBIAS   I—just want you to be happy. You and, um—

KIM   Jason?

TOBIAS   You and Jason, and your mother—I just want you to be happy. I'm sorry I've been such an egregious failure as a father . . .

KIM   *(Incensed)*   No, you're not, Daddy! You're a fantastic father, all my girl friends have crushes on you, for God's sake!

TOBIAS   If it's your dream to "go into the theatre"—why, then, it's . . . it's . . . *(Choking on the words)* . . . fine with me. Terrific!

KIM   Wow, thanks! It's O.K., then about Venice Beach Rep, too?

TOBIAS   What's that?

KIM   I need to fly out for the audition, y'know, in Los Angeles, Mom's been having a cow about it, but I thought, I mean going all that distance, I should, like, stay a few days? not just turn around and come back?—O.K.?

TOBIAS   O.K.—what?

KIM   *(A quick hug)*   Daddy, you're the greatest. *(Self absorbed, she draws away from TOBIAS and opens one of her books)* Tell me how this sounds, O.K.?—it's Ophelia. Sol Schwartz says I have a natural gift for classic theatre because of my "ethereal quality."

Kim postures a bit, then recites the following. She is surprisingly talented.

KIM   O, what a noble mind is here o'erthrown!
      The courtier's, the soldier's eye, tongue, sword,
      The' expectation and rose of the fair state,
      The glass of fashion and the mould of form,
      The' observed of all observers, quite, quite, down! And I,
      of ladies most deject and wretched . . .

Midway through this speech, TOBIAS exits like a man in a dream.

KIM   *(Glancing around)*   Daddy? Where are you? *(Snapping book shut in petulance)* Oh, Daddy! *(But she takes up another book, leafs through it, preens a bit, excited)* Hedda's more like it: *she* takes charge.

KIM *is about to practice her Hedda Gabler speech when* WILLY REBB, *looking disheveled, enters the room with a loud rap on the already opened door.* REBB *is flush-faced, perspiring, his bowtie askew.*

KIM   Oh, hi, Willy. You can be my audience.

REBB *(Breathing hard, embarrassed)* Is . . . your mother anywhere around?

KIM   Mom and Dad just sort of drifted off . . . maybe they're dressing for the banquet. You look sort of, er, excited, Willy. Is anything wrong?

REBB I guess, um, you haven't heard . . . ?

KIM   Heard what?

REBB *(Awkwardly trying to make light of it)*   There's a ridiculous rumor— a typically distorted Mount Orion rumor—that I, er, committed suicide.

KIM   Wow, that's cool, Willy! How'd you do it?

REBB *(Annoyed)*   I didn't do it—obviously. *(Rubs throat, chagrined)* The damned beam broke.

KIM   You really did try?—*you?*

REBB Why not me?

KIM   You, um, don't seem the type. You're kind of . . .

A vague gesture whose meaning is transparent: he's too hefty.

REBB *(Indignant)*   Endomorphs despair, too—we experience the Dark Night of the Soul, too. *(Pause; then complaining)* The beam in the family room wasn't real oak—at the price we paid! Damned thing turns out to be papier-mâché, with fake worm holes.

KIM   *(With schoolgirl earnestness)* They say carbon monoxide is more reliable. But overdosing on pills, which is what the majority of suicidal women try, is *not.*

REBB *(With glum irony)*   Thanks. I'll remember that.

KIM   Gas ovens used to be a favorite method but now there's microwave—that'd be too messy.

REBB *(Backing off)*   Is your mother just possibly upstairs? No one answered the door, I just walked in. *(Calling)* Paula? PAULA?

REBB exits.

KIM   *(Calling after)*   Willy, wait—have you consulted the Hemlock Society Handbook?

Lights out.

SCENE 4

Lights up. Shortly afterward, at NEDRA's *rented house. In old clothes, barefoot,* NEDRA *is hurriedly packing. There are boxes on the floor, the photographs and posters have been removed, much of the furniture is gone.*

A knock at the door.

NEDRA *opens the door, and it is* TOBIAS *in his tuxedo, carrying a single long-stemmed flower of some coarse but colorful weedy variety, trailing roots and bits of dirt.* TOBIAS *is disheveled, flush-faced, animated and assertive; the most vital we've seen him.*

NEDRA   Tobias! My God! You! But—why are you *here?* Isn't your induction tonight?

TOBIAS *(Cheerfully, a bit wildly)*   In twenty minutes. I'm not going. *(Hands* NEDRA *the flower)*

NEDRA   What do you mean, you're not going? How can they induct you as Director without *you?*

TOBIAS *advances upon* NEDRA, *who backs away clutching the flower.*

TOBIAS *(Tapping his pocket)*   I have my speech—I'm all prepared—but—I'm not going.

NEDRA *(Frightened)*   But why?

TOBIAS   Because I can't be in two places at once. I'm *here,* thus not *there.*

NEDRA   But, Toby—

TOBIAS   Even if you send me away, Nedra, I'm not going to the Institute. They can proceed without me. Oh, Nedra! *(Embraces her)*

NEDRA   What's that weird sound?

TOBIAS   My teeth chattering.

NEDRA   But you're burning up.

TOBIAS   I'm burning up. *(Pause)* Nedra, a man tried to kill himself today, and I'm to blame.

NEDRA   My God! Who?

TOBIAS   My closest, dearest friend.

NEDRA   Oh, Toby, that's terrible!

TOBIAS   I didn't know him all that well . . . but I'm to blame. *(Glancing about)* Nedra, where are your things?—in that U-Haul outside?

NEDRA *(Quickly)*   I told you, didn't I—I'm leaving Mount Orion.

TOBIAS   You were leaving on Monday. This is Saturday.

NEDRA   I—wanted to get started early tomorrow. Sunday's the best day for driving.

TOBIAS *(Hurt, incredulous)*   You mean—you planned to leave without saying goodbye? And we'd never see each other again?

NEDRA *(Weakly)* I do what I . . . want to do. I come to a place, I see what I need, I . . . move on.

TOBIAS *(Passionately)* You'd do that to me? To both of us?

NEDRA Toby, this friend of yours who tried to kill himself—you're upset—is that why you're here?

TOBIAS No. I'm here because I love you.

NEDRA O God—I was afraid of that.

TOBIAS I'm here because I—can't be anywhere else. *(Pause)* That's why my teeth are chattering.

NEDRA You're not really resigning your job, are you?

TOBIAS My job has resigned *me*. I'm not the man they want.

NEDRA But your wife? Your family? You can't just walk away—

TOBIAS I must. I've got only one more week to live—maybe.

NEDRA Oh, Toby—not that. You don't really believe that.

TOBIAS No, no—of course not.

NEDRA That's superstition—you're not a superstitious man.

TOBIAS When I'm with you—no.

NEDRA You have to assume a future. You might change your mind later.

TOBIAS That's why I'm here now. So I can't change my mind later.

NEDRA But—what are we going to *do*?

TOBIAS Look, Nedra, do you love me?

NEDRA Yes, Toby.

TOBIAS Then that's it.

NEDRA It's this—simple?

TOBIAS It always is!

They embrace passionately.

JASON, *hair neatly combed, wearing a sport coat, enters; he sees* TOBIAS *and* NEDRA, *who do not see him.*

Lights quickly dim.

THE END